MORALITY AND CITIZENSHIP IN EDUCATION

0304701866

Also available from Cassell:

Avis et al.: *Knowledge and Nationhood*

Best: *Education, Spirituality and the Whole Child*

Bottery: *The Morality of the School*

Morality and Citizenship in Education

John Beck

CASSELL

Cassell
Wellington House
125 Strand
London WC2R 0BB

PO Box 605
Herndon
VA 20172

First published 1998

British Library Cataloguing-in-Publication Data
A catalogue record for this book is available from the British Library.

ISBN   0-304-70186-6 (hardback)
          0-304-70187-4 (paperback)

Typeset by BookEns Ltd, Royston, Herts.
Printed and bound in Great Britain by
Redwood Books, Trowbridge, Wilts.

Contents

He did not at that time see that mediaevalism was as dead as a fern leaf in a lump of coal; that other developments were shaping the world around him, in which Gothic architecture and its associations had no place. The deadly animosity of contemporary logic and vision towards so much of what he held in reverence was not yet revealed to him.

(Thomas Hardy, *Jude the Obscure*, 1895;
St Martin's Library Edition, p. 91)

What does it matter, when you come to think of it, whether a child is yours by blood or not? All the little ones of our time are collectively the children of all the adults of our time, and entitled to our general care. That excessive regard of parents for their own children, and their dislike of other people's, is, like class-feeling, patriotism, save-your-own-soulism, and other virtues, a mean exclusiveness at bottom.

(Thomas Hardy, *Jude the Obscure*, p. 283)

Acknowledgements

I would like to acknowledge permissions granted for the republication in this volume of two articles that have appeared previously in academic journals. My thanks therefore, first to Carfax Publishing Company for permission to republish as Chapter 1 of this book a paper which first appeared in the *Cambridge Journal of Education*, and secondly to Triangle Journals Ltd for their agreement to the republication of a paper which first appeared in *Curriculum Studies*, and which appears here as Chapter 5. I should also like to thank Homerton College, Cambridge, for a small research grant which enabled me to complete the writing of the text and prepare it for publication.

It will be clear to any reader that in writing this book I have drawn extensively on the ideas and insights of many different people. I would especially like to thank a number of colleagues, past and present, at Homerton College who have helped to shape my thinking and understanding of the issues this book addresses. In particular, I would like to acknowledge my indebtedness to John Ahier, Charles Bailey and Rob Moore, and also to Terry McLaughlin of the University of Cambridge School of Education. None of them, of course, bears any responsibility for the particular inflection that I may have given to their ideas in various parts of my discussion. Last, but not least, my thanks are due to Naomi Roth of Cassell for the interest and support she has given in preparing the book for publication.

Introduction

BLAMING TEACHERS FOR NATIONAL DECLINE

In recent years it has become fashionable to blame schools and teachers for much of what has gone wrong, or is thought to have gone wrong, in British life. Claims that the nation is in decline seem never-ending: the economy, family life, moral standards, educational standards, a sense of community, the nation's health, even our national sporting achievements – all these have been identified as areas in which things have been getting progressively worse. Although a moment's serious thought makes it seem highly implausible that educational institutions could really be responsible for so much decay, they have, nevertheless, been recurrently targeted and held accountable.

Just over twenty years ago, for example, Sir Arnold Weinstock (the then chief executive of GEC – later to become Lord Weinstock) wrote a short article in the *Times Educational Supplement* under the headline 'I blame the teachers' (Weinstock, 1976). In this piece, he attributed the lack of international competitiveness of British industry not to industrialists themselves and their well-documented shortcomings in the area of training, but to the nation's schools and especially the teachers. Schools were said to be producing school-leavers who had low levels of literacy and numeracy, poor attitudes to work discipline, and who were 'over aspired' – i.e. they were not excited by the prospect of monotonous shop-floor jobs and wanted better for themselves. The situation with academically successful pupils was, if anything, alleged to be even worse. Here, schooling was charged with perpetuating an anti-industrial culture which went right back to the mid-Victorian period, and which produced attitudes of disdain if not outright contempt towards manufacturing industry. Teachers transmitted this kind of outlook to their pupils with the result that the best and brightest chose careers in the City, the civil service and the professions – but not manufacturing industry – thereby helping to ensure continuing industrial decline. The teaching profession, Weinstock proclaimed, was due for a culture change and needed to be re-educated to see that it was the duty of teachers to promote respect for wealth creation and the values of free enterprise. Twenty years later, we witnessed the spectacle of the Prime Minister of the day, John Major, blaming teachers for, of all things, a decline in the nation's sporting achievements – the nadir of which was the lowest gold medal tally for twenty years in the 1996 Olympics! Looking back to 'the good old days' of the sort of grammar school he himself attended, when teachers voluntarily coached and refereed school games of all kinds, he lamented the decline in this kind of commitment among today's teachers – and hinted at the need to make compulsory team games part of the National Curriculum. It would be superfluous to describe the response of an already over-burdened teaching profession to this particular piece of silliness!

'Declinism', to borrow a term from the historian David Edgerton (Edgerton, 1996a), has become something of a national preoccupation; indeed it is arguable that the *real* 'British disease' is this addiction to lamenting alleged national failings. Nowhere, of course, has the chorus of lament been louder or more sustained than in relation to our supposed *moral and spiritual* decline: we are not the people we once were; traditional values have been eroded to a dangerous degree – undermining social cohesion and weakening our sense of national identity. Those who offer this diagnosis do not really, of course, blame it *all* on schools and teachers. The list of alleged causes is a long one, including: the moral permissiveness ushered in by that deplorable decade 'the sixties', the decline of religious belief and observance, the break-up of stable communities, the influence of cultural diversity and multiculturalism, relativistic currents in intellectual life – most recently, postmodernism, etc. Nevertheless, the role of schools and educators *has* been seen as pivotal – both in terms of responsibility for the descent into moral crisis and also as a potential means of reversing the trend.

Nor do teachers in schools stand condemned alone. A favourite resort of traditionalist cultural critics is the claim that teachers have been misled – by a variety of malign intellectual influences (for example, feminism, Marxism, liberal theology, post-modernism) and also by teacher-trainers. A common feature of complaints of this order is the contention that potentially sensible and responsible teachers have, in different ways at different times, been exposed to too much *theory*. Kenneth Clarke, when he was Secretary of State for Education in the mid-1980s, coined the unforgettable phrase 'barmy theory'. He used it to highlight his claim that what society needed was for trainee teachers to get into the classroom and be given a good dose of common sense instead of a load of progressive, half-baked theoretical twaddle! The language of this kind of diatribe is familiar enough and it would be foolish to deny either its effectiveness or its popular appeal. Moreover, there is of course *some* validity to criticisms of 'theory' within teacher education – an issue which we shall consider in more detail shortly. But what is crucial when considering this dichotomy of 'theory' versus 'common sense' is the point made by Rob Moore – that this so-called common sense is actually a *competing* theory in disguise (Moore, 1994b). For all their populist rhetoric, what people like Kenneth Clarke were really saying was that we needed to go back to a *different set* of theories – ones that favour more traditional styles of teaching, less permissive ideas about authority relations, subject-based conceptions of school knowledge, psychometric models of intelligence, pencil-and-paper tests, etc. The idea that we can ever really have a system of education which is theory-*free* is strictly for readers of the *Sun*!

If we are *properly* to understand the profound social currents that are reshaping societies like our own, what we actually need is not less theory (let alone *no* theory) but rather, more and more relevant theory. Furthermore, we need to draw *together* a range of theoretical insights derived from different disciplines. One reason why theory within initial teacher-training became discredited was that the different education disciplines (philosophy, psychology, sociology, history) remained too enclosed within their separate subject boundaries. Students were too often left to their own devices when it came to *integrating* the insights which these disciplines potentially offered (not to mention relating them to practice).[1] For academic *writers*, of course, there is a similar temptation to play safe and stay within subject boundaries. A certain confidence, even temerity, is necessary if one sets out to write across the boundaries of several disciplines. After all, no one can any longer be an expert in even one of the sub-fields of educational or social-scientific theory and research. Moreover, the academic pressures resulting from recent developments in higher education, notably the competitive assessment of research publications as part of the Research Assessment Exercise (RAE), heighten this tendency towards self-protective academic specialization. As Noel Malcolm has recently pointed out, one main outcome of the RAE is the accumulation of more and more specialized papers, each one read by fewer and fewer people (Malcolm, 1996).

Yet it is arguable that there has never been a time when it has been *more* important for 'theorists' to engage in dialogue with 'practitioners' – and to do so in a language which is accessible without being simplistic.[2] The dominant rhetoric of 'common-sense' and 'classroom practice', as well as the current preoccupation with pragmatic issues like effective school management or coping with school inspections, threatens to drown out proper consideration of more complex and 'esoteric' issues – for example, questions to do with the kinds of civic and moral education we should be offering to young people as we approach the twenty-first century. To that extent at least, we should all be grateful to people like Dr Nicholas Tate, Chief Executive of the government's School Curriculum and Assessment Authority (hereafter SCAA), who has played an energetic and high-profile role in keeping questions about the state of the national culture, the moral health of the nation, etc. in the public eye.

TRADITION AND MODERNITY

How is our society changing as we approach the millennium and what are the implications of such changes for education? The essays in this book explore two contrasting kinds of answers to these questions. On the one hand, there is what I have already called 'declinism': the view that the pace and character of change is destabilizing society, contributing to a crisis of values, creating a situation in which a clear sense of identity becomes increasingly problematic as people lose their moral bearings and sense of direction. For supporters of this kind of analysis, the appropriate response is seen in terms of a clear 'need' to reassert *tradition* – and this is often linked to calls to revive a sense of pride in our *national* identity. The key terms are thus 'nation', 'heritage', 'tradition', and 'shared values'. A less familiar kind of analysis of what is happening to us and where we may be going has recently been developed by a number of sociologists who have for some time been interested in the phenomenon of 'modernity' – notably

Anthony Giddens in the UK and Ulrich Beck in Germany (see, for example, Giddens, 1992; Beck, 1992). In their view, economically affluent and technologically advanced societies right across the world are undergoing a transition from 'industrial' to 'post-industrial', from (mere) modernity to 'late modernity'. These changes are taking place in a context of increasing 'globalization', for example, in terms of the influence of multinational firms in manufacturing and commerce, the ever widening scope and power of global financial markets, the world-wide dissemination of 'Western' media and lifestyles, increasingly rapid global communications, etc.

Less obviously, but perhaps even more fundamentally, human *knowledge* is increasingly organized and disseminated in new ways. Most significantly, the knowledge initially generated by 'experts' of various kinds (scientists, the medical profession, the legal profession, dieticians, beauticians, therapists, even sociologists!) 'leaks' back into everyday life and is increasingly drawn upon by ordinary people attempting to make sense of their lives and the situations in which they find themselves. As a result, we all come to understand ourselves in new ways: we draw at second hand, as it were, upon an increasing range of (often competing) 'theories' to understand our problems and dilemmas. The availability of these ways of understanding ourselves opens up (at least to thought) wider horizons and possibilities than were even thinkable for previous generations. Not surprisingly, all of this is associated with an intensification of *individualism*. Each of us unavoidably faces a life of choices – choices which will affect the lives not only of ourselves but also of others (closer and more distant). And paradoxically, we are not free *not* to make choices: they are increasingly thrust upon us by the way society is organized. The counterpart of all this is that the grip of tradition is decisively weakened, as is the authority of localized and traditional cultures or subcultures and hence, also, the authority of traditional 'community leaders'. The other face of the process of ongoing modernization, then, is *detraditionalization* (see Heelas, Lash and Morris, 1996).[3]

It is tempting to think of the traditionalist analysis as pessimistic and the accounts of modernization as optimistic. To do so would, however, be over-simple. Traditionalists, after all, believe not only in the desirability but also the *possibility* of reclaiming and reinvigorating the traditional values and standards that, as they see it, are in danger of being lost. This is one reason why they are so inclined towards 'needs talk': the endless use of the would-be inclusive language of 'our' nation, 'our country's needs', 'our' schools , 'our' heritage, etc.[4] The analysts of late modernity on the other hand, despite the generally positive tone of their writing, draw attention to various problems which they see as part and parcel of the changes they describe. Most importantly, they are much preoccupied with the analysis of *risk* as a distinctive phenomenon of late modernity. This, very significantly, includes a range of risks that are generated by humanity itself rather than by nature. Among these are what Anthony Giddens calls 'high consequence risks' – like the dangers posed by nuclear weapons and nuclear power generation, or global warming, or oil spills. Risk, in this sense, is itself one of the things that has become increasingly globalized (see, for example, Giddens, 1990, esp. pp. 124–34). But no less significant, in the lives of ordinary individuals, are the risks that are inseparable from facing a life of unavoidable choices and calculations, for example: the uncertainties now surrounding marriage or cohabitation, the question of whether working to obtain a degree will really turn out to be worthwhile in the sense of ensuring access to the job market at an appropriate level, etc. The key issue at stake between these competing overall accounts of our current social predicament, then, is not one of an optimistic versus a pessimistic outlook. It is, simply, which of the two accounts is the more convincing?

STRUCTURE AND CONTENT

This book has been written intentionally as a set of separate but inter-linked essays dealing with a range of related topics.[5] It is therefore possible to read each chapter independently of the rest and in any order. The essays have, however, been grouped into two main sections and the book as a whole is designed to have an overall coherence and a developing line of argument.

Part One deals with the wider context – historically and socially, outlining and situating the competing analyses of contemporary social change discussed above. The first chapter focuses on the themes of nation, identity and alleged cultural crisis: it examines a range of criticisms of contemporary Britain expressed by writers associated with the Conservative New Right, and sets this against the background of a much longer and in many ways more self-consistent tradition of conservative cultural criticism which can be traced back at least to the eighteenth century. Certain enduring weaknesses in this whole corpus of writing are then analysed. The second chapter focuses more closely on claims and counter-claims about alleged *moral* decline in Britain today. A 'traditionalist' analysis of the country's current predicament is juxtaposed against a more developed discussion of Anthony Giddens' and Ulrich Beck's account of late modernity.

Part Two is concerned more directly with the school curriculum – and particularly with those aspects most commonly brought together in schools under titles like 'Personal and Social Education', 'Education for Citizenship', etc. – though its key focus is on moral and civic education in a changing society. What is offered is not a set of practical recipes. The aim, rather, is to stimulate fundamental *thinking* about the aims and changing social context of these curriculum areas. Almost everyone agrees (at least in theory) about their importance and contemporary relevance; nevertheless it is also widely, if tacitly, acknowledged that Personal and Social Education remains something of a Cinderella subject – indeed, according to a recent article by a *Guardian* educational correspondent, it is 'widely despised by pupils' (MacLeod, 1996, p. 8). Although issues of curriculum structure are very important in this broad area, the discussions in Part Two focus almost entirely on questions of aims, justification, and content. To a significant extent, these need to be clarified first – before issues of curriculum structure (which is in any case likely to vary considerably between schools) are addressed.

Part Two begins with a consideration of that fraught and perplexing domain commonly designated as 'the spiritual and the moral'. Following an analysis of the overlapping and confusing ways in which the term 'spiritual' has been used in recent debates, it is recommended that the term is, where possible, put aside as far as curriculum planning for moral and civic education is concerned. This is not, however, to seek to marginalize religious education: indeed, Chapter 3 contains a sustained critique of recent proposals by David Hargreaves that would have precisely this effect in mainstream schools (Hargreaves, 1994). Chapter 4 discusses moral education and civic education; it identifies a range of reasons why the two should be closely linked, even though the overall scope of moral education is far broader. Much of the discussion is concerned with an analysis of different positions within the broad area of liberal political theorizing. Although this initially sounds forbidding, clarification of issues here turns out to be essential if discussions about moral education are to proceed with clarity and candour. The chapter concludes with a critical examination of the proposals about values education put forward by the National Forum for Values in Education and the Community, which was established by SCAA in 1996. The more specifically *political* aspects of citizenship education are then examined in the following chapter. Here it is argued that citizenship as a *political* concept is 'essentially contested'; it therefore follows that schools cannot endorse any particular, fully developed view of citizenship, against any other. Education *for* citizenship, therefore, has significant limits; but one important task which remains for schools is to educate *about* citizenship, developing students' knowledge and understanding of the competing conceptions of citizenship on offer, as well as equipping them with a range of skills which might heighten their capacity to participate in 'political' processes – from the micro to the macro level. The concept of 'enterprise' is another area of contestation both within and beyond education. Chapter 6 explores some of the main dimensions of these debates, with particular reference to the role of the notion of 'enterprise culture' (and its counterpart 'dependency culture') in recent New Right thought and politics, both in this country and in the USA. The issues at stake in these debates raise fundamental questions relating precisely to competing conceptions of citizenship – and of moral responsibility – in a context of broader economic and political change. For these reasons, it is concluded that any simple notion of education *for* enterprise raises serious problems. The chapter also considers the impact of what is sometimes called the 'new managerialism' on the wider ethos of schools and other state-funded institutions, including its possible significance in the shaping of new understandings of professionalism – initially proposed by government agencies but now supported by a growing number of professionals themselves. All this is seen as having somewhat contradictory implications for the values and ethos of schools considered as 'communities'.

THE POLEMICS OF TRAVESTY?

The tone of the discussion in this book is in places somewhat polemical and occasionally adversarial. Most of the chapters begin by citing recent statements by high-profile individuals generally recognized as 'traditionalist' in outlook. Although the commentary which follows is often critical of the views expressed, it is important to stress that these opening statements are primarily intended as points of departure for what is, hopefully, constructively critical dialogue. Because of the position he has occupied, it has been impossible to ignore the many public pronouncements by Dr Nicholas Tate – concerning matters such as the state of our national culture, the crisis in public and private morality, etc. It is, therefore, worth noting that Dr Tate has, when referring to his critics, several times warned against what he has called 'the polemics of travesty', and he has recommended, as a basis for constructive debate, 'the principle of charity' proposed by the philosopher Donald Davidson:

> By this, one responds to points of view with which one disagrees by saying: 'This sounds like someone who is trying to get at the truth. I can't understand why they are taking up this position. But let's assume they are rational. Let's listen to their reasons. Then I can decide whether our views really are incompatible and, if they are, which of us is right.' (Tate, 1996c, p. 18)

I hope that, in some measure at least, the spirit of this approach is preserved in the arguments developed in this book.[6] In the present circumstances of educational policy debate, however, *some* element of polemic is neither misplaced nor unjustified. The most recent Conservative administration presided over by John Major (to say nothing of the preceding years of Thatcherite rule) was not notable for encouraging open, reasoned, public debate about education. Indeed, at virtually every opportunity, vigorous attempts have been made to exclude dissenting voices and to belittle competing ideas rather than to engage with them seriously. Ever since 1979, the usual recourse has been to what Stephen Ball has aptly called 'discourses of derision' (Ball, 1990). And more recently, to take just one example, Her Majesty's Chief Inspector of Schools, Chris Woodhead, has seemed not merely to be deaf to those whose views differ from his own but increasingly to revel in a posture of intransigence. Apparently troubled by no doubts, his manner with those who oppose him has seemed to many observers arrogantly dismissive. In his Second Annual Lecture as Chief Inspector, for instance, he announced that criticism is the sincerest form of flattery, commenting that: 'the more intense the criticism, the more vociferous the cries that we have compromised our independence, the more confident I will be that we are, as the Citizen's Charter put it, in touch with the interests of the people who use the service' (quoted in Gardiner, 1996, p. 3). In a context in which the heads of the new educational quangos have been given extensive executive powers to implement major policy changes, sometimes of a highly controversial and debatable character, certainty of this order is deeply disturbing.

Within teacher education, to take another area where similar processes are operating, those forms of educational theory with the potential to be critical of the *status quo* have been largely 'written out' of the professional preparation of new teachers. Again, one main reason seems to be an ideological determination to silence possible dissent. As a result, those entering the profession are not receiving the kind of grounding in the appropriate concepts or relevant empirical evidence which would equip them to engage seriously with debates about values, culture, morality, religion, politics and citizenship. In some cases, students' first degree studies will provide some of these foundations; but in other cases not at all. Young teachers as a whole are thus increasingly poorly educated in these matters – which is not a criticism of the teachers but of some aspects of the way in which their training has been restructured.[7] It is ironic indeed that in the very article in which he complained about his own views being travestied, Nicholas Tate should have written: 'bad "theory" has been allowed to discredit the place of ideas in teacher-training for far too long' (op. cit.). The term 'bad' here, however, seems to be no more than a device to marginalize (and dare one say travesty) those forms of theory of which Dr Tate disapproves. While it is indeed right, therefore, to take seriously his admonition that polemic should not go so far as to travesty the arguments which it opposes, nevertheless, vigorous and sometimes polemical engagement can be exactly what the situation calls for. Ever since the publication of the first *Black Paper on Education* (Cox and Dyson, 1969), the traditional Conservative right has, after all, conducted its own campaigns precisely through highly polemical pamphleteering, often with the less than impartial participation of powerful sections of the mass media. There is, therefore, a clear need at present for left-leaning polemical writing, a need which has been heightened as 'New Labour' seeks in various respects to outdo the Conservative Party in calculated populism and competition for the 'middle ground' of British politics. Really gifted polemicists like the late and great E. P. Thompson are sorely missed (see, for example, Thompson, 1980).

NOTES

1   It needs to be emphasized that this was not simply an issue of failing to relate theory to classroom practice – a criticism which has arguably been *over*stated. The value of educational theory in the preparation of teachers as members of a profession is by no means limited to its immediate classroom relevance – contrary to much contemporary rhetoric. A properly educated teaching profession needs to be better equipped to think seriously about a much wider range of issues than those centred on classroom competence – not least those which are the focus of this book: civic, moral and social education.

2   What is *truly* simplistic, of course, is to tell teachers that all they need is common sense and a 'mastery' of practical competencies.

3   It is important to appreciate that the processes of detraditionalization do not involve an all-round diminution in the significance of *ritual* in social life. In certain areas, new secular rituals may be developed – around sport, popular music, politics, etc. But such modern rituals are not vehicles for the authority of tradition, nor are their essential mechanisms those associated with ritual in *traditional* contexts (see Giddens, 1994).

An arresting *contemporary* example which vividly catches something of the essence of how ritual works within a framework of traditional beliefs and assumptions, is the following passage from Jeanette Winterson's novel *Oranges Are Not the Only Fruit*:

> The priest has a book with words set out. Old words, known words, words of power. Words that are always on the surface. Words for every occasion. The words work. They do what they're supposed to do; comfort and discipline. (Winterson, 1991, p. 157)

4   Prominent exponents of 'needs talk' in the UK are the members of that Holy Trinity of 'educational eminences' who have advised recent governments about the curriculum and assessment: Sir Ron Dearing (the government's chief curriculum adviser), Chris Woodhead (Her Majesty's Chief Inspector of Schools) and Nicholas Tate (the chief executive of SCAA). In much of their public discourse, rhetorical reiteration of a language of 'our needs', 'our civilization', 'our schools', etc. is used not only as a substitute for reasoned argument but also to conceal the actually controversial content or implications of many of the claims being made. For example:

(a) Sir Ron Dearing introducing a SCAA conference on spiritual and moral development:
'I wanted to hold this symposium because, like many other people, I have some deep concerns about the way our civilization is going...
It requires only a little evil to hurt and change the whole quality of our civilization...
In this our civilization has visibly decayed. And there is no more central need in a civilization than the safety of the individual member going about her, or his, affairs. Fundamentally, that is the greatest need we all have from a civilization...'
(Dearing, 1996)

(b) The conclusion to Chris Woodhead's well known 'Politea' pamphlet *A Question of Standards*:

'To return to the substantive question of what we want from our schools and colleges: the aspirations that we have for our children . . .'

(Woodhead, 1995a, p. 18)

(c) A paragraph from one of Nicholas Tate's conference papers on Spiritual and Moral Aspects of the Curriculum:

'As a society we no longer have this framework, at least in a form readily accessible to most people. We lack the everyday moral language that traditionally helped to maintain a moral structure to our lives . . . there is no doubt that we have lost the robust intellectual basis for our [sic] moral life we once had.'

(Tate, 1996a, para. 13 and para. 26)

5 An earlier version of Chapter 1 was published in the *Cambridge Journal of Education* (J. Beck, 1996a) and a version of Chapter 5 appeared in *Curriculum Studies* (J. Beck, 1996b).

6 As a further safeguard against misrepresentation, I have, at several points in the book, deliberately chosen to make use of *extensive quotation* from writers whose ideas I am discussing – particularly where I am taking issue with the views expressed. Such sources are fully documented so that the interested reader may pursue the arguments further.

In the light of all this, it is a little disappointing to discover that Dr Tate does not always live up to the standards which he so earnestly recommends to others. Quite by accident, it came to my attention that in a speech to the Independent Schools Association on 11 October 1996, Dr Tate had cheerfully ridiculed an extract from an article of mine published in the *Cambridge Journal of Education*. The article in question (as indicated in note 5 above) appears in a modified form as Chapter 1 of this present book and the specific passage can be found on pp. 19–20: it comprises the whole of paragraph (c) except the final sentence. The matter was brought to my attention by Chris Benfield, a reporter on the *Yorkshire Post* who had published an account of Dr Tate's talk and who had the decency to contact me to see if I wished to respond (Benfield, 1996a). Subsequently, I obtained from the SCAA Press Office a copy of the speech in question. Dr Tate's method is instructive – at least for those interested in the finer points of the polemics of travesty! Without either having the courtesy to obtain my agreement and without identifying me as the writer, he read out the extract (taken out of context from a 12,000-word article) and rubbished it as a piece of incomprehensible and educationally irresponsible jargon: 'I hope you followed that. I didn't . . . Come again! I have read it five times and I am none the wiser . . . etc.' (Tate, 1996e, pp. 7–8). He then went on to similarly attack the work of 'another teacher trainer' (also anonymous), and concluded:

> I could go on. My point is that many of these intellectuals are letting us down. Instead of getting to grips with the issues facing hardworking teachers, they are engaging in self-regarding activities of the kind I have illustrated. I do not wish to disparage ideas. Far from it. But ideas need to be comprehensible. They also need to be harnessed in support of the kind of social reality the rest of us can feel committed to spending our short lives trying to promote – rather than the pipe dreams of Left Bank deconstructionists. (ibid., pp. 8–9)

My point is this. Not only is Dr Tate's posture of indignation on behalf of 'hardworking teachers' thoroughly unconvincing but his entire *modus operandi* in this instance is disappointing – particularly in the light of his own warnings about the polemics of travesty. Academic writing of the kind being discussed here is not intended for reading aloud at public school conferences and the like. It is designed primarily for an academic readership – as well as for a wider audience which is prepared to engage seriously with unfamiliar ideas. Belittling 'theorists' for employing the specialist languages of their disciplines is a trick as familiar as it is cheap – and it completely fails to advance constructive dialogue. Similarly, to simply disparage poststructuralism and postmodernism contributes nothing to serious debate. In any case (as any impartial reader of Chapter 1 will discover), the overall stance of the chapter is not one which by any means endorses a postmodernist stance – 'Left Bank' or otherwise.

7   These observations should not be construed as a wholesale condemnation of recent developments in initial teacher-training. Good-quality partnership schemes between schools and higher education have, in important ways, significantly improved many aspects of teacher-training courses. Moreover, teachers in higher education and in schools have derived mutual benefit from the closer contacts and collaboration involved. Many students on such courses express high levels of satisfaction. However, there is no *necessity* for good school-based (as opposed to school-centred) initial teacher-training to be thorough-goingly anti-theoretical – though constraints on time constitute a serious problem.

Part One
Tradition and Change:
Is Britain in Cultural and Moral Decline?

Chapter 1

A Nation in Decline? The Limitations of Conservative Cultural Pessimism

INTRODUCTION

The proposals of the final Dearing Report leading to the introduction in September 1995 of the Revised National Curriculum proved to be a stimulus to a further round of debate about the wider purposes of the school curriculum in England and Wales. Two aspects of Dearing's proposals were particularly significant in this respect; first, the radical slimming down of the statutory requirements at Key Stage 4 and second, the 20 per cent of time at Key Stages 1 to 3 which (at least officially) was allocated for individual schools to determine their own curricular priorities.

On a single day in July 1995, the national press, radio and television carried reports of high-profile interventions seeking to influence schools in shaping these priorities. On the one hand, powerful voices from the vocationalist lobbies continued the process of making more concrete the somewhat tentative proposals in the final Dearing Report, for occupational and vocational 'pathways' for some school students from age 14 onwards (Dearing, 1994, pp. 27–49). Sir Ron Dearing himself unveiled his interim report outlining a new framework of courses and qualifications for education and training for all 16 to 19-year-olds – aimed at achieving the national targets for education and training for the year 2000 set out in the Competitiveness White Paper *Forging Ahead*. And in an initiative clearly timed to coincide with this, Gillian Shephard, who had been recently confirmed in her new role as Minister of the new combined Department for Education and Employment, announced plans for taking a minority of pupils out of full-time education at the age of 14 and providing them with new-style 'apprenticeships': 'there is a case for having closer integration and more workplace-based education for certain groups of young people if, thereby, we can avoid demotivation and do something useful for employers at the same time; I believe we can be quite radical in the sorts of programme we offer from 14 onwards' (*The Times*, 19 July 1995).

On the same day, most newspapers as well as the BBC's *Today* programme carried reports of a speech delivered some days previously by Dr Nicholas Tate to a gathering of headteachers. Perhaps with an eye on the publicity likely to be given to the new vocational initiatives, Dr Tate suggested that in addition to economic ends, there were other and perhaps even more important purposes which a national curriculum should serve:

> As a nation, we spend a lot of public money on education and tend to see it in terms of developing individuals' life chances and the country's economic competitiveness. If we included other fundamental purposes such as the transmission of our culture and social cohesiveness, we would end up with a very different national curriculum. (*Daily Telegraph*, 19 July 1995)

The element in Dr Tate's speech which proved controversial was that he explicitly linked these themes of culture and social cohesion to the idea that the curriculum should foster a clear sense of *British* cultural identity, and he indicated that it was a mistake to respond to cultural diversity with 'some kind of watered down multi-culturalism' – provoking headlines such as 'Curriculum chief backs Britishness' (*Daily Telegraph*, 19 July 1995) and 'Teach children to be British idea stirs up a storm' (*Guardian*, 19 July 1995). Dr Tate, who 'appeared to be taken aback by the reaction', was, when interviewed, at pains to emphasize that he was 'not suggesting for a moment that the different ethnic and cultural identities that pupils have should be neglected'; indeed, he stressed, 'they should be respected' (ibid.). Nevertheless, he did quite clearly stand by his basic view that 'the teaching of the majority culture, with the emphasis on the English language, English history and literary heritage, and the study of Christianity and the classical world' were 'at the heart of our common culture and our national identity' and should be a central part of the education offered to all pupils in order 'to develop a sense of where they are as people living in Britain' (ibid.).

Dr Tate's surprise at the vehemence of the reaction is perhaps more understandable once one appreciates that there was actually nothing new in all this. A year earlier, at the time when SCAA was launching the consultation exercise on the revised National Curriculum proposals, he had rehearsed very similar ideas in an article in the *Times Educational Supplement*, where he compared English lack of cultural confidence in these respects with the situation in France 'where the national curriculum is explicitly designed as a way of maintaining unity within an increasingly diverse society' (*Times Educational Supplement*, 29 July 1994). In this article, he had decisively stated, in terms strikingly similar to his 1995 speech, that:

> [T]he SCAA recommendations come off the fence on this issue. The proposals for British history, standard English and the English literary heritage are designed to reinforce a common culture. A national curriculum, we imply, is more than just a recipe for meeting economic needs, vital though these are; it is more than just the means to facilitate the infinitely varied life choices of collections of isolated individuals. It also plays a key part in helping society maintain its identity. (ibid.)

Not only, then, were such views not novel in 1995, but the basic ideas which Dr Tate was seeking to promote amount to little more than a reiteration (in rather moderate terms) of some of the core arguments of the mainstream of the neo-conservative wing of the New Right – thinking which has had wide currency and no little influence on curriculum debates in the UK since at least the publication of the first *Black Paper on Education* (Cox and Dyson, 1969) – and in some respects for very much longer than that. Moreover, this corpus of thought and writing, in its popular and polemical as well as its more scholarly forms, has been subjected to extensive critical commentary and analysis during this same period (see, for example: Ball, 1990; Donald, 1992; Gilroy, 1987 and 1992; Jones, 1989; Lawton, 1994; Whitty, 1990). In the light of such extensive analysis, one might well ask: 'Is there more to be said?' Perhaps there is, or at least it may be said rather differently.

The tradition of neo-conservative writing which Dr Tate's remarks represent, typically identifies certain kinds of inter-dependencies between five main elements:

- nation
- culture
- identity (individual and collective)
- social cohesion
- educational curricula.

However, both in neo-conservative writing itself and in critical commentary upon it, these elements and the relationships posited between them are rarely analysed *systematically*. More commonly, neo-conservative writers tend to presume (or to assert) that these elements are all mutually interdependent (not least because such writers tend to conceive of a healthy state of culture and society in terms of some kind of integrated and organic whole), while critics of such writing, for all their perceptiveness, often focus upon particular *aspects* of these posited interconnections – often because the primary focus of much of this critical work is the analysis of specific policy developments (such as the introduction of the National Curriculum) and/or the discussion of specific and currently controversial issues (such as anti-racism). Thus, for example, although references to nation, national identity, Britishness, English culture, national heritage, Britain's imperial past and neo-colonial present, etc. are ubiquitous, relatively little has been written which connects these debates systematically to analyses of the nature of nations and of nationalism as general phenomena. This essay will attempt a highly preliminary sketch – which will seek to identify some of the main questions which a somewhat more systematic examination of these issues would need to address. In the course of the discussion, various lines of critique of neo-conservative assertions and argument will be developed and discussed.

NATIONS, NATIONALISM AND SOCIAL COHESION

Nation and nationalism are contested, perhaps even 'essentially contested' concepts. In much recent writing, particularly in the fields of education and cultural studies, Benedict Anderson's notion of nations as 'imagined communities' has been very influential (Anderson, 1983; and see, for a critical discussion in relation to the concept of racism, Gilroy, 1987, pp. 44–6). For our purposes, however, Ernest Gellner's examination of these concepts in *Nations and Nationalism* (Gellner, 1983) is particularly pertinent, not least because of the interconnections it makes between the emergence of successful nationalisms, the imposition of a 'high' (literate) culture, the development of a centralized educational system within a defined (national) territory, and the role of this educationally transmitted culture in holding together the atomized individual members of impersonal modern societies. These, of course, are also in a sense the themes of much neo-conservative writing. However, Gellner's analysis is developed on the basis of assumptions which are significantly different. Whereas neo-conservative thinking tends to be backward-looking, seeing national identity and social cohesion as depending essentially on the effective transmission and internalization of a set of extensively shared cultural *beliefs and values* as well as meanings inherited from the past, Gellner focuses upon a literate culture primarily as an indispensable means of *communication* – required first and foremost for the effective functioning and administration of modern, industrial (or industrializing) economies and polities. Such a culture does indeed confer membership and a necessary minimum of identity, perhaps most significantly in relation to other nations, but it does not imply the existence of nor the necessity for a powerful and extensive central value system: Gellner's analysis may in a sense be functionalist – but it is not a species of normative functionalism.

> Industrial society... has engendered a new *kind* of division of labour: one requiring the men [sic] taking part in it to be ready to move from one occupational position to another, even within a single life-span, and certainly between generations. They need a shared culture, and a literate sophisticated high culture at that. It obliges them to be able to communicate contextlessly and with precision with all comers, in face-to-face ephemeral contacts, but also through abstract means of communication... The maintenance of this kind of inescapably high (because literate) culture required protection by a state, a centralised order-enforcing agency...
>
> In general, each such state presides over, maintains, and is identified with, one kind of culture, one style of communication, which prevails within its borders and is dependent for its perpetuation on a centralised educational system supervised by and often actually run by the state in question, which monopolises legitimate culture almost as much as it does legitimate violence, and perhaps more so. (ibid., pp. 141 and 140)

Thus, on Gellner's analysis, the emergence of nations occurs in the context of modernization, when predominantly agrarian and localized societies, with 'a complex structure of local groups, each sustained by folk cultures reproduced locally by the micro-groups themselves', face economic and other pressures which act as stimuli to create more inclusive forms of cultural organization as well as more impersonal forms of social organization. The nationalisms that emerge, Gellner suggests, commonly represent themselves as the assertion of 'the pristine, vigorous life' of the people (the *Volk*). But the national culture which actually emerges is emphatically not a simple continuation of one of these local folk cultures; rather, a successful nationalism 'revives, or invents, a local high (literate, specialist-transmitted) culture of its own', albeit one which draws selectively on earlier folk styles, dialects, and other traditions: 'it was the great ladies at the Budapest Opera who really went to town in peasant dresses, or dresses claimed to be such' (ibid., p. 57). A national culture of this kind does confer a sense of collective distinctiveness and self-recognition upon its members and this is of crucial yet limited significance; but these individuals are also and necessarily members of societies characterized by a high degree of anonymity and impersonality as opposed to community (*Gemeinschaft*). Gellner notes that in societies which have successfully become nation states, it is this national culture and not community which 'provides the inner sanctions' – but he adds somewhat sardonically: 'such as they are'! (ibid., p. 140). A national culture transmitted in part through centralized educational institutions is then, on this kind of analysis, not *principally* significant as a source of collective identity and social cohesion – even though it plays an irreducible part in this respect. A *functioning* national culture including the maintenance of social stability and a non-precarious sense of national identity is, especially in contemporary advanced societies, entirely compatible with a significant degree of pluralism at the level of beliefs and values in many respects, and with a considerable diversity of self-identifications (in terms of religious, sexual, ethnic and other identities) on the part of individuals and groups within these societies.[1]

Neo-conservative thinking, however, characteristically asserts the opposite; this has nowhere been clearer than in discussions since the 1960s of the 'threat' to social cohesion and national identity posed by the presence in Britain of culturally 'alien' minorities (who also happen to be conspicuous on account of their 'racial' difference). A classic statement of such thinking was Enoch Powell's attempt in 1968 to draw a sharp distinction between the legal status of citizenship and 'true' belonging within a national culture: 'the West Indian does not, by being born in England, become an Englishman; in law, he becomes a United Kingdom citizen by birth; in fact he is a West Indian or an Asian still' (Powell in Gilroy, 1987, p. 46). In similar vein, attacking local education authority policies of anti-racism and multicultural education in the 1980s, members of the influential neo-conservative 'think tank' the Hillgate Group asserted that nothing was more important than to 'reconcile our (ethnic) minorities, to integrate them into our national culture, and to ensure a common political loyalty independent of race, creed or colour' (Hillgate, 1987, p. 4). Ten years before this, the last of the Black Papers on education had contained an even more highly coloured diagnosis of the dangers that could be expected to result from the undermining of the stable transmission of 'our' culture by cultural pluralism – especially when endorsed by fashionable liberal relativism. Edward Norman, then Dean of Peterhouse College, Cambridge, warned: 'the values of this country are under threat; society discloses advanced symptoms of moral collapse ... a great moral chaos will accumulate within a few decades if the whole absurdity is allowed to go on that long' (Norman, 1977, p. 103). As this writer saw it, the existence of a diversity of faiths in Britain, associated with the presence of ethnic minorities from the Caribbean and the Indian subcontinent, had been seized upon by the religious education 'establishment' as a pretext to endorse a trendy form of multi-faith RE whose aim was to substitute for the authoritative transmission of the Christian religion and its moral teachings the 'exploration' by young people of the beliefs of major world faiths and also of various 'non-religious stances for living', the aim being to equip young people to arrive at reasoned choices among this diversity of beliefs and lifestyles. In Norman's opinion, the influence of such pernicious doctrines could lead only to 'moral anarchy' (ibid., p. 101). Norman's analysis is of continuing interest and relevance in that it displays two contradictory characteristics which can be found more widely in recent neo-conservative cultural criticism. There is, on the one hand (even for work that is avowedly polemical), a tendency greatly to exaggerate the threat to cultural transmission and social cohesion. As Bridges has pointed out, the arguments of such writers are often greatly weakened by a tendency for their polemics to be directed against 'the most extreme instances (their) reading and imagination can muster' (Bridges, 1986, p. 23). On the other hand and contradictorily, there is a desire on the part of many neo-conservative analysts to insist that these relativizing and subversive forces are *not* fundamentally characteristic of English society and culture:

For England is *not* a pluralistic society, except in a most qualified sense . . . Children don't naturally reject inherited values: they are being taught to think like that . . . Working-class and lower-middle-class society shows few signs of religious or moral diversity . . . A large majority of parents . . . expect their children to be taught Christianity in schools. (ibid., p. 100)

As Ken Jones has demonstrated (Jones, 1989, pp. 44–5), Norman in this way managed to deny that the moral crisis, for all its alleged seriousness, was fundamental. Rather, it resulted from a hopefully temporary interruption to the orderly transmission of traditional values and beliefs – and there was reason to believe that this could be reversed: 'in the end, perhaps, it will be possible still to count on the values of the home winning against the influence of the teachers of morals' (Norman, op. cit., p. 104). The cause of the crisis, Norman argued, was the influence of a national intelligentsia (including leading churchmen and theologians) which had lost its nerve and also lost touch with ordinary people: 'Society discloses advanced symptoms of moral collapse as the opinions of the intelligentsia seep downwards. Nations of high morale and with confidence in their values never allow children to "choose" their "stance for living"' (ibid., p. 103).

For neo-conservatives, the attractions of a *trahison des clercs* thesis are considerable. Insofar as a contemporary crisis in the kinds of moral and cultural authority which neo-conservatives champion can be attributed to a temporary aberration, then the essential underlying continuities of the culture can seem both strong and capable of recovery. Indeed, the neo-conservatives' programmatic aim of extending their control over educational curricula (as in their campaigns to influence the National Curriculum) can only appear viable as a mechanism of cultural restoration insofar as current challenges to 'traditional' beliefs and values can, with *some* degree of plausibility, be represented as relatively short-lived and pathological episodes in an underlying narrative in which cultural continuities persist. (Margaret Thatcher's demonization of 'the sixties' as a decade of pathological permissiveness performed a somewhat similar role in relation to the project of reasserting so-called Victorian values in the 1980s.)

Convinced neo-conservative thinkers and writers appear to have an abiding need for this kind of ideological comfort. Margaret Thatcher herself, as an ambitious and pragmatic politician, may or may not have been taken in by her own racist rhetoric in her television interview prior to the 1979 general election when she stated that: 'people are really rather afraid that the country might be rather swamped by people of a different culture; . . . and if there is any fear that it might be swamped, people are going to react and to be rather hostile to those coming in' (Thatcher in Hardy and Vieler-Porter, 1990, p. 196). But serious neo-conservatives do appear to take it as axiomatic that a democratic society cannot maintain social cohesion or stability unless that society is integrated around an authoritatively transmitted national culture which enshrines a set of common beliefs and values. According to Sir Keith Joseph, for example, one of the most important reasons why all pupils should study history in schools was so that they should 'understand the development of the shared values which are a distinctive feature of British society and culture and which continue to shape private attitudes and public policy' (Joseph, 1984).

NON-NORMATIVE SOURCES OF SOCIAL INTEGRATION

Yet, as many other writers have persuasively contended, such beliefs border on the metaphysical. The sociologist John Thompson, for example, has pointed out that this view of shared values as a kind of indispensable social cement which stabilizes society by binding its members together is highly questionable:

> There is little evidence to suggest that certain values and beliefs are shared by all (or even most) members of modern industrial societies. Moreover, there is little reason to suppose that the stability of complex industrial societies requires or depends upon a consensus concerning particular values and norms. Insofar as societies are 'stable' social orders, this stability could just as easily be the outcome of a diversity of values and beliefs, a proliferation of divisions between individuals and groups, a lack of consensus at the very point where oppositional attitudes might be translated into political action. (Thompson, 1990, p. 8)

To elaborate briefly:

(a) Social institutions have powerful non-normative means of securing their own reproduction: industrial and commercial organizations, for example, have definite legal and political as well as economic conditions of existence. Such institutions also wield impressive power which very effectively constrains the actions of individuals and groups – whether as employees limiting their trade union militancy for fear that new investment will be channelled elsewhere, or as consumers whose 'free choices' are structured and sometimes even manipulated from boardrooms in Tokyo or New York or the City of London, etc.

(b) The remarkable orderliness of quite ordinary, everyday social interaction does not rest primarily on a sharing of *values*. As ethnomethodologists demonstrated in the 1960s, such orderliness is indeed a kind of miracle – and it is dependent upon deeply taken-for-granted 'trust' and 'background expectancies'. (Harold Garfinkel brought these hidden sources of stability and predictability to light – for example, by encouraging his students to engage in calculated acts of *disruption* of these expectancies – such as trying to haggle over the price of toothpaste at a super-market checkout! (Garfinkel, 1967).) These everyday performances, moreover, are *active* accomplishments, always potentially open to modification and innovation, whereas theories of normative order tend to depict individuals as essentially passive – waiting (and *needing* as a guarantee of their psychic integration) to internalize society's core values and beliefs.

(c) Social action and interaction is, of course, to a significant degree shaped and even determined by a whole range of *discourses* which are part of cultural experience. However, such discourses (as well as the institutional practices associated with them) are not unified, nor are they ultimately traceable or reducible to some 'core' of fundamental common beliefs. Quite the contrary: they are multiple and in many ways contradictory. The writings of Michel Foucault have been of decisive importance in demonstrating the ever-widening significance of the discursive regulation of social action and individual identity in modern societies (for example, Foucault, 1972 and 1976; see also Fairclough, 1992, ch. 2). The work he has inspired is, however, in important respects different from theories which employ the concepts of normative order or (at least in some instances) dominant ideology. In particular, although, for

Foucault, discourses create regimes of 'truth', and although they do not merely regulate but in important ways actually *constitute* social subjects, the power exercised through them has no unified location or basis. It is not the property of any social class, nor are discourses a set of instruments which can be appropriated by (or work in the interests of) any one section of society. Rather, power is capillary; it 'has the character of a network; its threads extend everywhere' (Sarup, 1993, p. 74). As a result, the 'subject positions' which this multiplicity of dispersed, de-centralized discourses creates are inevitably *contradictory* to some degree. These contradictions are one key source of change and challenge to those discourses which may be dominant in particular parts of society at particular times. It follows that for poststructuralist analysis, there can be no subjectivity *outside* of these multiple discourses – and therefore no access to a human subjectivity which is the ultimate author of its 'own' acts. Our actions are the products of processes much less unified and much more contradictory than any theory of internalization of a system of common values would suggest.

There are, then, many reasons for scepticism when faced with assertions that a nation's social cohesion and stability, let alone its moral 'health', will be imperilled if its educational institutions fail to transmit effectively a clear sense of that nation's common cultural heritage and shared values.[2] To recognize this, however, does not involve denying that historically it has very often been the case that national educational systems and their curricula *have* served as powerful ideological mechanisms in the definition and maintenance of highly selective (and often self-serving) representations of national culture and an associated sense of national identity. There have been and there continue to be vigorous and sometimes bitter struggles to define and control definitions of national identity and culture, and to enshrine them in schools and elsewhere. Raymond Williams' concept of the 'selective tradition' (Williams, 1961, pp. 67–76), with its central insight that 'we tend to underestimate the extent to which the cultural tradition is not only a selection but also an interpretation' (ibid., p. 69), has been a particularly powerful influence upon historical and sociological studies of curricular knowledge, since at least the emergence of the 'new sociology of education' in the early 1970s (Young, 1971). Subsequent work has, however, problematized some of the most basic assumptions of a proportion of this research, in particular, its tendency to employ undifferentiated notions of an essential national culture and to regard school curricula and texts as 'expressions' of such a culture, also its conceptualization of children as passive individuals who are unproblematically socialized into internalizing the hegemonic values and representations of a culture of this nature (see Ahier, 1988, pp. 6–8). Introducing his own study of the significance for national identity of elementary/primary school history and geography textbooks which were in use in England in the period from 1850 to 1960, John Ahier set out an alternative approach which highlights the problematic and always incomplete character of even very persistent educational endeavours concerned with the constitution of a sense of national identity in children:

> Instead of assuming that a psychologically and socially undifferentiated child-reader imbibes such a national world view, this (study) tries to suggest an ideological labouring of national construction, an ever-problematic enterprise of locating children and readers within the territory and boundaries of the nation-state. Instead of the idea that children become socialised into the (in this case) ruralist values of the state the suggestion here is

that some readers may 'find themselves', either within the national chronologies of the history books, or within the maps of the homeland in the geography texts, *and others may not.* (ibid., p. 8, my italics)

Ahier's conclusion reinforces the point: 'the texts … did not exist as expressions of some *previous* national culture, but as attempts to project or construct that upon which the whole enterprise of universal state schooling and its textbooks depended, i.e. an *assumption* that there was a naturally integrated distinct people existing within given boundaries' (ibid., p. 175, my italics). This advice surely points the way towards more profitable research. Instead of lamenting (with certain neo-conservatives) the supposed dissolution of the national culture as expressed in the school curriculum, or deploring (with certain industrialists and politicians[3]) the supposed *power* of this same curriculum to continue to transmit an anti-industrial, gentlemanly and quintessentially English culture imbued with the values of anti-urbanism and rural nostalgia, it might be more profitable to explore the more complex and interesting questions which work like Ahier's proposes. One aspect of this, for example, is to examine the interdependence between particular historical representations of the nation, its past and its place in the world and the *pedagogic* conventions and discourses of the same historical period (ibid., esp. ch. 2).

'BRITISHNESS' AND NATIONALISM

Finally, what of the kinds of feeling about nation and culture conjured up by the term 'nationalism'? The formation of most nations was accompanied by various complex combinations of spontaneous and incited expressions of popular feeling around potent symbols which came to express the identity of the new nation. Such symbols could be historically deep-rooted or they could be highly synthetic: in suitable circumstances either could be sufficiently potent. In some cases, successful assertions of nationhood involved the overthrow (at least politically) of external (sometimes imperial or colonial) oppressors. Whatever the mechanisms in particular cases, on Gellner's analysis, the development of 'a world in which national identity … took precedence over the many other historical forms of allegiance or communal feeling' was inevitable and universal – 'a necessary condition of tolerable modernization' as the tide of modernization swept the world (Nairn, 1988, pp. 129–30). For a particular stage of its development, the world has been, as it were, condemned to nationalism, though it is possible that this epoch is now approaching its end as certain kinds of supra-national developments, organizations and perhaps identifications become more significant – notwithstanding the development in the late twentieth century of what Hobsbawm terms an 'ethnic identity politics' whose tragedy was 'that it could not possibly work' (Hobsbawm, 1994, ch. 19).

The peculiar character of *British* nationalism has been interminably analysed and debated. Moreover, the awkward and inauthentic feel of 'Briton' and 'Britishness' as terms with which UK citizens can comfortably identify has been often remarked upon. Tom Nairn cites Fowler's *Dictionary of Modern English Usage* to illustrate this point: 'it must be remembered that no Englishman, or perhaps no Scotsman even, calls himself a Briton without a sneaking sense of the ludicrous, or hears himself referred to as a

Britisher without squirming' (Fowler in Nairn, 1988, p. 176). The language of this example of 'modern usage' may be pre-feminist but it does substantiate the long-standing awkwardness of 'Britishness' used in these ways. National identifications which feel subjectively authentic, insofar as they remain significant to modern UK citizens at all, are more likely to relate to the component (or competing?) UK nationalisms of Scottish, Welsh and English[4] – while the one remaining *British* identification which remains strong – that of a diminishing band of Northern Irish unionists[5] – now constitutes a source of irritation (as well as deep concern) to many other UK citizens – and an embarrassment to a growing section of the English Conservative Party.

A somewhat similar ambivalence about speaking of nationalism in so many words is detectable also in the work of many neo-conservative writers. For all their rallying cries to be more like the French in unashamedly emphasizing national identity and culture within the curriculum, such writers fight shy of actually calling for a strengthening of nationalist sentiment. The reasons for this are perhaps not far to seek. The language of nationalism can, in our times, hardly help but sound divisive: we live in a century in which nationalism has taken and is still taking pathological, even monstrous, forms. 'Ethnic cleansing' is but the latest and widely publicized euphemism for genocide carried out in the name of national self-assertion. Who therefore, in our time, could explicitly advocate teaching children to be nationalistic? One of the virtues (and vices) of the wonderfully elastic word 'culture' is that it can serve as a coded means of saying the otherwise nearly unsayable. In a similar way, Paul Gilroy and others have argued that in the 1980s Britain saw the emergence of a 'new racism' which links a range of discourses including those of Englishness, Britishness, patriotism, xenophobia to give 'race' a new contemporary meaning: 'these themes combine to provide a *definition of 'race' in terms of culture and identity*' (Gilroy, 1987, p. 43, my italics). Mrs Thatcher's reference, quoted earlier, to 'people' (implicitly *white* people) being fearful of being 'rather swamped by people of a different *culture*' (implicitly *black* people) was a particularly blatant instance of the use of such ostensibly deracialized discourse for clearly racist purposes.

NATIONAL CULTURE AND IDENTITY IN CONSERVATIVE CULTURAL CRITICISM

Another writer who sought to define 'our National Character' by making connections to a highly selective reading of aspects of the national culture and its past was Stanley Baldwin. According to Bill Schwartz, Baldwin was at pains to avoid creating what he termed, in a very revealing phrase, 'an ugly nationalism' and preferred to appeal instead to what he saw fit to call 'the natural devotion to the land and people of one's birth' (Baldwin in Schwartz, 1984, p. 14). Schwartz demonstrates that this construction of nation and culture not only depended on an unquestioned racism ('it was, by definition, white and superior'), it also 'wove together a highly particular reading of English literature, history and geography' (ibid., p. 14). For Baldwin, the greatness of the most important English writers resulted, in part at least, from their ear for the language of the ordinary people. In a passage of characteristic nostalgia for the supposed loss of the organic society of localized communities which allegedly produced such writers, he wrote:

> I regret that the dialects have gone, and I regret that by a process which for want of a better name we have agreed among ourselves to call education, we are drifting away from the language of the people, and losing some of the best English words and phrases which have lasted in this country through the centuries, to make us talk one uniform and inexpressive language. (ibid., p. 14)

In Baldwin's case, this very familiar rural retrospect for a social order seen as only just, within living memory, having been finally lost (see Williams, 1973, esp. ch. 2) was accompanied by another tendency in which (in Schwartz's words) he 'ultimately transposed history to the *natural* world, eternalising the ideology of Englishness' through inordinately detailed images of unchanging rural landscapes (ibid., p. 15, my italics), and further naturalizing the English character by means of appeals to allegedly innate (albeit also culturally inherited) characteristics of 'our English race':

> [N]othing can be more touching than to see how the working man and woman after generations in the towns will have their tiny bit of garden if they can, will go to gardens if they can, to look at something they have never seen as children, but which their ancestors knew and loved. The love of these things is innate and inherent in our people. It makes for that love of home which is one of the strongest features of our race. (ibid., p. 16)

Constitutionalism was a further element in his characterization of the common heritage of the English. Thus, the famously 'unwritten British Constitution' was depicted as the product of centuries of gradual accretion, being more like a natural growth than a human creation, while Magna Carta marked a key point in the development of a parliamentarianism which 'was the natural outcome, through long centuries, of the common sense and good nature of the English people' (ibid., p. 15). The speeches containing this mystifying rhetoric were part of a calculated strategy, on Baldwin's part, of bolstering his own political position *vis-à-vis* critics within his own party, as well as serving a pragmatic purpose of combating the endemic social unrest of 1920s Britain. So that, at the time of the General Strike for example, he 'could broadcast to the nation "I will not surrender the safety and security of the British Constitution" – and then sit tight' (Schwartz, 1984, p. 14).

However, other Conservative cultural critics, whose portrayals of English culture have certain similarities with Baldwin's, were, nevertheless, part of a tradition which had a much more authentically *critical* purpose within the long history of English Conservatism. One of the best known of these writers, and a contemporary of Baldwin, was the famous poet and critic T. S. Eliot. In 1931 Eliot contributed an article to *The Criterion* in which he attacked those on the right who, in the 1930s, sneered at Bolshevism as an economic system which was condemned to fail because it could not even succeed in feeding the masses:

> But perhaps the present government of Russia *will* succeed, and what then?... The Bolsheviks at any rate believe in something which is equivalent for them to a supernatural sanction; and it is only with a genuine supernatural sanction that we can oppose it. The only hope is a Toryism which, though not necessarily distinct for parliamentary purposes, should refuse to identify itself philosophically with that 'Conservatism' which has been overrun first by deserters from Whiggism and later by businessmen. And for such a Toryism not only a doctrine of the relation of the temporal and spiritual in matters of

church and state is essential, but even a religious foundation for the whole of its political philosophy. (Eliot, 1931)

Eliot's appeal for a restoration of traditional and Christian Conservative values and his attack on the inadequacy of a Conservatism rooted merely in the self-interest of the business class resonates with a very long tradition of thought and writing which may be labelled as broadly Conservative – aspects of which have recently been analysed by the historian Nigel Everett in *The Tory View of Landscape* (Everett, 1994). Everett draws attention to the very long-standing character of the debate within Conservatism between, on the one hand, supporters of economic liberalism and economic individualism and, on the other, a competing set of beliefs claiming to be more authentically Conservative/Tory. In the late seventeenth and eighteenth centuries one important focus for such debates was precisely the landscape of England itself. Discussing the foremost topic of concern of mid to late eighteenth-century debates about the landscape, the 'improvement' of many country houses and landed estates to create new or rebuilt mansions set in 'natural' parklands, Everett examines many aspects of the disagreements between supporters of what he chooses to call 'the Whig idea of landscape' and its Tory critics. At the heart of the Whig view was a tendency to redesign both country house and the surrounding landscape so that it became 'a place' – the conspicuous private possession of a single individual or family. Thomas Whately, for example, one of the main theoreticians of landscape gardening in the later eighteenth century, advised his clients how the reach of such 'improvement' could be extended even beyond the boundaries of the park, for example by planting avenues of trees along ordinary highways so that 'a kind of property may in appearance be claimed even there'. In pursuit of such improvement, many landowners removed and only sometimes relocated 'unsightly' buildings and even entire villages or small towns – a particularly notorious example being Lord Milton's development of his estate at Milton Abbey in Dorset, which involved not only the obliteration of a market town of 120 houses but also the forcible relocation of the town's grammar school (established for local scholars) to Blandford Forum, six miles away – all in the teeth of vigorous local opposition. Conservative *reactions* to such 'improvement' include the subtle irony noted by Raymond Williams in Jane Austen's accentuation of the tell-tale word 'place' in 'the improving talk of Henry Crawford in *Mansfield Park*':

> 'By such improvements as I have suggested . . . you may give it a higher character. You may raise it to a *place*.' (Austen in Williams, 1973, p. 153)[6]

A less restrained protest is cited by Everett in the language of a sermon delivered in 1777 by a country parson, the Reverend James Ibbetson, who denounced the 'new plans or systems of improvement' then being proposed as in the public interest as really schemes to serve the 'sole emolument of a few pragmatical men', reminding such men that 'they are only our Betters who do *more* good than we' (Everett, 1994, p. 61).

One aspect of Everett's discussion which is of particular interest is his analysis of the work of the contemporary legal theorist William Blackstone whose *Commentaries on the Laws of England* were published between 1765 and 1769. On Everett's account, Blackstone created a version of English law which, precisely through its evocation of *tradition*, was a basis for a deeply critical stance on certain contemporary changes relating to such issues as enclosures, the expropriation of small landowners and tenants, poor relief, game laws and the abuse of settlement laws. Blackstone in part drew sustenance for his view of English law from Locke, in particular the view 'that all units of property, however small, are to be defended'; but most distinctively, he sought to argue that 'the true, antient, indisputable rights of Englishmen' were protected within a tradition of common law embedded in the British Constitution. His favoured image of the constitution was that of an 'ancient pile': 'the ancient edifice manifests the accumulated wisdom of past ages, and the nation is bound by ties of nature, honour and religion to transmit it intact to posterity' (ibid., p. 59). Similarly, the common law was depicted by Blackstone as 'a venerable edifice of antiquity' and, significantly, as 'somehow mystically embodying the customs and universal agreement of the whole community, as being as Sir John Davis had put it, "connatural" with the nation' (ibid., p. 59).

By the first two decades of the nineteenth century, the context of the debate had shifted in major ways. The increasing hegemony of 'the English system of thought' (a blend of utilitarianism and political economy), as well as rapid industrialization and the growth of an urban working class, 'produced something of an impasse for the Tory view, stuck between its theoretical benevolence and its fear of democratic levelling impulses' (ibid., p. 204). In particular, the representatives of 'a responsible, cultivated landed interest', for example the seventh Earl of Shaftesbury, were too few – and the remainder of that class too compromised – to carry forward the Conservative critique of what were seen as the socially disintegrative effects of unfettered economic liberalism. The task was, instead, increasingly assumed by 'men of letters', most significantly, in the first three or four decades of the nineteenth century, certain of the Romantic poets including Wordsworth, Southey and Coleridge. Coleridge attacked the 'overbalance of the commercial spirit' and argued, as Everett puts it, that 'the idea of a nation as a historical continuity and community', with 'generation linked to generation' by common values, had given way to the 'superstitions of wealth and newspaper reputation'. Coleridge also diagnosed *philosophical* causes of the 'hectic of disease' from which society was suffering – in the materialistic philosophy of John Locke, which tempted people 'to throw off all show of reverence to the spiritual and even moral powers of the soul' (quoted in Mathieson and Bernbaum, 1988, p. 137). In all these respects, Coleridge's ideas are very clearly part of the Conservative tradition we have been describing: and J. S. Mill said of him that he had revived 'the idea of trust inherent in landed property'. Also significantly Conservative in tendency was the marked ambivalence on the part of both Coleridge and Wordsworth towards forces promoting *democratic* change. Although both, at times, argued that the ordinary people were less corrupted by the rising tide of selfishness than were their social superiors, Wordsworth and Coleridge were, nevertheless, very far from believing that either rural labour or the urban working class were unequivocally progressive forces.

Moral connectedness could only be restored, Coleridge believed, through a strengthening of the influence of the Christian religion. He proposed that this should be accomplished through the creation of 'nationalized' institutions – most famously in his proposal for 'a national clerisy'. As he envisaged it, this clerisy would be composed of two elements: an elite who 'would remain at the fountain heads of the humanities, in cultivating and enlarging the knowledge already possessed, and in watching over the interests of physical and moral science' and the remainder, instructed by this minority, whose members would eventually make their way into society 'so as not to leave the smallest integral part or division without a resident guide or instructor' (Coleridge quoted in Mathieson and Bernbaum, 1988, p. 139). Mathieson and Bernbaum go on to argue that the most important legacy of Coleridge's proposals lay in the complementary role he envisaged for *literature* (especially poetry) and religion in this re-education of the nation: both poetry and religion, he contended, had as their primary aim 'the perfecting and the pointing out to us the indefinite improvement of our nature, and fixing our attention upon that' (Coleridge, 1930, pp. 111–12). This linkage, Mathieson and Bernbaum contend, had a double effect: first in helping to orientate the curriculum of the reformed mid-Victorian public schools (and subsequently of the state grammar schools) towards an emphasis on the liberal and above all literary education of Christian gentlemen (guaranteeing an antipathy to industry, technology and even science), secondly, in inspiring a tradition extending from Thomas Arnold through Matthew Arnold and T. S. Eliot and down to F. R. Leavis which invested in a literary elite the guardianship of what was held to be the most significant and perishable part of the nation's cultural heritage.

Despite the longevity and the deep moral seriousness of this 'Tory' critique, however, many critics have argued that it is fatally flawed in one key respect. Everett's general characterization of the overall 'Tory' point of view displays the problem very clearly:

> The Tory idea of landscape described here is a point of view opposed to a narrowly commercial conception of life and *associated with a romantic sensibility to the ideas of continuity and tradition* felt to be embodied (*inter alia*) in certain kinds of English landscape. In a simple form it is expressed perfectly in Ford Madox Ford's hero Christopher Tietjens, 'the last Tory'...Tietjens assumes, like many before him, that some older sense of conscience, tradition and manners has given way to a generalised selfishness, coarseness of sentiment, and specious habits of reasoning used to justify self-interest. He links together imaginatively his values of cultivated Anglicanism, accuracy of thought and the responsible ownership of land, with English church towers, 'quiet fields', 'heavy-leaved timbered hedgerows', and 'slowly creeping ploughlands, moving up the slope'. *The landscape has outlived the values that are imagined to have created it – 'the land remains' – but the total triumph of the new over the old must soon lead to its destruction.* (ibid., p. 1, my italics)

This is an almost perfect example of that nostalgic rural retrospect which looks back to a happier, more settled, more caring, more socially integrated past in which the dominant social groups, guided by religious precept and principle, willingly accepted the responsibilities of wealth and the guardianship of the continuity of what was most precious and most perishable in the shared culture of the nation. As Raymond Williams demonstrated, in some cases but by no means all, a long succession of the writers who have portrayed the past in these terms have also seen it as having only just, within their own lifetimes, passed finally away beyond recall (Williams, 1973, esp. ch. 2).[7] Others, like T. S. Eliot, could still seriously argue, at the mid-point of the twentieth century, that it would be better for society if the great majority of human beings could remain in the settled rural communities where they were brought up – a claim which led Raymond Williams to make the uncharacteristically caustic comment: 'the great majority, of course, excludes a man who moved not only from one place but from one continent to another' (ibid., p. 106). As we have seen, within this 'Tory' tradition, there was no simple myth of a *single*, happier, more integrated rural past: the various writers concerned were not only too sophisticated for that but also far too concerned about the changes occurring in their own time. Nevertheless, the underlying conception of English society and culture which is repeatedly appealed to does contain elements of a persistent myth: it has at its heart what Simon Schama, speaking of the pseudo-wildernesses created within the parks owned by eighteenth-century country gentlemen, calls a 'poetic lie': 'the new arcadias were really poetic lies about their relationship to land and labour, just like the sunken, brick-lined "ha-ha": the trench that made the garden and the park seem continuous while keeping the animals off the lawn' (Schama, 1995, p. 539). At the centre of this enduring myth is the idea of *loss of community*. The past, which may either be seen with regret as finally gone, or alternatively as capable of restoration, is in either case conceived as a time of harmonious social integration in which class relations involved mutuality of respect and care. From the onset of industrialization and urbanization, a characteristic move within this structure of myth was to represent the rural as a place where such values persisted and to attribute what could then be seen as their 'breakdown' to the 'unnatural' ways of living and working associated with urbanization and industrialization. Williams shows that such a tendency extended to many writers who were clearly *not* conservative in their overall outlook or political affiliations: George Eliot is a case in point. In his discussion of this type of contrast in George Eliot's novel *Felix Holt*, Williams comments:

> A natural country ease is contrasted with an unnatural urban unrest. The 'modern world', both in its suffering and, crucially, in its protest against suffering, is mediated by reference to a lost condition which is better than both and which can place both: a condition imagined out of a landscape and a selective observation and memory. (Williams, 1973, pp. 219–20)

Williams goes on to argue that this becomes the basis of a particular critical sensibility evident in the writings of certain of the so-called Victorian moralists (most conspicuously Henry James) and in the criticism of F. R. Leavis. Within this structure of feeling, '*value* is in the past' and the focus of 'great literature' becomes narrowed so that what is left is a 'class England' and 'a set of personal relationships and of intellectual and moral insights in a history that for all valuing purposes has disastrously ended'. The touchstone of true judgement then becomes 'the sensibility – the bitter and frank sensibility – of the isolated moral observer', who is part of no socially and politically organized (and therefore 'morally' compromised) movement for social improvement – and who has, moreover, little belief that genuine moral benefit or growth can come from such movements.

NATION AND CULTURE IN CONTEMPORARY CONSERVATIVE CULTURAL DISCOURSE

What then of contemporary neo-conservative writing on the themes of nation and culture? In some ways there are marked similarities with elements of the older conservative tradition outlined above. For example, Roger Scruton, in an essay published almost forty years after T. S. Eliot's *Notes Towards the Definition of Culture*, characterizes the national culture in significantly similar terms. British culture is pictured, in a manner akin to Eliot's 'continuous gradation of cultural levels', as containing various elements: from the 'high culture' in which aesthetic values are paramount; through the 'deep' customs and beliefs of religion; the 'political culture' including a sense of law and justice; down to the 'shallow' customs which include feasts, ceremonies, manners, etc.; and finally the sphere of popular entertainment (Scruton, 1987). Although Scruton does not use the term 'organic', culture is, for him, above all else the key and indispensable source of social unity; indeed he *defines* it in these terms: 'a culture is a pattern of social unity' (ibid., p. 132).

> All the activities mentioned have this in common: that they serve to bind people together in a common enterprise. To put it another way, they are ways of 'belonging' to the larger world of human society, and affirming one's reality as a social being. Unless people acquire the habit of 'belonging' they cannot live peacefully together, nor can they be happy. (ibid., p. 129)

The process of coming to 'belong' obviously requires that the core of values, beliefs and practices which make up the culture is handed on to the next generation, in other words that the core cultural traditions are preserved and transmitted. Now, as we have previously argued, there are many reasons to *question* definitions and assertions of this kind – and there is no need to repeat those arguments. Of more interest is to examine Scruton's view of the role of religion – since this is an area where he differs somewhat not only from T. S. Eliot (and the long conservative tradition) but also from many of his contemporary allies (such as Baroness Cox, also a member of the Hillgate Group, who played a key role in amending the 1988 Education Reform Act to include mandatory acts of worship in schools and a dominant position for the teaching of Christianity within Religious Education). Scruton accepts that in modern societies, religious belief and ritual cannot be the *primary* source of social cohesion – though it can still play an important supporting role and orthodox Christianity should therefore be supported. As Jennifer Somerville has pointed out, religion for Scruton is not important for its truth value so much as:

> for its role in reinforcing values generated initially within the family, stable family relationships being seen as essential to the development of those 'human bonds' without which abstract values are powerless to sustain ties of social obligation – and indeed, it is this combination which, Scruton claims, 'produces in people a natural conservatism'. (Somerville, 1992, pp. 105–6)

Differences of this kind within neo-conservatism *could* be represented as little more than matters of emphasis. However, in view of the tradition of which it is part, the question of the *truth* (as against the function) of Christian teaching should, perhaps, not be quite so easy for neo-conservatives themselves to overlook. As we have seen, for Coleridge as for Eliot, it was the truth of Christian teaching that was the fundamental source and sanction supporting their vision of the good society – and it was the transcendent nature of that truth and those teachings which gave coherence to their projects of cultural restoration. Although this is not an issue likely to detain many people in our strongly secular contemporary society, it is, nevertheless, a far from trivial ambivalence within modern neo-conservatism.

Having cast religion in a supporting role, Scruton looks to *the law and the constitution of Britain* as a major carrier of the core values of the culture and thus of national identity. Briefly acknowledging that his brief discussion raises 'large questions of political philosophy and sociology', he nevertheless asserts:

[W]e can at least see that the *law* of England, and the parliamentary procedure through which it is developed and enacted, are as much parts of the public culture of Britain as is the Christian religion. Any attempt to impart British culture to the children (or the grandchildren) of immigrants quite reasonably involves an instruction [sic] in the nature of, and the feeling for, English law: in the *Rechtsgefühl* (the feeling for law and justice) of England, upon which the 'English peace' is ultimately founded. (ibid., p. 130)

It is an amusing irony that in his search to define the *geist* of English culture, Scruton has to resort to German. More seriously, it is the underlying impulse to identify some supposed enduring essence at the heart of English law (and of English attitudes *to* the law) that strikes one as so questionable. As we saw earlier, William Blackstone in the eighteenth century constructed a version of English law which claimed a similarly essentialist warrant grounded in an appeal to tradition – but which was used as the basis for a stringent critique of the legal and parliamentary practices of the time. Everett makes the point with great precision:

[S]*electing* from laws, customs, and precedents, *while insisting all the time that he was replacing innovation with tradition*, Blackstone created a version of English law on which a deeply critical stand could be taken against such things as slavery, compulsory workhouses, the game laws, the abuse of the settlement laws and virtually all capital punishment. (Everett, 1994, p. 59, my italics)

Perhaps 'immigrants' and their grandchildren should be invited to study Blackstone!

A third major area of difference between contemporary neo-conservatism and the long tradition of conservative cultural criticism discussed above has to do with their relationship to economic liberalism and economic individualism. As has been shown, the 'Tory' tradition was characterized, perhaps above all else, by the seriousness and consistency of its critique of the socially and culturally disintegrative effects of morally unregulated market forces. However, those associated with contemporary neo-conservatism have appeared significantly more ambivalent in their attitudes to the ideology of the neo-liberal strand of New Right thought. Whitty, for example, has analysed some of the ways in which the educational policy ideas of the Hillgate Group drew upon neo-conservative *and* neo-liberal repertoires, and he interprets this not as muddle but as deliberate strategy:

Heavily influenced by neo-conservative critiques of progressivism, members of the Hillgate Group are attracted by the idea of prescription at the level of the curriculum in order to defend traditional standards and values. However, they also see parents as a potent force against progressivism and embrace – and indeed wish to extend – the government's espousal of market forces in open enrolment, opting out, and so on, as the best way of improving educational standards. (Whitty, 1990, p. 24)

A key attraction of unleashing market forces in education was, as Brian Simon first pointed out, that the atomizing effects of policies such as opting out, local management of schooling, new contracts of employment for teachers, etc. undermined the power and marginalized the influence of the two main *organized* forces supportive of collectivism: the local education authorities and sections of the teaching profession (Simon, 1987, esp. ch. 1). This rendered both groupings less effective (though, as things have turned out, far from wholly *in*effective) in resisting attempts to reinforce 'tradition' through the National Curriculum.

It is still too soon to attempt any overall estimate of the extent of *rapprochement* that may be emerging or that may be possible between neo-conservative and neo-liberal strands within the developing agenda of the New Right – not least because issues of economic and cultural change operating on a *global* scale are of central importance in any such endeavour. It is, however, now almost a commonplace to observe that this world-wide progress of free-market economics, exerting influences extending well beyond the boundaries of any nation state, is everywhere deeply subversive of tradition. As David Marquand has recently pointed out:

> The global market place which the new-style Tories celebrate is cold and hard; in a profound sense, it is also subversive. It uproots communities, disrupts families, mocks faiths and erodes the ties of place and history. It has created a demotic global culture, contemptuous of tradition, hostile to established hierarchies and relativist in morality. Above all, it has made a nonsense of national sovereignty, at any rate in the economic sphere. (Marquand, 1995)[8]

Interestingly, Marquand goes on to argue that notwithstanding this diminishing in the *real* importance and independence of sovereign nations and indeed even because of it, the British Conservative party, with its historical attachments to nation and tradition, is caught in a contradiction: 'they are for the sovereign market, and they are also for the sovereign state; they cannot have both at once'. In this situation, he suggests, assertions of national independence are however, for some Conservatives, even more necessary: such assertions having a psychic coherence even where they lack intellectual cogency: 'the gap between creed and reality makes the creed more inspiring and its devotees more zealous' (ibid.).

'HIGH CULTURE', NATIONAL CULTURE AND THE CURRICULUM

Finally, let us turn to the question of 'high' culture and its relationship to national culture and the curriculum. 'High' culture has no unitary, generally accepted meaning. Even a single writer may use it in more than one sense in the space of one short essay. Roger Scruton is a case in point. In the essay we have already been discussing, 'The myth of cultural relativism', Scruton initially characterizes high culture in terms reflecting what is probably its most common usage: those aspects of the culture of a society 'in which aesthetic values are paramount' (Scruton, 1987, p. 127). Later in the argument, however, he shifts to a broader definition which seems to include what might be called the whole of the intellectual culture and this, he suggests, forms the basis of 'what has been called a liberal education, but which might just as well be called an education in the high culture of our civilization' (ibid., pp. 133–4). Earlier, we have also noted Ernest Gellner's use of 'high culture' which is, in many ways, similar to this second sense indicated by Scruton though, as we have also seen, in Gellner's usage the term has a more functional inflection.

A vexed area of debate concerns the relationships between 'high culture' (in its various senses) and 'other cultures', notably the cultures of the most significant ethnic communities living within a country such as the United Kingdom. It was sensitivities in this area which were associated with the most critical of the responses provoked by Dr Tate in the incident referred to at the beginning of this chapter, and it is in this area too that the interventions of neo-conservative writers and lobby groups have generated particular controversy. Once again, Scruton's 'The myth of cultural relativism' essay provides a useful focus for discussion, particularly if read in conjunction with the Hillgate Group's pamphlet *The Reform of British Education* which was published in the same year. Scruton acknowledges that '*all* cultures contain a principle of internal criticism' but he goes on to argue that British and Western European cultures are characterized by an exceptional degree of 'openness' (op. cit., p. 131), this being even more true in relation to the 'high' culture of these societies which exhibit such openness 'at its most developed' (ibid., p. 133). This openness of high culture is, in part, said to be intrinsic *to* high cultures – because they constitute 'a sphere of maximum exposure to what is strange and interesting' (ibid., p. 134). The exceptional openness claimed for British culture, however, has a second source, the *Rechtsgefühl*, that feeling for law and justice which, as we have seen, is held to be 'a dominant principle' of the culture as a whole, not only its high culture. This enables Scruton to offer the following observation – remarkable for its combination of ethnocentrism and complacency:

> The child brought up in the British way of doing things is encouraged to question and to criticise, to seek fair play and impartial judgement, and to receive as doctrine only that which he [sic] has independent reason to believe to be true. A child brought up in such a culture does not *need* the presentation of 'alternatives' which so many educators wish to foist upon him. (ibid., p. 132)

As our earlier discussion has suggested, as soon as the Hillgate Group and Scruton turned to curricular *prescription*, this ostensible openness became heavily qualified. In the first place, as Ken Jones has noted, Scruton's insistence that a culture is in its essence a unifying force requiring the sharing of meaning, beliefs and values, carried the implication that it was the duty of educators to transmit not only the 'feeling for *justice*' which is a part of the *Rechtsgefühl* but also to engage in authoritative 'instruction... bound explicitly to particular notions of the rule of law that have served as the legitimising foundation of the British state' (Jones, 1988, p. 57). As both Jones and Pat White have pointed out, this involved the Hillgate Group in a rather evident self-contradiction. On the one hand, they vehemently attacked what they called the 'politicization' of the school curriculum, but on the other hand, their own curricular prescriptions were themselves revealed as no less politicized and also as 'closed' – not least in their support for what White calls 'a limited and deferential moral education' alongside very traditional 'religious instruction' (Jones, op. cit., p. 56; White, 1988). A second consequence of Scruton's over-integrated conception of culture and society is that conflicts over meaning and/or values tend to be seen as pathological, with the further implication that such conflicts tend to be 'ascribed to differences *between* cultures' with a resultant tendency to 'classify some meanings as alien intrusions into a culture' (op. cit., p. 57). Within a culture whose 'openness' they celebrate, therefore, the education which the Hillgate Group proposed to offer to 'immigrants' and their 'offspring' turns out to be uncompromisingly assimilationist! To admit 'other' cultures to 'our' curriculum is to admit the dangerous and alien virus of *relativism*: 'Our culture – being part of the universalistic culture of Europe – must not be sacrificed for the sake of a misguided relativism, or out of a misplaced concern for those who might not yet be aware of its strengths and weaknesses' (Hillgate, 1987). What, however, really appears misguided in this is the Hillgate Group's own exaggerated *fear* of cultural diversity.

Following his appointment as chief executive of the School Curriculum and Assessment Authority, Dr Nicholas Tate seemed to become similarly preoccupied with the issue of relativism. In a series of contributions to SCAA conferences throughout 1996, he repeatedly warned that both the cultural identity and moral well-being of the nation were under attack from the forces of relativism. And he increasingly seemed to identify himself with the task of leading the forces of resistance to these perceived trends. It was time, he robustly declared, to slay this 'dragon of relativism'. (These arguments will be discussed in more detail and with particular reference to moral decline in Chapter 2.) It is important to acknowledge that Dr Tate's tone – especially in relation to other cultures – was less uncompromisingly assimilationist than that of some of the writing discussed above. For example, in 1994, having, as he himself put it, 'come off the fence' in terms of indicating that SCAA's support for the revised National Curriculum was unambiguously associated with the aim of reinforcing a common culture and sense of national identity, he nevertheless added: 'the proposed curriculum aims to do this in ways that respect other traditions, including those outside our common culture' (Tate, 1994). A similar recognition of the legitimacy of a limited kind of multiculturalism was contained in his introductory comments to the SCAA conference on 'Curriculum, Culture and Society' held in February 1996, where he acknowledged that Britain had not always been strong in recognizing the positive contributions of other cultures: 'Traditionally, one of our failures in this country has been that we have not made young people sufficiently aware of the richness and diversity of some of these other cultures and traditions' (Tate, 1996b, para. 22). For all that, however, his fundamental message at this SCAA conference, as elsewhere, was that relativism in the sphere of culture was creating a rootless society without a clear sense of identity and that those responsible for the curriculum of our schools must stand against these relativizing currents and support a curriculum 'proudly based in a cultural heritage that has its roots in Greece and Rome, in Christianity, and in the many-sided traditions of European civilization' (ibid., para. 19).

Despite this qualified acknowledgement of the 'contributions' of 'other cultures', then, the basic premise of Tate's position is that it remains legitimate to understand the condition of culture in modern Britain in terms of an 'inside' and various outside 'others' – and also to constitute that 'inside' as some kind of unity rooted in 'our' (and not 'their') cultural heritage. Yet, as James Donald has made brilliantly clear, the precarious unity that can be constructed through the notion of 'national culture' can never be other than a *fictional* unity:

> A nation does not express itself through its culture. It is culture that produces 'the nation'...[but] what is produced is neither an identity nor a single consciousness, but hierarchically organised values, dispositions and differences. This heterogeneity is given a certain fixity as 'the nation' [which] differentiates it from other cultures by marking its boundaries. This integrity can only constitute a fictional unity of course, because the 'us' on the inside is itself always differentiated. (Donald, 1992, pp. 50–1)

We need, therefore, to replace the falsifying idea of culture and nation as a stratified yet organic and essentially harmonious unity, with a recognition of two essential things:

(a) that this 'hierarchy of organized values, dispositions and differences' which constitutes the national culture is the complex effect of a multiplicity of only partially integrated but also partially contradictory discourses and practices; and

(b) that these discourses are inseparable from the operations of *power*, as well as the multiple oppressions and antagonisms of class, gender, race, spatial exclusions, etc. which actually constitute 'our' shared past as well as 'our' present.

Without retracting any of these criticisms, it is important to insist upon one element in the Hillgate Group's analysis which surely *is* valid. This is the stress placed on a certain kind of openness within 'high' culture – so long as 'high' is understood as embracing the whole of that intellectual culture which had its origins primarily *though by no means exclusively* in Europe and which is, in any case, now increasingly *global* in its sources and influence. At the heart of this openness is *critical* reason – with its relentless interrogation of what Descartes called 'custom and example' – and where, in Ernest Gellner's words,

> there are no privileged knowers, no organization is allowed to claim cognitive monopoly, there are no privileged events or objects. Logical cogency and evidence are king. Explanations are required to be symmetrical, and they are subject to tests not under the control of the system of ideas that is under scrutiny. Belief systems are not allowed to set up closed circuits, in which a sacred and privileged background picture leads privileged validators to perceive and recognize sacred evidence, which then reconfirms the initial Picture. (Gellner, 1992, p. 146)

These are the core imperatives which lie at the heart not only of what Gellner calls Cognition but also of liberal education, even if they are not the only ones. This spirit of critical reason is able, in principle, to interrogate *all* fundamentalisms (and it is not itself a fundamentalism whatever certain kinds of fashionable postmodernism may claim). A liberal education grounded in such principles is the form of education most likely to liberate people's minds from the limited horizons of *whatever* more localized cultures they are born into – to liberate them *from* what Charles Bailey calls 'the present and the particular'. As Bailey reminds us, *educators* also need to ask what it is that the liberally educated person is released *for*. The core of his answer is that a liberally educated person is released *for* 'a kind of intellectual and moral autonomy, ... the capacity to become a free chooser of beliefs and actions – in a word, a free moral agent' – adding that the key idea at the heart of this notion of autonomy is not anarchy but self-*government* (Bailey, 1984, pp. 20–2). If these were the principles which guided education within the National Curriculum, and if they were in place at the heart of the training and education of teachers (instead of being increasingly *dis*placed), there would be less need to agonize over how many examples of plays by Shakespeare or novels from someone's version of the canon of English Literature should be required reading for 'British' children. As knowledge and cultural production expands at a rate which it has become fashionable to describe as exponential, the aspiration of laying down a definitive list of essential 'great works' becomes increasingly futile as well as self-defeating. It is the fundamental *principles* that need to be addressed – and it is this level of principle which, once again, was almost wholly neglected in the effective but nevertheless pragmatic 'fix' which was the Dearing Review of the National Curriculum (Dearing, 1994).

NOTES

1 Gellner's views on these matters are, of course, contested – and not only by neo-conservative writers. Anthony Smith, for example, represents one of the polarities in recent debates about nationalism. He is among those scholars who lay greater emphasis than does Gellner himself on 'the persistence of ethnic ties and cultural sentiments which in some cases date back to pre-modern times' and who tend to stress the significance of 'ethnic nationalism' as a source of cultural revolt against the 'territorial nationalism' of established nation states (Smith, 1995, p. 19; see also Smith, 1991). This division of opinion was summarized by Gellner himself, in one of the last lectures he ever delivered:

> Anthony (Smith) and I tend to be pitted against each other on opposite sides of what has become the major dividing line in the study of nationalism – the line between what I call 'primordialists' and 'modernists'. The primordialists say that nations were there all the time (or some of them were, anyway), and that the past matters a great deal. The modernists such as myself believe that the world was created at about the end of the 18th Century, and nothing which happened before makes the slightest difference to the issues we face. (Gellner in Smith, 1995)

2 This discussion should not, of course, be understood as seeking to suggest that shared values and identifications play no part at all in the maintenance of social cohesion, stability and a sense of identity in modern pluralistic societies. At least within functioning democracies, there must be an irreducible minimum of shared values – those, for example, which underpin certain basic rights of democratic citizenship, for example: freedom of conscience, freedom of association, freedom from arbitrary arrest, freedoms to participate in political institutions, etc. And underpinning these, there is likely to be some generally shared (though by no means universal) subscription to more abstract and general values such as respect for persons, the importance (within certain limits) of toleration, etc. However, a sharing of values of this kind is, amongst other things, likely to be a basis for well-founded *opposition* to attempts to impose or 'restore' more comprehensive and more 'closed' versions of normative order. These questions will be addressed more systematically in Chapters 2, 3 and 4.

3 A succession of industrialists and politicians has displayed remarkable persistence, or simply ignorance, in reiterating *uncritical* versions of the so-called Correlli Barnett/Wiener Thesis (Barnett, 1978 and 1986; Wiener, 1981) which blames certain allegedly pervasive and endemic features of British academic culture for the long-term relative decline in Britain's industrial competitiveness. A significant early example was Sir Arnold Weinstock's intervention in 1976 (Weinstock, 1976) which was an important influence on James Callaghan's famous Ruskin College speech of the same year. A fairly recent instance comes from an interview given by the former Conservative minister and Chancellor of the Exchequer Sir Geoffrey Howe, in which he castigated 'people like William Blake' who

> contrasted the dark, satanic mills with England's green and pleasant land. There has been a kind of cultural gap between educationalists, who want to remain green and pleasant, and our entrepreneur-industrialists, who work in the dark, satanic mills. (*International Herald Tribune*, 1991, p. 2)

Such confident and recent assertions take little or no account of the extensive critical discussion that has accumulated around this thesis (see, for example, Ahier, 1988; Gunn 1988; Rubinstein, 1977 – and for an illuminating recent analysis of the whole debate, Hickox, 1995).

4 Recent evidence to support these claims is admittedly scant. However, in a very recent small-scale study based on interviews with a sample of twenty-four 13 to 14-year-olds drawn from two contrasting comprehensive schools, Paul Goalen found that almost none of these young people saw themselves primarily as 'British':

> One of the most striking features of our research was how few pupils saw themselves as

British. Nineteen of the interviewees when asked their nationality responded without hesitation that they were English, and only two said they were British. Of the remainder, one claimed to be half Scottish and half English, one Mexican, and the other Indian. Excluding the Mexican and the Indian, only eight of the remaining twenty two appeared to understand the difference between being British and English with fourteen not understanding the difference or expressing some uncertainty. (Goalen, 1996)

5 A fascinating glimpse of the ways in which a context of contested nationalisms (reinforced by religious antagonisms) can sustain what might otherwise (and elsewhere) appear to be an anachronistic and stereotypical kind of identification with 'Britishness' is provided by a set of case-studies of children from Northern Ireland, assembled by the American psychiatrist Robert Coles. One of the children whom Coles interviewed was a 10-year-old Protestant girl:

A Protestant child in Belfast, sitting under a picture of Queen Elizabeth, told my wife and me that:

the Queen is our mother: she holds all her subjects together, my Granny says, and if you're not one of her subjects, you'll be a girl who has lost her mother, and that's the saddest girl in the world. So we have to stay part of Great Britain; it's our homeland, my Granny says.

The girl's earliest memory (as recounted to Coles) was of her father singing to her:

I was very small; I can't even see my father, but it was, I know, I think I know because I smelled the tobacco on him . . . and he's singing to me, and I say 'again', and he sings it again, 'God Save the Queen'. . . . That's the first thing in my life I can recall now. My granny said the Queen would love to know I was her subject so soon in my life – hearing my father's singing of the anthem. (Coles, 1986, pp. 56–7)

What has to be insisted upon here, however, is precisely the exceptional character of such subjective identifications for contemporary UK citizens as a whole. Such ways of thinking and feeling, as well as what might be called the 'folk' or community-based modes of their transmission, need to be seen as the product of the specificities of the adversarial situation in the province of Northern Ireland. Northern Ireland, of course, provides a classic illustration of Ralf Dahrendorf's thesis that the intensity of conflicts within a society tends to be positively correlated with the degree of superimposition of conflicts – in this case, a tendency for class, religious and nationalist antagonisms to be superimposed (Dahrendorf, 1959, esp. pp. 214–15).

6 Rather curiously, in view of the very extensive overlap in subject matter between Everett's book and Raymond Williams' *The Country and the City*, Everett makes almost no reference to Williams' seminal study, although it is included in the bibliography. The explanation may be that Everett is explicitly writing from a standpoint broadly in sympathy with the Tory views he is describing and he perhaps wished to avoid engaging in debate 'on a second front' with a writer known for his Marxist sympathies.

7 Williams, of course, analysed a much broader variety of retrospects within this overall structure of feeling, showing, for example, how very different kinds of retrospect were constructed from different positions within the class structure as well as at different points in history, and devoting considerable attention to the persistent tradition of rural *radicalism* represented by writers like Stephen Duck, Crabbe and Cobbett. (For an illuminating commentary on Williams in these and other respects, see Ahier, 1988, pp. 24–37.)

8 How far Marquand is correct in attributing such changes primarily to 'the global market place' may be debatable. Anthony Giddens, for example, sees changes of this kind as the result of a far more extensive and complex set of developments, associated with what he terms 'reflexive modernization' and the transition to a state of 'high modernity' (see, for example, Giddens, 1994a; Beck, Giddens and Lash, 1994). However, there is little doubt that the growing influence of free-market ideologies and institutions has, at the least, played a significant role in *accelerating* such changes. Giddens' discussion of tradition in his essay *Living in a Post-Traditional Society* is particularly pertinent (Giddens, 1994b).

Chapter 2

Millennial Moralism, Tradition and Modernity

MILLENNIAL MORALISM

> When you have a society in which unbelief has become the norm and practising Christianity a minority pursuit, then you have to raise the question, what are the shared values that hold us together?...We have lost a sense of community and I have been warning against the loss of the sense of shared values that used to bind us together... (Dr George Carey, Archbishop of Canterbury, quoted in Marr, 1996, p. 14)

> I am conscious that our civilization is being damaged...by a gradual loss of the invisible ties that safeguard...respect for one another. The invisible bonds to which I refer are the bonds that came naturally in a much more stable society than we have today. They came from (extended) families who often lived their lives in one town; from neighbours... from the doctor, the parson, the headteacher...being long part of one community...and by their lives setting standards, in particular, for young people. By contrast today, we are a highly mobile society. Those tentpegs of my childhood have largely gone, especially in our cities...
>
> Today most women have a care about walking along a lonely street in the evening. Parents are fearful of letting their children play out of sight. Old people are fearful of opening the door to a stranger. In this, our society has visibly decayed. (Sir Ron Dearing, 1996, paras 8, 9 and 13)

Analyses of this kind, from public figures of some eminence, have recently been the springboard for various initiatives designed to combat the moral decline which is allegedly so evident a feature of the present state of British society. Thus, in the interview from which the first extract above is taken, Dr Carey announced his intention to use the anniversaries of the coming of St Augustine to Canterbury in 597 and the death in that same year of St Columba on Iona, to launch a pre-millennial crusade: 'I think the church must grab the opportunity of the Millennium' – one of the aims of such a crusade being to help create a 'partnership between the school, parents, government, and the media to return Britain to the good society, founded upon the principles which I regard as essentially Christian' (op. cit.). Similarly, the statement by Sir Ron Dearing, the then government's chief advisor on the school curriculum, was part of a keynote speech which set the scene for a SCAA conference held in January 1996, which led to the establishment of a National Forum to examine 'the role of spiritual and moral values in education and the wider community' (SCAA, June 1996a, p. 3)[1] and to assess how, as Dearing himself put it, 'we in education take on the responsibility for renewing civilization, in particular with parents' (Dearing, op. cit., para. 19).

In a speech at this same conference, Dr Nicholas Tate, the Chief Executive of SCAA, offered a similar but more detailed diagnosis of the nation's moral and cultural ills. As with Sir Ron's contribution, the analysis of *contemporary* ills, making reference to recent instances of high-profile lawlessness including the murder of headteacher Philip Lawrence, was counterpointed against images of a more cohesive, more integrated past in which stable local communities, underpinned by the values of a shared cultural and religious heritage, were the basis for the effective transmission to the younger generation of clear moral guidelines:

> At the heart of the traditional educational enterprise – both in schools and in the home – was the transmission of a set of rules, precepts and principles. Many were pithy and memorable: the Ten Commandments; the seven deadly sins; the seven principal virtues, together with all those common sayings – 'do as you would be done by', 'common decency' – that Richard Hoggart still found on the lips of elderly people in Leeds in the late eighties. (Tate, 1996a, para. 12)

Dr Tate went on to argue that today 'we no longer have this framework' and 'we lack the everyday language that traditionally helped to maintain a moral structure to our lives' (ibid., para. 13). The shared moral language has, he argued, been undermined by the spread of 'an *all pervasive relativism*' that has come to '*dominate our consciousness*' (ibid., paras 14 and 20, my italics) – a relativism so pervasive that it had even affected Richard Hoggart's elderly women in Leeds: 'at some point in their re-statement of the rules they have lived by they stop themselves and say "but that's only my opinion"' (ibid., para. 14). The outcome may be, Dr Tate suggested, that we as a society, and especially those involved in education, are increasingly morally disabled – lacking the confidence to give a moral lead on any matter which might appear contested or controversial. He identified four reasons why moral relativism has apparently come to have such a hold over the nation's consciousness. First, there is an exaggerated political correctness accorded to groups 'who in the past have been discriminated against or excluded', which allegedly makes the younger generation, and particularly younger teachers, reluctant to 'do anything which might suggest that they are imposing ethnocentric, class or gender values on their pupils' (ibid., paras 17 and 21). Such thinking is, Tate contended, reinforced by a more general *cultural* relativism which denies that cultural products can be judged as superior or inferior to one another. This argument was amplified in a speech to a subsequent SCAA conference held in February 1966:

> We are not in the business of simply developing young people's skills, introducing them to 'an array of cultural delights'... and then leaving them to make their own cultural (or indeed moral) choices... *That would be to reinforce our current sense of rootlessness and confusion of identity.* (Tate, 1996b, paras 17 and 18, my italics)

A second cause of the spread of relativism is identified as the decline of religious faith: 'as the Archbishop of Canterbury has recently said, people ever since the

Enlightenment "have been living off the legacy of a deep, residual belief in God; but as people move away from that, they find it more and more difficult to give a substantial basis for why they should be good" ' (Tate, 1996a, para. 23). The third source of relativism is identified as the pernicious effect of certain wider intellectual currents which have transformed academic disciplines such as English studies, history and sociology – culminating in the destabilizing and dispiriting influence of postmodernism. Fourthly, 'relativism cannot be dissociated from consumerism: if large numbers of people are going around thinking that there is no difference between morality and taste, consumerist pressures within our society must partly be to blame' (ibid., para. 25).

So much for the diagnosis; what about remedies? Here, it is becoming increasingly clear that Dr Tate has very deliberately decided to use his position as SCAA's Chief Executive to promote widespread public discussion focused upon certain issues and 'problems' which he (and no doubt government in certain respects) have identified as particularly significant:

> Over the next couple of years SCAA will be monitoring the implementation of the slimmed-down National Curriculum and reviewing fundamental issues as a staged process. This will help us to advise Ministers on whether there is a case, as we approach the millennium, for making changes to our current curriculum, and if so, in what the direction of change might be. (Tate, 1996b, para. 5)

This, of course, is in itself a sensible and responsible course of action – not least because, as he acknowledged in this same paper, there is very general agreement that 'the original debate on the National Curriculum in the late 1980s did *not* get to grips with some of the basic issues' (ibid., para. 4, my italics; and see, among many examples, Chitty, 1988; Pring, 1989, ch. 5; White, 1988). What has given a number of commentators some cause for concern is the suspicion – and indeed the evidence – that Dr Tate has been seeking to give a rather strong steer to this process of curricular debate. In a series of speeches and newspaper articles in the last two years, the central thrust of his concerns has become increasingly evident. His stance is essentially neo-conservative and the direction of change he personally strongly supports is a 'back to the future' project of restoration of 'our' national (and Western European) cultural, religious and moral 'heritage': 'there is no doubt that we have lost the robust intellectual basis for our [sic] moral life we once had. If ever a dragon needed slaying, it is the dragon of relativism' (Tate, 1996a, para. 26). In the broader cultural sphere, the conclusion is that certain 'national' elements of the National Curriculum should be more vigorously affirmed to enable young people to recover a clearer sense of their identity in the face of these relativizing influences:

> In this country, the cultural dimension of the curriculum needs to be firmly and proudly based in a cultural heritage that has its roots in Greece and Rome, in Christianity...The curriculum seeks to introduce young people to this heritage, give them a sense of its past achievements, and help them to see the relevance of these to the present day. That is why our statutory curriculum places emphasis on the centrality of British history, Britain's changing relations with the rest of the world, the English literary heritage and the study of Christianity... (Tate, 1996b, para. 19)

As part of this emphasis on the national cultural heritage – within literature and the arts, the call is for a restoration of a literary canon, a musical canon and an artistic canon as central points of reference for the school curriculum (ibid., paras 25 and 26).

And finally, in the sphere of *morality,* two complementary educational strategies are suggested as a basis for the task identified by Dearing as 'renewing civilization' (no less!). First there is the promotion of Religious Education – apparently on the basis of an assumption that, somehow, religion remains, for all of us, the real (even if unrecognized) basis of morality. Citing Dr Carey's claim that as people move further away from sharing a deep residual belief in God, they find it increasingly difficult 'to give a substantial basis for why they should be good', Dr Tate adds the following remarkable and revealing comment:

> This is one reason why religious education must continue to be a vital part of every child's curriculum...It is also a reason why children's spiritual development is so important, as the origin of the will to do what is right. (Tate, 1996a, para. 23)

This is later amplified in a way that indicates that it is the teaching of Christianity in particular which is vital in this respect: 'there are now encouraging signs that religious education is poised to recover the place it has lost: through a reassertion of the central place of Christianity within the RE curriculum, alongside the study of other religions' (ibid., para. 35). Secondly, he has called for a more explicit formulation of a statement of shared, fundamental values which should form the basis of *individual* moral conduct and which 'society' should authorize all schools to teach on its behalf. He is quite clear in stating his own view that *public* virtue 'can only be achieved on the basis of private virtue' (ibid., para. 31).

As this discussion has shown, Dr Tate and Dr Carey have repeatedly picked up upon and reinforced one another's public interventions. In early July 1996, the archbishop introduced what *The Times* called 'an unprecedented debate on morality' in the House of Lords (*The Times*, 5 July 1996, p. 9). The terms of the debate were unchanged: first, the damage to social cohesion and our way of life resulting from the corrosive effects of relativism, and secondly the need to reassert the cultural and moral authority of our traditional institutions. Welcoming both the SCAA consultation on moral values and the strengthened focus on moral and spiritual development in OFSTED school inspections, Dr Carey stated:

> I believe that the fight back against moral and cultural relativism is under way. There is now a reaction against moral relativism, a growing mood in favour of a more truthful and more constructive way of describing the things that bind us together. (ibid., p. 9)

He 'replayed' the familiar themes of the need for schools to teach all pupils a clear set of moral rules, argued that the British had been given a set of such rules – the Ten Commandments – but that few children now knew more than two or three of them, and that we were in danger of 'squandering our inheritance'. He also deplored the fact that only 20 per cent of secondary schools hold a daily religious assembly. Finally, the familiar reference to the permissive follies of the 1960s was included via a quotation from Dr Jonathan Sacks, the Chief Rabbi:

> [I]t is as if in the 1950s and 1960s we set a time bomb ticking which would eventually explode the moral framework into fragments...the human cost has been colossal but the cost has been far wider in terms of the loss of authority, institutions in crisis, and the loss of a public sense of moral order. (ibid.)

UNREAL RETROSPECTS AND FALSE DAWNS

Analyses and prescriptions of the kind outlined above are, of course, by no means wholly misplaced and misdirected. For example, it *is* important to recognize that there are strong arguments to support the view that at least certain moral principles are relatively objective and have a transcultural application, and that one of the most important aims of liberal education is to help young people to become, in some degree, rational and autonomous moral agents (recognizing that this is an ideal and that as such, it can never be attained).[2] Similarly, encouraging national debate about moral education, religious education, education for citizenship, etc. under SCAA's auspices is to be welcomed. For better or for worse, SCAA now has the status of 'lead body' in the development of the school curriculum in England and Wales, and its leadership is acting wisely and responsibly in initiating wide-ranging discussion in these inevitably controversial but also vitally important areas.

Nor is the social analysis of our 'millennial moralists' wholly misdirected. The social bases of identity have indeed changed fundamentally in advanced so-called 'post-industrial' societies. As sociologists such as Anthony Giddens and Ulrich Beck have pointed out, the anchoring of identity in stable local communities, in the sub-cultures of social class, in the stability of a job for life or a professional career, has been extensively undermined by the economic and technological changes associated with what Anthony Giddens calls 'late modernity'. Similarly, gender relations and identities have been radically transformed (U. Beck, 1992; Giddens, 1990 and 1991). (We shall elaborate upon these issues in the next section.) Nevertheless, it is important to insist that the *overall* social order and continuity of modern democratic societies does not depend principally upon the maintenance of an extensive set of common values internalized by all members of those societies. As has already been argued in Chapter 1, social stability and continuity in such societies is the outcome of multiple and *contradictory* conditions and processes which include: the very unequal distribution of wealth and power (among individuals and corporate entities); the multiplicity of ideological (or discursive) determinants of individual action – which have no overarching ideological unity; and the daily routines and unconscious 'background expectancies' (as Garfinkel termed them) which sustain order and predictability in everyday social interaction (Garfinkel, 1967). To recognize this is, however, not to deny the crucial significance of a limited but fundamental set of 'public values' which do underpin certain rights of citizenship in most developed liberal democracies – and which are codified in the law in such states. These mainly have to do with the protection of certain liberties of the individual against arbitrary infringement by civil or religious powers, by other citizens, or by corporate entities. The most important of these rights include: freedom of conscience, freedom of expression, freedom of association, freedom from arbitrary arrest, formal equality before the law, certain political rights associated with democratic citizenship, etc. Even in these respects, however, the relationship between such rights and general *values* is not one of direct correspondence. Such rights were won through struggle (at least in part) and they have to be constantly protected against those forces *within* such societies which would abridge them if they could. (These rights do not persist simply because they are underpinned by supporting values; it is the fact of their institutionalization in law which is a crucial protection *of* those values.) The extent and the character of support for certain other values – which can certainly in a sense be termed 'public values' – is more problematic to assess. At a rather abstract level there clearly is a readiness on the part of most people to subscribe to certain 'official' values of this kind: for example, democracy, equality of opportunity, tolerance, individual liberty, etc. But the extensive 'sharing' of even these values may be possible *only* at this highly abstract level. As soon as there is a need to consider their *application* – in specific social, institutional and political conditions – much of the consensus tends to disappear, and people's attachment to other values and goods, notably property and privilege, tends to introduce disagreements of quite fundamental kinds. (These issues are discussed more extensively in Chapter 4.)

Now, the plausibility of the moral crisis analysis of our 'millennial moralists' depends upon these complex realities being disregarded in favour of certain potent but simplifying myths – myths which are rooted in a generalized disposition to regard modernization as pathological. Two myths have proved particularly significant in this respect: the myth of the better past; and the myth that the essential character of that better past can be restored – through a reassertion of tradition and a reaffirmation of our common national heritage and shared identity.

Let us begin with the first of these myths. Raymond Williams, in his book *The Country and the City* (Williams, 1973), employs the image of an escalator, moving backwards through time. The traveller on this escalator first encounters the literary critics F. R. Leavis and Denys Thompson deploring the philistinism and commercialism which they saw as associated with mass production and mass civilization in the 1930s; they look back to a better 'Old England' and lament that 'a whole culture that had preserved its continuity from the earliest times had now received its quietus' (Leavis and Thompson, 1933, quoted in Williams, ibid., p. 18). The point about Williams' escalator, however, is that as it moves back further and further into the past, the traveller encounters a whole succession of such laments for a better, more integrated, more morally responsible community – which, on each occasion, is seen as having only just, often within living memory, passed away irretrievably. Williams traces this back as far as Magna Carta but points out that in one sense, the ultimate point of reference is Eden! In many nineteenth- and twentieth-century versions of such idealizing retrospects, a present which is *urban* is contrasted with a past that is *rural* – so that a profound ambivalence about urbanization and urbanism is one important tendency shaping the images of the idealized past. One of the most interesting features of the essentially similar laments of our 'millennial moralists', however, is that their main point of reference is typically to a better *urban* (as well as national) past. The references, as we have seen, are to 'Hoggartian' working-class communities of extended families which are bound to one another and to a wider national identity by a sense of common decency, a shared past, the residual but still effectual influence of Christianity – all reinforced by informal mechanisms of social control.

Now, it is important to emphasize again that such images are not wholly misplaced. But it is equally necessary to stress that they *are* selective and idealized. They omit, for example, the whole long history of recurring middle-class anxieties and periodic panics about the moral state of the urban working class – which can be traced right back to the beginnings of the growth of industrial towns in the UK. David Reeder, for example, has pointed out that 'a paradoxical feature of Victorian reformist effort was that . . . the family and the community became more and more idealised'; and 'the argument for popular education in early and mid-Victorian Britain was frequently underpinned by a desire to restore the relationships of community in the new industrial urban society' (Reeder, 1977, p. 76). Reeder goes on to examine a whole range of concerns about 'the urban child' taken up by various different groups of social reformers around the end of the nineteenth century: these included, to take just one example, the efforts of the Nonconformist minister J. B. Patton to arrest what he saw as the moral deterioration of young people by 'working for the salvation of the unfit in mind and body' – which led him to found the Boys' Life Brigade (1899), Guilds of Courtesy, and the Young Men's Brigade of Service (ibid., p. 82).

In more recent times too, numerous depictions of certain kinds of working-class urban localities highlight not their stability and moral integration within an overarching national community of common values but precisely opposite characteristics. For example, a number of sociological studies of families in Liverpool's dockland area in the 1950s, summarized in Josephine Klein's *Samples from English Cultures* (Klein, 1965), paint a picture of dislocation and alienation. Absent fathers abound: in one of John Barron Mays' samples of 66 families, 'thirty-one (boys) had fathers away at sea, dead, or gone, or chronically ill' (ibid., pp. 42–3). Mothers are no less a problem: 'he (Mays) notes the premarital and promiscuous sexual intercourse, the illegitimacy without stigma, the mothers up too early after confinement, haphazard feeding in infancy, . . . the toughness of children towards each other, their irritability and violence, etc.' (ibid., p. 43). Another study of this locality cited by Klein is Madeleine Kerr's study of 'Ship Street', an area which, although disadvantaged, was not severely socially dislocated: 'the genuine Ship Streeter has been in the area for two or three generations' (ibid., p. 50) and 'relatives beyond the immediate family are in and out of the house all the time' (ibid., p. 51). Kerr claims that in this locality, the sense of moral obligation became progressively attenuated as groups became larger and more remote. As Klein summarizes the argument:

> No obligations are felt to the remotest and largest groups. This is very well brought out in Kerr's discussion on crime. Two words are used to describe taking things which belong to others: thieving and robbing. The former is permitted, the latter strongly condemned. Thieving is taking things from an employer 'who'll never miss it', or from the large stores in the city . . . Robbing, on the other hand, is taking things from one's own group, from friends or relatives, and this is strongly condemned. (ibid., p. 50)

Paul Willis' well-known account of 'shop floor culture' and the school counter-culture of 'the lads' in a secondary modern school in Wolverhampton in the early 1970s paints a similar picture of the lack of moral integration of a certain section (but not a criminal section) of the working class into wider social values. His work also highlights the persistence *and longevity* of attitudes of disrespect not only for employers and their representatives, but, for example, for women and non-whites among young males in such localities (Willis, 1977). All these accounts, and many more which could be cited, may well be portraits of what were once called the 'rough' rather than the 'respectable' sections of the working class – and the accounts we have are, of course, refracted through the theoretical presuppositions of the various researchers involved. Nevertheless, they are an important antidote to the idealized retrospects favoured by some of our 'millennial moralists'.

A final point about these idealized retrospects is that they can sometimes carry an implicitly racist message – particularly in cases where they are linked up to attacks upon multiculturalism as a disintegrative influence in our society. The stable, socially cohesive communities of yesteryear which are celebrated are, implicitly, *white* communities. The latent (and usually unintended) message, therefore, can become that the supposed slide into cultural and moral disintegration followed the arrival of those cultural 'others' who did not share 'our' way of life – many of whom were black as well as 'foreign'.

The second potent myth, that a strong assertion of traditional values can recover key elements of this 'world we have lost', is in many ways a corollary of the first. The basis of the second myth is that society's moral decadence is ascribed primarily to a deficiency of moral responsibility on the part of *individuals*, and this in turn is attributed to the failure of parents, schools, religious leaders and other agencies of socialization to provide clear moral guidance and discipline, and to produce a well-founded sense of identity. Their ineffectiveness in this regard is said to result largely from the influence of false values and false prophets: the catalogue, as we have seen already, includes indulgent parents, single parents, trendy progressive teachers, teacher trainers who have infected students with 'barmy theory', liberal theologians who have diluted the stern message of orthodox religious teaching, relativistic intellectual currents in the arts and social sciences, the gay and feminist lobbies, ethnic and cultural diversity and the multicultural lobbies, etc. The narrative is very familiar; it has been almost endlessly recycled – and amplified by sections of the right-wing media – over the last twenty years and more. And yet, and yet – supporters of this sort of analysis have looked in vain for the bright day of a widespread return to traditional values. Instead they have seen only a succession of false dawns.[3] The fundamental explanation of this failure lies, I believe, in the inadequacy of the underlying account of how and why society is changing. Far from it being the case that we need to turn away from 'barmy theory' in favour of sound common sense as supporters of tradition sometimes advocate, what is actually needed is a more adequate theoretical analysis – which not only recognizes current changes for what they are but also provides a more comprehensive and convincing explanatory account of them. As Rob Moore has convincingly argued, this kind of dichotomizing of 'theory' as against 'common sense' is in any case, a piece of politically opportunistic mystification: 'the argument against theory is *itself* a theory' (Moore, 1994b, p. 36).[4] However, before moving on in the next section of this chapter to examine some recent sociological writing which seems to me to meet this requirement of offering a more comprehensively and convincingly theorized account of current changes, I want to briefly consider the widening *political* appeal of 'millennial moralism' – or at least certain aspects of it.

I suggested earlier that Nicholas Tate's overall position on values, culture and identity can be located within the broader frame of neo-conservative thinking – and I have attempted in Chapter 1 to analyse some of the continuities and discontinuities between recent neo-conservative writing and a much longer tradition of Conservative cultural criticism represented by writers such as T. S. Eliot, Matthew Arnold and Coleridge. However, it is increasingly clear that at least some aspects of the neo-conservative analysis of our contemporary cultural and moral predicament are by no means confined to that narrow political constituency. For one thing, the current occupant of the throne of St Augustine is not politically aligned in that way. For another, as New Labour shifts ever rightwards in an effort to capture the so-called 'middle ground' of British politics (actually of course an ideologically shifting ground), we may speculate that the appeal of analyses whose political implications are in the direction of blaming complex social problems on *individual* moral inadequacies is likely to be considerable. This is particularly likely to be the case given the increasing impotence of national governments when it comes to dealing with many of the real causes of contemporary behavioural changes. New Labour in office might indeed be 'tough on crime' but it might also lack not only the freedom of economic manoeuvre but also the political will to be similarly and effectively 'tough on the causes of crime'.

Of greater *intellectual* interest, perhaps, is the stance of some on the centre-left who differ radically from most of those contemporary neo-conservatives who managed to achieve, under the auspices of 'Thatcherism', some degree of accommodation with *neo-liberal* ideas and policies – notwithstanding the significant philosophical tensions between these twin strands of New Right thought. A case in point is A. H. Halsey's Foreword to Norman Dennis and George Erdos, *Families Without Fatherhood,* published by the New Right 'think tank' the Institute for Economic Affairs (Dennis and Erdos, 1993). The book summarizes research which indicates that divorce and single parenthood damage children – and that this damage is not *simply* the result of the poverty which marital breakdown often brings in its train.

Halsey's Foreword begins as follows:

> Modern society has strange suppositions. I think the central one is the belief that if ego maximizes his or her choices we are all better off... The family is the age-old disproof of this collective nonsense. The traditional family is the tested arrangement for safeguarding the welfare of children. *Only a post-Christian country could believe otherwise.* (ibid., p. ix, my italics)

Halsey goes on to link a defence of the traditional family and parental responsibility to a vehement attack on what he considers to be excessive individualism of the 1980s and the policies which have fostered it. He ascribes what he symptomatically calls 'the individualist *doctrine*' (my italics) to two main causes: first the triumph of technology over nature which tends to conceal the family's continuing role in the creation of collective wealth; secondly, 'the developing assumption, so rampant in the 1980s, that the adult ego is self-sufficient'. The combined result, he says, is an outlook that proclaims that children are commodities which adults can choose to have or not, simply as a matter of sovereign consumer preference, while 'marriage becomes a mere contract'. He comments that this is already imminently leading to a situation in which rich societies face declining populations and warns apocalyptically that 'the individualized as distinct from the socialized country eventually and literally destroys itself' (ibid., p. x). His alternative is a tough-minded combination of traditionalism and collectivism. *Moral* support for stable two-parent families (and for other-regarding altruism within such families) needs to be re-emphasized. He consequently deplores the dismantling in the 1980s of the (never adequate) institutional supports such a policy requires – in terms of public health, education and social services, which would enable 'quality children' to be produced, 'women... to have freedom to combine motherhood with a career', and 'men... to take a fuller part in domestic rearing of their offspring' (ibid., p. xi). Halsey concludes by ascribing responsibility for this state of affairs *jointly* to Margaret Thatcher and those fractions of the educated middle class whom he sees as devoted to libertarianism and 'lifestyle choice':

> Mrs Thatcher inadvertently found her central principles powerfully supported in this crucial area by quite other social and personal forces in the creation of a new and indeed unprecedented wave of pro-individual, anti-social development of economy, polity and community. (ibid., p. xii)

REFLEXIVE MODERNIZATION

Professor Halsey is, of course, far too scholarly and clear-sighted a sociologist to subscribe to any simple myth of a better past. He is quite explicit about this:

> It is not that I see a golden age of traditionalism. Material deprivation, and inequality between the classes and the sexes were integral to British society in the first half of the century. There was no utopia. There was cruelty, a double standard of sexual morality, incest and child abuse, savage treatment of unmarried mothers, desertions and separations. (ibid., p. xi)

Moreover, in analysing Halsey's position, we should not lose sight of the fact that an objective appraisal of the available evidence does strongly suggest that he may be right to endorse the view that marital separation is, taken overall, seriously damaging to many of the children involved. Neither feminists (nor men!) do well to try to rationalize this away. Nevertheless, I suggest that even Halsey tends to underestimate the complexity and intractability of the problems he identifies – and especially their causes. Arguably, the situation cannot be adequately explained in terms of the abdication of individual moral responsibility and the influence of a 'doctrine' of unqualified consumer freedom – even when these are set in the context of the damaging social consequences of the free-market orthodoxies and institutional changes which have occurred since the 1980s.

A more comprehensive sociology of change in modern 'post-industrial' societies is available in the intriguingly convergent work of Anthony Giddens in Britain, and Ulrich Beck (and Elisabeth Beck-Gernsheim) in Germany. Their work was initiated quite independently, and from significantly different theoretical starting points, but what has emerged is an impressively similar and comprehensive diagnosis of the major directions and determinants of change, as these societies move into what both writers see as a new phase of modernization. The overall corpus of writing now available is substantial and it will not be possible to summarize it in anything like its full scope – which includes, for example, a preoccupation with global 'risk' and a range of environmental concerns.[5] What I shall attempt here is the briefest outline of the core ideas – especially as they relate to the issues of tradition and change, values and beliefs, and questions of self, identity and interpersonal relationships.

A multiplicity of terms has been used by social analysts of various kinds, to try to capture what many agree in seeing as the *transformative* character of the changes which are currently reshaping the world's most economically and technologically advanced societies: for example, 'post-industrial', 'post-Marxist', 'post-modern', 'post-Fordist' – while others have suggested that we are witnessing 'the end of ideology', etc. The term which Giddens and Beck employ to characterize these fundamental changes is rather forbidding and jargonistic: 'reflexive modernization' – and this may help to explain why it has not 'caught on' to the extent that some of the other phrases certainly have. It is probably *not* helpful to begin by trying to offer a succinct definition of reflexive modernization! A better approach may be to outline what Giddens and Beck see as the fundamental causes of all this complex change. At risk of considerable over-simplification, then, I shall suggest that three major 'motors' of change (to use Beck's term – 1992, p. 92) are seen as fundamental: first, 'the accumulation of reflexively organized knowledge' (Giddens, 1994a, p. 79); second, globalization; and third, the labour market. Giddens seems to place strongest emphasis on the first of these terms while Beck gives greater prominence to the last, but all three components of the analysis are significant for both writers. We shall consider each in turn.

Causes

(1) The accumulation of reflexively organized knowledge

Several major social theorists have regarded the accumulation of human knowledge as one of the principal determinants of social and economic as well as cultural change. Most famously, perhaps, the classical German sociologist Max Weber analysed the emergence and development of industrial societies partly in terms of the spread of scientific and legal-rational modes of thought and calculation, and he saw these as crucial not only to what he called the 'disenchantment' of the world but also to the development of capitalist modes of economic calculation and the inexorable spread of bureaucracy and legal-rational modes of domination (Weber, 1968). A more recent theorist whose work gave even greater prominence to the significance of Cognition (as he termed it) for social change was Ernest Gellner – whose analysis of 'the structure of human history' effectively ended up by suggesting, as Perry Anderson has argued, that 'the transformations of knowledge become to all intents and purposes the prime mover of historical change' (Anderson, 1990, p. 70; Gellner, 1988). As Anderson also points out, the significance of Cognition is, if anything, even greater in Gellner's analysis of *late* capitalism, where he considers a world in which material consumption may reach some kind of saturation level while 'Cognition...would advance with undiminished, even accelerating momentum' (ibid., p. 72). While Giddens seldom makes reference to Gellner, his overall conceptualization of reflexive modernization seems in many ways indebted (at least indirectly) to Gellner's work – and it too certainly accords a central place to the role of the accumulation of knowledge in propelling social change.

   Now Giddens is, of course, by no means the only contemporary writer to recognize that human knowledge and the applications of that knowledge have become ever more powerful – for example in enabling human beings to control and manipulate 'nature' in ways that were almost unimaginable until relatively recently. What is genuinely original in Giddens' discussion, however, is what is picked out in the phrase '*reflexively* organized knowledge'. The idea at the heart of 'reflexivity' is that of human self-awareness. For Giddens, humans are *intentional* beings, that is, they act according to their own consciously identified purposes, and they reflect upon and monitor their own thought and action, and modify their behaviour accordingly. This is a key reason why wholly deterministic accounts of human action are inadequate. The distinctive character of reflexivity in late modern societies, however, goes beyond this – and it is, Giddens argues, best grasped by contrasting these societies with those in which tradition was much more powerful. In traditional societies, large areas of social life and action were relatively *un*reflective: things were done in certain ways precisely because of the sanction of tradition: 'this is how it has always been'. In modern societies by contrast, the authority of tradition *qua* tradition is undermined; the grounds of social action are systematically interrogated by reference to current (and often expert) knowledge. This does not mean that tradition is wholly superseded; as Giddens says, 'tradition can be justified, but only in the light of knowledge which is not itself authenticated by tradition' (Giddens, 1990, p. 38). What is more, this interrogation by the critical questioning of expert knowledge comes to affect virtually *all* areas of modern life – from the most highly institutionalized (e.g. global financial transactions, investment decisions by multinational corporations) to the most personal and intimate. Thus, almost all areas of social life become permanently open to processes of critical questioning – which is directed back reflexively on to them, demanding constant reappraisal and reorientation: 'The reflexivity of modern social life consists in the fact that social practices are constantly examined and reformed in the light of incoming information about those very practices, thus constitutively altering their character' (ibid., p. 38).[6] The core of reflexivity, therefore (as Gregor McLennan has so clearly summarized it), is 'increasing self questioning, together with proliferating sources of *information*' (McLennan, 1992, p. 344). And the core of reflexive modernization is the development of a whole social order in which such reflexivity becomes pervasive and governs virtually all major processes of social change. Except episodically – or within self-insulating enclaves – there is no way of returning from this state back to tradition.

(2) Globalization

The fact that this form of reflexivity is increasingly *global* in its reach is the second key element in Giddens' and Beck's analysis. In terms of culture, one of the most powerful solvents of the authority of tradition (of whatever kind) is the increasing awareness on the part of quite ordinary people (as distinct from experts), and across the whole world, of lifestyles, values and world-views which are at variance with those which have previously been *locally* dominant (and in some cases virtually unquestionable). The extension of Western modes of education, of electronic communications, of tourism, of consumerism, even of warfare, undermines localism and delegitimizes forms of domination which depend upon localized and traditional belief systems and the sanctions which have upheld them. We are, Giddens suggests, 'the first generation to live in a thoroughly post-traditional society... a global, cosmopolitan order' (Giddens, 1994a, p. 83). Not only this, across the more economically advanced societies, we have also seen a kind of 'cultural diaspora' in which what Scott Lash calls 'transnational communities of taste, lifestyle and belief' can co-exist *and* influence one another across a range of locations that are highly dispersed geographically (Lash, 1994, esp. pp. 146–53). Thus the link between localism and shared ways of life is further undermined. Moreover, these spatially separated but culturally common ways of life exist – and can only exist – within the broader context of a cultural and value pluralism that is also increasingly global in its reach. One ironic effect of this same phenomenon is that it can act as a stimulus to active attempts to re-invigorate local cultural identities and to assert various kinds of fundamentalism – particularly those associated with nation, ethnicity and religion. However, the very multiplicity of these attempts – as well as their international visibility through the media – tends to undermine their credibility.

Globalization is, of course, not confined to the cultural sphere. The globalization of the operations of financial markets, the increasing power and influence of multinational corporations, the design and manufacture of cars, household appliances, electronic consumer goods, etc. for a global market place – all these are commonly recognized aspects of the phenomenon. A less obvious instance discussed by Giddens is *food*. In the more prosperous economies, for example, vegetarianism is an increasingly significant 'alternative' lifestyle choice for a growing minority of people – especially women. But this has been made a *palatable* alternative (in the literal as well as the metaphorical sense of the term) by the development of a global market in vegetable produce – one of whose consequences is that almost any kind of fruit or vegetable is available in the best supermarkets at almost any time of year. As Giddens points out, the implications are manifold. 'Nature' is increasingly transcended: localized diets and natural restrictions on diet are displaced by consumer choices – choices whose satisfaction requires, *inter alia*, the increasing development of cash crops in developing economies (sometimes at the expense of the most basic local dietary needs), international wholesale and retail operations in the marketing of food, etc. Moreover, as Giddens observes, all this applies not only to the affluent: 'few are exempt as most food becomes industrially produced' (Giddens, 1994a, p. 224).

An interesting recent example of the ways in which the cultural and economic effects of globalization may reinforce one another – to the consternation of those who may see themselves as moral guardians – was provided by a report on film violence published late in 1996 by the British Board of Film Classification. The publication of the report came shortly after the Conservative government's National Heritage Secretary, Virginia Bottomley, had launched an action plan against violence on television. The burden of the BBFC report was that censorship operating at the level of nation states was relatively powerless to influence a global culture of screen violence which had its roots in the economic priorities dictated by the leading American film producers and the business interests which supported them. James Ferman, the Director of the BBFC, pointed out that many of the most commercially successful superstars featured in the most gratuitously violent films, and that cutting the most objectionable elements did little to counteract the overall culture of the film if, as a whole, it was dedicated to violence:

> These are the films – films about strong men with the power to control the world – which everyone wants to see, including British audiences ... The real solution is for Hollywood to wake up with a conscience. But I have my doubts. There's too much money at stake. (*Independent*, 12 December 1996, p. 6)

(3) The labour market

This brings us to the third of Beck's 'motors of change': the labour market. For Beck, the primary significance of the operation of labour markets in contemporary advanced societies is that they increasingly propel people towards an intensified form of *individualism*. The underlying idea – that there is a close connection between the advance of the division of labour in the occupational sphere and increased individualism – is, of course, not new. Emile Durkheim, writing at the end of the nineteenth century, famously analysed the development of industrializing societies from precisely this standpoint and he identified certain 'pathological' effects in terms of 'exaggerated' forms of individualism (egoism and anomie) – which, he believed, resulted from individuals being cut adrift from the morally regulating influence of society (Durkheim, 1964). Later theorists such as the American, Talcott Parsons, similarly laid great emphasis on the *interdependencies* between the division of labour in the occupational sphere, and the character of the social roles and the kinds of individual motivations developed within institutions such as the family and schools (see, for example, Parsons, 1959). The essence of Beck's argument is that in the current stage of development of advanced societies, three aspects of the labour market, each of which has profound consequences for individualism, have assumed increasing importance. These are: the heightened importance of *education and skills*; the demand for increased geographical and social *mobility;* and the increased pressures of *competition* within the labour market (Beck, 1992, pp. 92–5). Furthermore, each of these is complicated (and its effects made more far-reaching) by its relationship with the changing character of *gender* relations in modern society.

The importance of education and training, both for initially gaining employment as well as for career progression, increases, Beck argues, for a range of reasons. The proportion of well-paid semi- and unskilled occupations in the advanced economies is declining – especially those relatively well-paid and full-time jobs (managerial as well as manual) in manufacturing industry which have until very recently been mainly a male preserve. This is occurring as a result of international competition, automation, 'downsizing', etc. Employers are prepared to pay premiums for scarce skills but the under-educated and unskilled find it increasingly difficult to find work which provides either a living wage or job security. At the same time, a significant expansion in educational opportunity for girls and women since the 1960s has resulted in increased numbers of more highly qualified females entering the labour market. Furthermore, the labour market they are entering is itself changing in ways which place these more highly educated women at a comparative advantage – notably as a result of the growth of service sector occupations. This itself is one factor intensifying labour market competition; another is the *international* competition affecting less-skilled occupations in manufacturing – with certain kinds of employment being transferred to low-wage economies. Various factors intensify the demand for individuals to become increasingly *mobile*: increasing job insecurity itself renders individuals less able to negotiate if their employer decides to relocate them or their work; reluctance to accept relocation can be perceived as a lack of commitment to the organization; the increasingly common experience of redundancy forces individuals to consider relocating themselves in pursuit of alternative employment, etc. Moreover, these developments are, as Beck says, 'by no means independent of one another; rather they reinforce one another and only thus ... do they cause the process of individualization' (ibid., pp. 94–5). The pressure for individuals to be cast back upon their own resources is further intensified by the weakening role and effectiveness (even in Germany) of trade unions and other collectivist forces. Instead there is an increasing 'juridification of labour relations' and labour law: this leads to 'an individualization of interests which no longer depend upon highly aggregated interest groups' (ibid., p. 95).

Some consequences

For our purposes, the most significant effects of the operation of all three of these 'motors of change' concern individualism and identity. Traditional, socially ascribed identities of all kinds – whether grounded in the solidarities of social class or locality or gender roles or religious allegiance (or the interrelations of all these) – no longer provide stable or relevant points of anchorage and reference. The extent to which this is so varies considerably of course, as between, say, metropolitan centres and the most remote rural localities. But everywhere, the authority of traditional cultural prescriptions and expectations is being undermined: and the very possibility of living according to them is being rendered increasingly problematic for more and more people. Now *of course* individual choice enters into this. It is, for example, individual women who are choosing careers over motherhood, or electing to be 'child-free' (as against feeling psychically incomplete because they are 'child-less'), or deciding that marriage is not a necessary precondition of living in a committed relationship, or choosing (more frequently than men) to end their marriage and seek fulfilment elsewhere. And one kind of popular explanation of what is going on is to place the blame for all this 'instability' on the self-absorbed self-indulgence of the individuals themselves:

> In many people's view the answer is obvious. The individualists themselves are the problem, their wants and discontent, their thirst for excitement and diminishing willingness to fit in with others, to subordinate themselves or do without. A kind of universal *Zeitgeist* has seized hold of people, urging them to do their own thing... (Beck and Beck-Gernsheim, 1995, p. 3)

But as we have already seen, these patterns of behaviour are precisely that – *patterned*. They certainly *are* the product of individuals' choices. But the fact of having to structure one's life as a whole succession of complex (sometimes agonizing) choices between highly uncertain, risky possibilities is not optional for increasing numbers of people. In crucial ways, individuals are as much the victims of these developments as they are their originators. Moreover, such choices have to be actively negotiated within a risk-laden and formidably complex framework of institutional rules, regulations, resources – with associated rewards and penalties. As Beck and Beck-Gernsheim have put it:

> Individualization in this sense, therefore, certainly does not mean an 'unfettered logic of action, juggling in a virtually empty space'; nor does it mean mere 'subjectivity', an attitude which refuses to see that 'beneath the surface of life is a highly efficient, densely woven institutional society'. On the contrary, the space within which modern subjects deploy their

options is anything but a non-social sphere ... (and) ... the decisive feature of these modern regulations and guidelines is that, far more than earlier, individuals must, in part, supply them for themselves, import them into their own biographies through their own actions ...

To simplify: one was born into traditional society and its preconditions (such as estate or religion). For modern social advantages, one has to *do* something, to make an active effort. One has to win, know how to assert oneself in the competition for limited resources – and not only once, but day after day. (Beck and Beck-Gernsheim, 1996, p. 25)

To an extent that is historically unprecedented, individuals are *forced* to make choices in more and more spheres of their lives. Instead of running along the safe tramlines of culturally prescribed ways of doing things, modern individuals inhabit a world in which complex bodies of expert knowledge have displaced the prescriptions and recipes of tradition. Knowledge and information about *health* is a good example – which Giddens has discussed at some length (see, for example, Giddens, 1991, pp. 99– 114). There are multiple pressures to adopt a more healthy lifestyle: from medical experts, from dieticians, from fashion 'gurus' (another kind of 'expert'), from family members ('cut down on your smoking, Dad'), etc. However, at any particular moment when choices have to be made, there is no unanimity among these experts. Even scientists who are trying to be objective disagree about matters such as the effects of cholesterol, while various well-financed lobbies and interests seek to persuade us that red meat is good for us, that sugar is (or is not) harmful, that we should patronize expensive private gymnasia, etc., etc. There has also emerged a range of new pathologies linked to the dissemination of all this knowledge concerning health and desirable body shape – for example, eating disorders such as anorexia and bulimia. Much of this knowledge is knowledge about various *risks*; but the indeterminacy and contested nature of the knowledge also means that an element of risk is likely to exist however one interprets and acts upon it. Yet we have no choice but to take account of it and act upon it in *some* way. These bodies of socially distributed 'expertise' structure our horizons of action, just as ritual, ascription and custom framed human action in more traditional societies. And this brings us to Giddens' main point: what is going on is a general expansion of what he calls 'institutional reflexivity' in which 'expert', specialized bodies of knowledge are socially disseminated and (necessarily) actively interpreted by ordinary people as a basis for choice and action in their everyday lives:

It is institutional, because it is a basic structuring element of social activity in modern settings. It is reflexive in the sense that terms introduced to describe social life routinely enter and transform it – not as a mechanical process, nor necessarily in a controlled way, but because they become part of the frames of action which individuals or groups adopt. (Giddens, 1992, pp. 28–9)

Because of this, individual biographies increasingly take the form of an active process of a conscious *making* of the self, in a world in which 'in many situations, we have no choice but to make choices' (Giddens, 1994b, p. 187). One's biography becomes a consciously structured (and restructured) reflexive *project*. This certainly means that as compared with previous generations, many individuals experience greatly expanded choices – but many of these choices must be made in contexts of much greater uncertainty.

When two or more of these biographies have to be negotiated *together*, the complexity and tensions involved potentially multiply. This is at the heart of the dilemmas and tensions of contemporary family life. The recipes, sanctions and constraints of the past have been greatly weakened – particularly for women, for reasons that have already been partially discussed. As a result of the dissemination of effective birth control, few women in modern societies are any longer at the mercy of nature (and men) in the sense of being condemned to a lifetime of child-bearing. As life expectancy extends, the child-bearing years are, in any case, a smaller and potentially less significant fraction of the life cycle. Although the phenomenon of women's employment is not new, what has changed is the proportion of well-educated women who can earn enough over a lifetime to be economically independent if they choose to be – and this includes for some the possibility of single parenthood combined with career progression. The existence of certain welfare provisions has, in many societies, meant that this choice of supported single parenthood is also open to much poorer women – albeit at a significant cost to them as well as the state. The advance of biotechnologies has made virgin birth a real possibility; parents can increasingly choose the sex of their child; and 'single individuals and same sex couples can have children of their own' (Giddens, 1994b, p. 189). Against this changing background, women's desires and aspirations have changed and expanded in ways which the traditional institution of marriage finds hard or impossible to accommodate – not least because *men*, understandably, show little inclination to make the sacrifices or assume the role traditionally allocated to wives and mothers. Househusbands exist (in small numbers) but, as the Becks ironically point out, according to the available research 'the househusbands suffer from the house*wife* syndrome: invisible achievements, lack of recognition and lack of self-confidence' (Beck and Beck-Gernsheim, 1995, p. 21). Ulrich Beck has argued that the entire process of capitalist industrialization was structurally dependent upon an occupational and domestic division of labour which he (perhaps misleadingly) terms 'feudal'. Within marriage, women were in significant ways unfree; and their roles in biological and social reproduction were prescribed: '. . . status-based marriage rules dominated as imperatives (the indissolubility of marriage, the duties of motherhood, and the like). They constructed the scope of action, to be sure, but they also obligated and forced spouses into togetherness' (Beck, 1994, p. 15).

But these arrangements – which we have inherited in a weakened form – seem increasingly unsustainable as well as ethically obnoxious to some. Today, there is no single sanctioned model of marriage. There are *negative* models, for example those which require women to maintain independent educational and professional careers of their own 'because otherwise they face ruin in the case of divorce and remain dependent upon their husband's money in marriage' (ibid., p. 15). There are models in which neither partner is prepared to sacrifice promotion possibilities and so the 'family' ends up living apart. These, and many other variants, tend to 'not weld people together but break apart the togetherness and multiply the questions' (ibid., p. 15). More optimistically, Giddens suggests that marriage (or living in a committed relationship) is now less a *determinant* of commitment than 'a *signifier of commitment*' (Giddens, 1992, p. 192, my italics) and that this is in many ways positive. It requires individuals to negotiate their biographies in a spirit of greater equality and democracy. In particular, it requires both parties to allow one another considerable autonomy, to respect 'the personal boundaries of the other' and offers scope for 'the involvement of individuals in determining the conditions of their own association' (ibid., p. 189). These relationships depend upon what he calls 'active trust' rather than traditional sanctions. However, despite this more hopeful assessment (*and* his optimistic assessment of the possibilities of active trust more generally as a basis for institutional solidarity), Giddens does not seek to hide the potential fragility of relationships developed under such auspices. Such relationships are sustained primarily *for their own sake*, for the intrinsic satisfactions they provide. However, in the conditions of late modernity, such commitment is seldom likely to be more than provisionally invested. He suggests that even *filial* ties may in some cases take on something of this voluntary quality: 'the relationship depends on who the other person "is" rather than on a specified social role' (Giddens, 1994, p. 117). The fairly recent American phenomenon of children seeking to 'divorce' their parents is, perhaps, a limiting case here.

CONCLUSION

This chapter has examined contrasting accounts and evaluations of some of the most significant changes facing individuals and groups in British society as we approach the millennium. There is broad agreement that these changes are challenging and far reaching. There is much less agreement about how we should respond – whether as citizens or as educators. However, there can be little doubt that the issues are of such importance and complexity that no good purpose will be served by declining the challenge or by refusing to engage in serious debate – particularly debate with those whose views we do not share. It has sometimes been assumed too easily that the most important voices that should contribute to discussions about the most desirable forms of moral and 'spiritual' education in our society are, on the one hand, representatives of religious bodies and, on the other, philosophers – in addition, of course, to politicians! All these, of course, will have (and have had) much that is pertinent to contribute. However, as this chapter has tried to demonstrate, there is also a significant role for sociologically informed analysis and – what may be of greatest importance of all – a need for all these different voices to join in a dialogue that is as genuinely open as possible. In the light of this analysis, which of course does not at all pretend to be value free, I shall go on in the second part of this book to consider what forms of moral, civic and political education might be most justifiable and most relevant for schools to offer to those young people who will live most of their lives in the next century.

NOTES

1 The National Forum for values in education and the community was set up following SCAA's 'Education for Adult Life' Conference held in January 1996. It consisted of 'subgroups drawn from fields including teaching, business, the police, the judiciary, the trade union movement, teacher-training and the media'. The groups reported back to SCAA in June/July 1996 'with the aim of formulating broad proposals for the Authority to consider in the autumn' (SCAA, 1996a, p. 3). A discussion of the consultative report of the Forum, which was issued in November 1996, forms the final section of Chapter 4 of this book.

2 For what is still one of the best discussions of these matters see Bailey (1984), especially chapters 1–4.

3 It is symptomatic that on the day when all national newspapers carried reports – usually on

their front pages – of Dr Carey's House of Lords 'moral crusade' speech, other items of news included the following:

– evidence of what was widely construed as moral equivocation by Dr Carey himself in relation to the impending divorce of the heir to the throne and Princess Diana: pressed in a radio interview to condemn adultery (and by implication the adulterous behaviour of both parties in the royal divorce), Dr Carey chose to side-step the question, which led the *Sun* to comment, in a characteristic instance of editorial hypocrisy and bad faith:

> the archbishop refuses to condemn the adultery of the Prince of Wales. Now adultery is no different from stealing, lying or murder. It's either right or wrong with no grey area in between. If the head of the church can't see that, what hope is there for the rest of us? (*Sun*, 6 July 1996, p. 6)

– an announcement that 250,000 people were expected to march through London to Clapham Common in celebration of the 25th London Gay Pride event and to celebrate London's status as 'gay capital of Europe' (Walker, *Independent*, p. 17);

– an impressive piece of special pleading by John Garrett, managing director of the Recreation Division of the Rank Organization, urging greater deregulation of controls on gambling, and advocating specifically a relaxation of the provisions of the 1968 Gaming Act (to allow advertising and promotion) and also relaxation of planning regulations so as to permit companies like his own to 'respond' to the 'real demand for edge-of-town leisure developments'. All this was justified as necessary to enable the leisure industry to 'create jobs and boost earnings from tourism' and prepare the industry 'to become one of the great British success stories of the 21st Century' (Garrett, 1996, p. 28).

4   As Moore points out:

> What the attack on theory illustrates is the arbitrary and opportunistic way in which theory is incorporated into public debates and political rhetoric. This device operates by opposing theory with the alternative of common sense. The latter is implicitly taken as what any sensible person knows to be really the case. Theory by contrast is presented as self-indulgent, out-of-touch, unworldly and narcissistic . . . [but] the argument against theory is itself a theory . . . (Moore, 1994b, p. 36)

5   Ulrich Beck's discussion of environmental issues is most fully developed in his *Ecological Politics in an Age of Risk* (Beck, 1995). The key texts in which Giddens outlines his account of reflexive modernization are *The Consequences of Modernity* (Giddens, 1990), *Modernity and Self Identity* (Giddens, 1991), and *Beyond Left and Right* (Giddens, 1994). The last is probably the most comprehensive and accessible discussion yet available. Beck's overall analysis is most fully developed in his *Risk Society* (Beck, 1992). Texts which address the consequences of reflexive modernization in the sphere of sexuality, love and interpersonal relationships are Giddens' *The Transformation of Intimacy* (Giddens, 1992) and Ulrich Beck and Elisabeth Beck-Gernsheim's *The Normal Chaos of Love* (1995).

6   It is in this respect that Giddens' analysis seems most highly indebted to Gellner. The role of *critical* reason in the shaping and constant reshaping of modern life is a *leitmotif* of Gellner's entire *oeuvre* – exemplified nowhere more clearly than in *Reason and Culture*, whose final paragraph includes the following:

> In a stable traditional world, men had identities, linked to their social roles, and confirmed by their overall vision of nature and society. Instability and rapid change both in knowledge and society has deprived such self-images of their erstwhile feel of reliability. Identities are perhaps more ironic and conditional than once they were, or at any rate, when confident, unjustifiably so. (Gellner, 1992b, p. 182)

Part Two
Curriculum Implications:
Moral and Civic Education for
Twenty-first-Century Citizens

Chapter 3

'Spiritual and Moral Development' and Religious Education

MIXED MESSAGES: THE CONFLATION OF RELIGION, 'THE SPIRITUAL' AND 'THE MORAL'

> Although many can accept that truth in moral matters can be independent of God, the loss of the religious basis for morality has weakened its credibility. As the Archbishop of Canterbury has recently said, people ever since the Enlightenment 'have been living off the legacy of a deep, residual belief in God. But as people move further away from that, they find it more and more difficult to give a substantial basis for why they should be good'. This is one reason why religious education must continue to be a vital part of every child's curriculum ... It is also a reason why children's spiritual development is so important, as the origin of the will to do what is right. (Tate, 1996a, para. 23)

The Chief Executive of SCAA, here, as so often, can serve as a representative spokesperson of one particular approach to the contested question of what schools in contemporary Britain should do about transmitting moral values and promoting moral development in the young. The essentials of the traditionalist position are all there (either explicitly or implicitly) in this brief quotation:

- a seemingly rather reluctant recognition that for many people in contemporary society, questions of morality and moral truth are regarded as separate (or certainly separable) from questions of religion and religious truth;
- an unsubstantiated claim that, as a result of the decline of religious belief, more people now find it more difficult than in the past to find reasons for conducting themselves morally;
- a partially contradictory assertion that religious education is therefore vital for all children (and this turns out to be a kind of RE which gives priority to a traditional form of Christianity – whilst ostensibly acknowledging the value of other world faiths);
- a question-begging statement about the importance of something called 'spiritual development' as a fundamental source of 'the will to do what is right'.

Two essential assumptions seem to be involved in maintaining this stance: first a privileging of a particular kind of religiously based understanding of the term 'spiritual' (and 'spiritual development'); secondly, a reluctance, at least in the last instance, to accept that the religious/spiritual and the moral are, for many people, separable (and separated) domains. It is relevant to notice here that certain sorts of Christian conservatives have long seen it as their business (and indeed their responsibility) to fight to preserve these ways of thinking, and also the language and the institutional arrangements that have embodied them in official educational discourse. (In part this has been a specifically *Anglican* concern.) As is well known, a successful campaign of this kind was conducted by Baroness Cox and Graham Leonard, the then Bishop of London, in their efforts to amend the 1988 Education Reform Bill so as secure a more prominent position for RE as a formally designated 'basic subject' within the National Curriculum, and to require that new 'agreed syllabuses' should 'reflect the fact that the religious traditions in Great Britain are in the main Christian whilst taking account of the teaching and practices of the other principal religions represented in Great Britain'. The amendments also, of course, included the specification of the requirement for daily acts of collective worship 'wholly or mainly of a broadly Christian character'.

It is perhaps less widely known that the 1944 Education Act was the focus of similar interventionist efforts to secure official recognition for the category 'the spiritual'. The preamble to the Act includes the statement:

> ...and it shall be the duty of the local education authority for every area, as far as their powers extend, to contribute to the spiritual, moral, mental and physical development of the community by securing that efficient education... shall be available to meet the needs of the population of their area...

(A modified version of this wording, incorporating a reference to 'a broad and balanced curriculum which promotes the spiritual, moral, *cultural,* mental and physical development of pupils', is also part of the preamble to the 1988 Act.) However, as Peter Gilliat has pointed out, the term 'spiritual' was not part of the original draft of the 1944 legislation, being introduced in committee stage – again in the House of Lords. Viscount Bledisloe, proposing the amendment, argued that in view of the fact that, for the first time, both religious education and an act of worship were to become obligatory in state schools, 'surely we ought to incorporate in the Bill words which indicate our conviction that it is the Christian ethic and that it is spirituality which we want to advance in every stage of our national education if we want to promote morality as well as the other virtues of our race' (quoted in Gilliat, 1996, p. 162).

Significantly, we find here, once again, precisely the same conjunction we have previously encountered – of doctrinal Christianity, 'the spiritual' and the use of education to promote both 'spiritual development' and national moral virtue. The *locus classicus* of this kind of position is, probably, Matthew Arnold's *Culture and Anarchy* (Arnold, 1869). It is well worth taking a little time to consider Arnold's famous essay here – not least because certain phrases from it are so frequently cited by neo-conservative writers as a key legitimizing source for their overall vision of national cultural restoration. Nicholas Tate, for example, in a recent SCAA discussion paper on 'Curriculum, culture and society', cites Arnold in just this way:

> I am not suggesting that young people should spend all their time studying Jane Austen and Shakespeare or listening to Bach and Mozart. Far from it. What I am suggesting is that

we (their educators) should give these things their proper value as (in the words of Matthew Arnold) 'the best that has been known and thought'. (Tate, 1996b, para. 29)

This particular (and favourite) quotation is, in itself, one with which it is virtually impossible to disagree: who could seriously suppose that we should *not* value and make available in schools 'the best that has been known and thought' – always presuming that we could reach a well-founded agreement about what that *was*! However, Arnold's *actual* agenda in his celebrated discussion of culture is both more specific and more controversial than the popularly cited phrases 'sweetness and light' and 'the best that has been thought and said in the world' (Arnold, p. viii) might lead one to suppose. And what turns out to be especially interesting for our purposes here is the particular linkage which Arnold seeks to establish between the terms 'culture', 'reason' and 'the will of God' – and also between all these terms and national moral regeneration.

Culture and Anarchy proposes a very particular and *programmatic* definition of culture.[1] Arnold's 'culture' has work to do. The term is deployed to highlight and to combat what he regarded as the severe limitations and the disastrous consequences[2] of certain of the dominant ideological currents of his age: notably, self-satisfied non-conformity and free-market liberalism. In *this* respect, therefore, his idea of culture is far from being simply conservative – in either the literal or party-political sense of that word. He calls upon his readers to embrace 'culture' as the basis from which to critically interrogate these dominant 'stock notions' of the period. This is nowhere more clearly brought out than in the way in which the famous (and usually decontextualized) quotation about the 'best that has been thought and said' continues:

> The whole scope of this essay is to recommend culture as the great help out of our present difficulties; culture being the pursuit of our total perfection by means of getting to know, on all the matters which most concern us, the best that has been thought and said in the world; *and through this knowledge, turning a stream of fresh and free thought upon our stock notions and habits, which we now follow staunchly but mechanically.* (ibid., p. viii, my italics)

Culture and Anarchy sets out the cardinal deficiencies, as Arnold sees them, of the three great classes of mid-Victorian society, which he designates respectively as the Barbarians (the aristocracy), the Philistines (the industrial and mainly non-conformist middle class) and the Populace (the working class). He argues that the defects in the 'consciousness' of each of these social classes derived from the fact that their class-based perception of society was inevitably sectional and self-interested. In an expansionary era of change, the aristocracy, whose virtues, though real, were increasingly anachronistic, could no longer 'supply the principle of authority needful to our present wants' (ibid., p. 47). The middle class, meanwhile, were too strongly and too uncritically identified with the forces which were certainly transforming society but also disastrously undermining social cohesion: an uncritical belief in individual liberty, in free-market economic principles, and a pious non-conformity that was as blind to its own shortcomings as it was keenly aware of everyone else's. The Populace – sometimes misleadingly depicted as a 'playful giant' – constituted a threat to social order. This was partly because of the appalling squalor and poverty in which many working-class people were obliged to exist (largely as a result of the operation of laissez-faire economic policies), but it was also partly because they were being led astray by well-intentioned but deeply wrong-headed 'agitators'. The consequence of this overall situation was that social order and human well-being were threatened by the forces of *anarchy*.

Arnold's book proposed 'culture' as the most hopeful solution to these problems; it is primarily in this sense that his concept of culture may be termed programmatic:

> [T]he essence of an epoch of expansion is the movement of ideas, and the one salvation of an epoch of expansion is a harmony of ideas. The very principle of authority which we are seeking as a defence against anarchy is right reason, ideas, light. (ibid., pp. 45–6)

Arnold defines culture in terms of disinterested enlightenment produced by the exercise of reason – hence his frequent recourse to the well-known terminology of 'right reason', 'sweetness and light', 'the study of perfection', etc. Moreover, he suggests that the only institution in mid-Victorian Britain which could accrue to itself the authority necessary for the effective dissemination of this enlightenment was the State[3] – with a subordinate but crucial role being reserved for education – primarily because only the State could hope to embody disinterested reason:

> but the question is, the action of the State being the action of the collective nation and the action of the collective nation carrying naturally great publicity, weight and force of example with it, whether we should not try to put into the action of the State as much as possible of right reason and our best self, which may, in this manner, come back to us with new force and authority... (ibid., p. 84)

In this respect, Arnold was very directly writing in the tradition of Coleridge (see Chapter 1 of this book).

All this, in Arnold's own day and in Britain, was controversial enough – as he recognized with characteristic good humour.[4] But what was – and what remains – most seriously controversial in Arnold's concept of culture is the linkage with God and Christianity which is at its very heart. His consciousness of the ebbing of the 'sea of faith' expressed in what is now the most famous of his poems, 'Dover Beach', did not at all lead him, in the polemical writings of his maturity, to weaken his belief in the central importance of the Christian religion for right living and national salvation. In this respect he was very much his father's son. The 'enlightenment' which was at the centre of his notion of culture was a specifically Christian (indeed Anglican) form of enlightenment; similarly the 'right reason' was a reason exercised in accordance with the core doctrines of the Established Church. Symptomatically, on no less than eight occasions in *Culture and Anarchy*, the telling conjunction 'reason and the will of God' recurs at salient points in the argument[5] – and this is sometimes further reinforced by reference to an appeal to a religious sensibility which is seen as part of the *natures* of the 'best' representatives of humanity:

> But in each class there are born a certain number of natures with a curiosity about their best self, with a bent for seeing things as they are, for disentangling themselves from the machinery, for simply concerning themselves with reason and the will of God, and doing their best to make them prevail – for the pursuit, in a word, of perfection. (ibid., p. 69)

For all his zeal, therefore, in calling upon his contemporaries to employ culture and disinterested reason to critically reconsider the 'stock' assumptions of the age, it turns out that certain of these assumptions were given a privileged status.[6] A certain sort of Christianity was the sacrosanct source from which the critique effected by 'culture' most fundamentally emanated. Far from being universalizable, therefore, Arnold's programmatic conception of culture turns out to be a prisoner of the most fundamental assumptions of that long Anglican, conservative tradition of thought which he so capably represented in his own time. This is, of course, the tradition which was discussed more extensively in Chapter 1, and which was to continue from Arnold into the work of other 'men of letters' of similar distinction, most notably T. S. Eliot. In our own times, it is represented by less eminent but still influential figures such as the Prince of Wales, Baroness Cox, Lord St John of Fawsley, the Revd E. R. Norman, the Revd George Austin, Dr Nicholas Tate, etc.

'THE SPIRITUAL': POSSIBILITIES AND PROBLEMS

Against this background, it is perhaps easier to see why, for such contemporary supporters of cultural restoration, there is a vitally important *symbolic* battle to be fought to preserve (or where necessary reinstate) traditional ways of designating certain categories of official educational discourse. As the American sociologist Joseph Gusfield pointed out some years ago, the capacity to control the public *definition* of certain terms can be seen as highly significant in itself – even (or perhaps especially) in cases where actual social behaviour may be markedly at variance with these 'ruling' definitions (Gusfield, 1967). Gusfield himself discusses the issue of 'prohibition' in the USA as an example. For our purposes, a pertinent example is the question of school assemblies. As we have noted above, under the 1988 Education Reform Act, there is a legal requirement for schools to hold daily acts of worship of a mainly Christian character. In many secondary schools, this requirement is in fact widely disregarded – sometimes for reasons of practical difficulty but frequently because not enough teachers in a given school are prepared to support assemblies of this kind.[7] It is significant that opponents of the House of Lords' amendment which introduced the requirement – and these objectors included many Christians – argued that precisely this consequence would follow. Nevertheless, for certain kinds of traditionalists, the *symbolic* significance of such legislation, – carrying the officially sanctioned message 'this is still a Christian country' – is itself of strategic importance.

The category of 'the spiritual' is a second case in point. As we have seen, specific and calculated intervention was needed to inscribe the term 'spiritual' into the 1944 Education Act – and the sponsors of this change clearly intended that the connotation of the term should be religious – indeed specifically Christian. Nor was the carry-over of essentially the same formulation into the 1988 Education Reform Act merely a matter of course: early drafts of the Act did *not* include the preamble requiring schools to promote 'the spiritual, moral, cultural, mental and physical development of pupils' (Alves, 1991).[8] Since 1988, there have been a significant number of further official documents which have not only sought to highlight the importance of 'the spiritual' but which have also persistently sought to tie together 'spiritual and moral development' in a manner calculated to suggest that the two constitute an indissolubly linked double entity – like Siamese twins (see, for example, National Curriculum Council, 1993; OFSTED, 1994). Thus, within symbolically important official statements about these areas of education, first, a religious dimension is imported into the category of 'the spiritual'; and then secondly, it is suggested or implied that 'the spiritual' constitutes the real (even if unacknowledged) basis of the moral. In the statement by Nicholas Tate (quoted at the beginning of this chapter) this double move is unusually transparent:

'this is one reason . . . why children's spiritual development is so important, as the origin of the will to do what is right'. More commonly, the discourse of the documents is vague, platitudinous, and tends to mix unjustified assertion with equivocation. It is worth noting that the 1993 National Curriculum Council paper *Spiritual and Moral Development* has been trenchantly criticized on precisely these grounds – for example by David Hargreaves, who noted that 'among the platitudes is the renewed assertion of the particular importance of RE to moral development' (Hargreaves, 1994, p. 34) and by Pat White, who called the document's characterization of spiritual development 'a bizarre catch-all category', its discussion of moral development 'confused and deficient' – adding that 'the document increases the confusion in the section in which it lumps spiritual and moral development together' (P. White., 1993, pp. 7–8).

It would, however, be a mistake to see this mix of assertion and ambiguity simply as evidence of an inability to think and write clearly about these important matters. There is nothing politically innocent about it. Documents from bodies like the NCC or SCAA, unlike leading articles in, say, *The Times* or the *Daily Telegraph*, cannot quite come straight out and instruct teachers that their job is to indoctrinate children in favour of a particular sort of doctrinal Christianity or in favour of various traditionalist beliefs about matters which are in fact controversial in our society. But, on the other hand, because of certain political pressures operating upon them, neither can documents from these bodies easily address such issues openly and with candour – acknowledging not only the fact but also the *legitimacy* of moral debate in many of these areas. After all, for certain kinds of traditionalists within the Conservative Party and especially among some of those who seek to drive its policies ever further to the right, the whole point is that there *is* no legitimate debate! We are then, here, very much in the realm of the sayable and the unsayable. Official documents are constrained to sustain – at least to some extent – a *pretence* that within our culturally and morally pluralist society, we are all nevertheless 'really' in essential accord about the role schools should play in these areas – and that role is essentially to instil traditional beliefs and values. In a rather similar way, no Conservative MP seems to dare to publicly admit that he or she is irreligious – let alone that their beliefs are humanist or atheist[9] – notwithstanding the abundant evidence of how far the behaviour of a minority of these same MPs departs from the religious and moral precepts they collectively seek to enjoin on others.

All this is rather depressing – and it is far from clear how far the possible election of a New Labour government, many of whose leading members identify themselves with a form of Christian 'Socialism', may improve matters. Nevertheless, the serious task of seeking to clarify the key terms and issues in current debates about the school's role in moral education must not be abandoned. Clarity in such matters is a precondition of progress, even if considerations of political expediency suggest that such progress may be difficult to achieve in 'the real world'.

The category of 'the spiritual' had further educational legitimacy conferred upon it when, in the mid-1970s, it was included by a group of Her Majesty's Inspectors in a proposed new approach to constructing a common curriculum for secondary schools: the well-known HMI 'areas of experience'. In their document *Curriculum 11–16* (DES, 1977a), HMI listed eight such fundamental areas: the aesthetic and creative, the ethical, the linguistic, the mathematical, the physical, the scientific, the social and political, and the spiritual. This framework was (very approximately) evolved from Paul Hirst's well-known 'forms of knowledge' thesis (Hirst, 1974) – but it had a much less rigorous rationale, as is suggested by the fact that subsequently technology was proposed as a ninth area, while literacy was added to linguistic, and the ethical became the moral. It is significant and symptomatic that in the subsequent document, *Supplement to Curriculum 11–16* (DES, 1977b), which included attempts to define each of the original eight areas, HMI found it necessary when arriving at 'the spiritual' to offer not one but two definitions. The first of these was distinctly woolly: it suggested that the spiritual should 'be concerned with matters at the heart and root of existence' and that it had to do with 'inner feelings and beliefs'. The second definition was clearer – associating the spiritual unambiguously with experience 'derived from a sense of God or Gods' and it reinforced this unequivocally religious denotation by arguing that the spiritual in this second sense was 'a meaningless adjective for the atheist and of dubious use to the agnostic'.

Now, a binary distinction of the sort proposed in this HMI document clearly has some utility, but equally clearly, it considerably simplifies the range of meanings and associations which the term 'spiritual' actually carries in its full range of usages – including various 'everyday' senses of the term. Briefly, these include:

- Spiritualism: the apparatus of mediums, seances, communication with the spirits of unique individuals who are believed to have 'passed over', etc.;
- beliefs in existence of 'departed spirits': as in 'the communion of saints', individual saints, ancestors, etc. – often including (especially in popular religion) beliefs that communication, intercession, propitiation, etc. are possible and even necessary in respect of these beings;
- beliefs in intermediary spiritual beings who never lived on earth in human form: ranging from angels (currently the subject of various cults in the USA), demons, devils, etc.;
- beliefs in lesser gods: household gods, tutelary deities, the lesser gods of the Hindu pantheon, etc.;
- theistic beliefs in a Supreme Being: Jahweh, Allah, God, to which certain predicates may be attached such as omnipotence, omniscience, love, justice; the paradoxical Christian doctrine of the Trinity is an example of how the 'purity' of even these monotheistic conceptions can become qualified as religious traditions develop and evolve;
- deistic beliefs in a first cause, etc.;
- mystical experience of the kinds which Aldous Huxley sought to subsume under the title *The Perennial Philosophy* (Huxley, 1946), the heart of which seems to be a loss or merging of the independent self in 'the ground of all being'; a range of experiences which have been interpreted through a variety of metaphors and images within the different major religious traditions – and with some of these interpretations making no reference to a god or gods – for example the Zen conception of *satori*;
- a range of drug-induced 'mystical' experiences which are difficult and sometimes impossible to distinguish from hallucinations (see, among a vast literature, Castaneda, 1968; Huxley, 1954);
- profound *aesthetic* experience which is felt to reach levels of significance which are

beyond the powers of propositional language to express – listening to late Beethoven string quartets, to take a hackneyed but nevertheless enduring example of works of art which seem to have been recurrently capable of evoking subjective experience of this order;

- the capacity of human beings – some of whom may be atheists or agnostics – for acts of outstanding courage, fortitude, goodness, etc., as in the phrase 'triumphs of the human spirit'.

This list is obviously by no means exhaustive: it does not, for example, include magic, witchcraft beliefs (ancient and modern), or astrology and horoscopes (perhaps the most widely indulged form of popular flirtation with 'spiritual' influences in the everyday lives of a surprising number of people in Western societies – not least, it would seem, Nancy and Ronald Reagan, Boris Yeltsin, the late Princess Diana, etc.).[10]

What drawing up a list of this kind *does* demonstrate, however, is the lack of utility of a single category called 'the spiritual' for helping to clarify aims and objectives not only in moral education but also in relation to religious education. It is not merely that the list brings together so many diverse and heterogeneous ideas, beliefs, practices, etc. An even more serious problem is that the meanings and propositions which lie at the core of certain religious senses of 'the spiritual' are precisely the meanings and propositions which many humanists, rationalists and secularists most decisively reject. To construct a curriculum domain, therefore, which aspires to bring them all together seems worse than misguided. Similarly, to suggest that in some global and inclusive way 'the spiritual' should permeate the teaching of the art, music, literature, history, science, as well as being centrally represented by RE, seems a recipe for confusion and miscommunication. As far as achieving clarity in curriculum planning is concerned, we would, I conclude, do better to bracket-off reference to the category of the spiritual as a guiding concept for moral education. Even within religious education, where the category of the spiritual in some of its senses must clearly continue to have a central place, careful distinctions and clarifications will be necessary. Here, the plural usage – spiritualities – may offer ways of thinking about both similarities and differences.

It will not, of course, be easy to persuade people of this. For one thing, those groups discussed above, who aim to preserve at least the *symbolic* presence of the 'religious/spiritual' within our increasingly secular institutions, are likely to resist such a proposal. Others too, however, will be tempted to continue to have recourse to deliberately ill-defined and inclusive uses of the term 'spiritual' within education generally. For example, the requirement that schools must hold daily acts of worship (and for this to be a matter which OFSTED is charged to monitor) is a constraint which some senior teachers may feel can be accommodated if such assemblies are given a clearly (but loosely) 'spiritual' character – sometimes celebrating a diversity of religious ideas, festivals, etc.; and at other times offering narratives of human moral or physical courage, service to one's fellow men and women, celebrations of human creativity, etc.[11] And in this context, it is noteworthy that certain secular organizations such as the British Humanist Association have gone out of their way to endorse an inclusiveness of this kind. For example, the Association's pamphlet entitled *The Human Spirit* contains the following:

Religious believers and Humanists, theists on the one hand, agnostics and atheists on the other, agree on the importance of spirituality but interpret it differently. Despite these different interpretations, however, *all can agree that the 'spiritual' dimension comes from our deepest humanity*. It finds expression in aspirations, moral sensibility, creativity, love and friendship, response to natural and human beauty, scientific and artistic endeavour, appreciation and wonder at the natural world, intellectual achievement and physical activity, surmounting suffering and persecution, selfless love, the quest for meaning and for values by which to live. (British Humanist Association, 1993, quoted in J. White., 1996, p. 34, my italics)

In spite of the generous intent underlying such inclusive sentiments, it is difficult not to feel uneasy. The statement suggests too much common ground; it implies too easily that vitally important differences can be glossed over; it sacrifices clarity for the sake of an at least partially misplaced togetherness. The phrase italicized above highlights the problem: of course there is a sense in which we can agree that 'the spiritual dimension comes from our deepest humanity'. But that merely displaces rather than resolves the fundamental underlying *disagreements* over a range of further questions – about the sources of 'our deepest humanity'. Moreover, there is a sense in which it is not only the most elevated but also the most *evil* deeds of which human beings are capable that arise from their 'deepest humanity'. A romantic privileging of one side of our human nature is a further danger inherent in identifying a humanistic conception of the spiritual with the morally positive aspects of our existence. To call acts of human barbarism 'inhuman' is certainly an understandable temptation for certain kinds of humanistic thinking – but it is arguably unhelpful if our aim is to think seriously about the full range of our human potentialities. This tendency has long been recognized as a weakness of those idealist 'philosophical anthropologies' represented by thinkers like 'the young Marx', in which the negative aspects of human behaviour have to be explained away by resort to a theory that it is oppressive *social* conditions which bring about a state of 'alienation' in which human beings become estranged from their true and essential humanity (see, for example, Ollman, 1971).

RELIGIOUS EDUCATION

What are the implications of this discussion for the future of religious education in state schools? If we put aside 'the spiritual' as an unhelpful term in trying to clarify the aims of moral education (and even, in some respects, the aims of religious education itself) – what should we conclude about the future of religious education in state schools? One writer who has recently examined this issue is David Hargreaves in his 'Demos' publication *The Mosaic of Learning* (Hargreaves, 1994). Apparently despairing of the inability of government agencies to rise above platitudinous assertion and their tendency to blame schools for failing to transmit clear moral and religious values, Hargreaves argues that, in view of the stubborn persistence of 'this conflation of moral and religious education' (ibid., p. 34), the time has come to acknowledge that:

> attempts to bolster RE since 1988 have failed: that morality is not as closely linked to religion, especially the Christian religion, as in the past; and that moral education will in the future need to be more closely linked to civic education if it is to provide a common core of values shared across communities in a pluralistic society.

The notion of a non-denominational core RE to be offered in all schools as a buttress to moral education is becoming less and less viable and should now be abandoned. The multi-faith pick 'n mix tour of religions easily trivialises each faith's claims to truth. As an academic discipline it has little appeal to most children and comes before they are mature enough to engage in the necessary historical and philosophical analysis. (ibid., p. 34)

His proposed alternative has two main elements: that 'there should be more religious schools' and that *all* schools, whether religious or secular, should be required to provide 'a common core of civic education' including a significant element of *moral* education (ibid., pp. 34–5). Hargreaves offers several arguments in support of his proposition that we should permit, and indeed encourage, the establishment of Muslim, Hindu, Sikh, etc. state schools alongside existing Jewish schools and those of various Christian denominations. These include: first, the undeniable point that there is an element of contradiction if not hypocrisy in current policies of blocking the establishment of state Muslim schools while continuing to give public support to voluntary aided and controlled Christian schools; secondly, the equally undeniable fact that the creation of such schools would increase parental choice; and thirdly and most importantly, that 'such schools could confidently and without apology assert the fundamental link between morality and religious faith which is so prized by religious groups' (ibid., p. 35).

Secular schools would no longer teach religious education as part of a national curriculum, although *secondary* secular schools might offer RE to older pupils when they had developed the maturity necessary to understand 'a religious faith from the outside' (ibid., p. 38). Hargreaves does stipulate that religious schools would have 'a duty to teach their students that morality without religion is an intellectually defensible and socially respectable position' (ibid., p. 36). Nevertheless, the great strength he seems to see in such schools is that they would meet the deep desire of some parents to send their children to institutions whose ethos reinforced that of the home, and that in consequence of 'home and school being jointly committed to the transmission and living experience of a shared moral and religious culture', schools of this kind would play a key role in sustaining 'the very communities, including the family, on which (such) moral and religious convictions ultimately depend for their sustenance and development' (ibid., p. 35). These schools would, in short, provide a sense of identity and belonging to the young of the communities concerned. Hargreaves cites and endorses here Rabbi Jonathan Sacks' distinction between two 'languages': 'the first and public language of citizenship' and 'our second languages' – which Sacks characterizes as follows:

> our second languages are cultivated in the context of families and communities, our intermediaries between the individual and the state. They are where we learn who we are; where we develop sentiments of belonging and obligation; where our lives acquire substantive depth. (Sacks, quoted in Hargreaves, 1994, p. 37)

In this way, religious schools would also contribute to the maintenance of high standards of morality across society as a whole, both by sustaining a religiously sanctioned basis for morality among a significant proportion of the population, and by strengthening the authority of the leaders of local communities – not least their spiritual leaders.

How should we respond to this radical agenda – which proposes such an interesting mix of iconoclasm in some areas and cultural preservation in others? One obvious objection, which Hargreaves himself anticipates, is that religious schools of the kind proposed would be socially divisive. Hargreaves denies this – partly on the grounds (outlined above) that religious schools would strengthen individual moral responsibility and thereby actually *increase* overall social cohesion and stability. This defence certainly has some plausibility – particularly in the context of a wider society which succeeded in promoting significant toleration of cultural and religious diversity. It is difficult, however, to balance this claim against an opposite concern – that the *superimposition* of religious, linguistic, ethnic and in some cases class differences can, in certain circumstances, be a basis for the most entrenched and intractable of social conflicts – as in the former Yugoslavia or in Northern Ireland or in Quebec – to take only three very obvious examples.[12] No one is in a position to reliably predict which of these different outcomes – greater integration or increased divisiveness – is the more likely were we to move to a national system of religious and secular schools of the kind proposed.

There are, however, other important reasons why it would be a mistake to accept Hargreaves' agenda. The most important of these has to do with the rights and interests of the children and young people who are destined to grow up in the contemporary and rapidly changing societies of late modernity. It is not legitimate, on *educational* grounds, to consign children in such societies to schools whose *raison d'être* is that they can 'confidently and without apology assert the fundamental link between morality and religious faith' – or more accurately, between a *particular* morality and a *particular* faith. To do so could risk sacrificing the autonomy of these young people in favour of a misplaced respect for a reified and fossilized vision of the various 'communities' which make up 'late modern' societies. Once again, we encounter here the fundamental division between, on the one hand, those who wish, paternalistically, to bolster tradition and traditional authorities in the face of modernization and pluralism; and, on the other hand, those who believe that there can and should be 'no turning back' in these respects. At issue in such cases are questions of representation and authority. Who now can legitimately claim to speak on behalf of these actually increasingly diversified constituencies which certain traditionalists still like to think of as unified localized 'communities' based upon shared values and religious beliefs? It is very far from obvious that the appropriate answer is 'the accredited religious leaders' and those parents who support them. The doctrines and disciplines which some of these leaders may wish to instil may well become increasingly *un*acceptable to sections of the younger generation within such notional 'communities'. And this is not simply a question of the young being 'brainwashed' by 'Western' influences or the seductions of consumerism, etc. There are, and there will continue to be, *legitimate* divisions of thought and action – both between and within the generations in these 'communities' – over fundamental issues such as women's rights, marrying out of a faith community, 'church' attendance, the truth claims of the faith, the claims of secular world views, issues of personal and sexual morality, etc., etc. There is, furthermore, a clear possibility that among the parents who would most strongly wish to send their children to schools which would represent their own faith are some whose principal motivation would be precisely the desire to bring about orthodoxy and conformity in their offspring.[13] In *practice*, moreover, it is very difficult to see how, once religious schooling became a sanctioned and widely institutionalized alternative, proper and effective safeguards could be instituted against narrow and indoctrinatory forms of 'education' – particularly within a school system which was increasingly legitimized on the grounds of enlarging consumer choice between differentiated types of schools.

Finally, what of Hargreaves' other main reservations concerning RE in state schools? He identifies three main problems:

(a)   that parental support for RE is based on unrealizable expectations that the teaching of the subject can function as 'a kind of social antiseptic' to protect young people from moral danger;

(b)   that RE as an academic discipline has little intellectual appeal to most children as well as coming too early in the process of their moral and cognitive development;

(c)   that RE in state schools has, partly in response to pressures of multiculturalism, too often become 'a multi-faith pick 'n mix tour of religions (which) easily trivialises each faith's claims to truth' (ibid., p. 34).

Let us consider each of these arguments in turn.

(a) Hargreaves is clearly right to claim that most parents express support for RE. This is clearly attested by the available survey evidence. And he is probably also correct that the main reason for such support has less to do with a belief that it is important that children should understand something about *religion* specifically, than with the understandable desire of parents that, if possible, schooling should somehow morally inoculate children so they are less likely to succumb to 'the ubiquitous dangers of drugs, sex and crime' (ibid., p. 32). Hargreaves is also correct when he argues that RE *alone* is not equipped for this kind of task and that moral education should be part of a much broader educational endeavour that includes civic education. All this, however, would come as no surprise to most teachers of RE, very few of whom have ever sought to justify their subject in these terms! If significant numbers of parents support RE for the wrong reasons, the problem which is raised is that of *re-educating the parents concerned* –   not marginalizing or abolishing RE from the curriculum of the great majority of state schools.

(b) This brings us to the second contention – which is really two claims packaged into one. It may indeed well be the case that RE as a discipline has limited appeal to pupils. *Why* this is so is more debatable – but it cannot be unconnected with the low status of the subject in terms of credible educational credentials. We should note, however, that RE is not alone in this respect. Personal and social education, as well as citizenship education, notoriously suffer from a similar problem – such courses being perceived by many pupils as occupying valuable curriculum time which could be devoted to 'proper subjects' – i.e. subjects which lead to additional GCSE grades. The root problem here is the entrenched *instrumentalism* of many pupils and parents – an instrumentalism which is likely to be further reinforced by the growing preoccupation of the two main political parties with raising 'standards', the use of performance indicators, and the like. The strategy which Hargreaves advocates, of *replacing* RE with civic and moral education, therefore seems unlikely to overcome this problem of perceived irrelevance. *All* such subjects are likely to be seen as largely irrelevant if judged by such narrow criteria. But this is not a good *educational* reason for neglecting them.

The claim that RE is introduced too early, before most children 'are mature enough to engage in the necessary historical and philosophical analysis' (ibid., p. 34), raises rather more complex issues. Hargreaves is surely correct that there are significant difficulties in coming to understand a complex 'form of life' such as a religious faith 'from the outside' (ibid., p. 38). Nevertheless, what he seems to fail to recognize is that such problems are by no means unique to religion. For example, coming to an 'inward' understanding of the culture of, say, mediaeval England, or (to take a more limited example) French Impressionist painting, also poses formidable challenges. Anything approaching a *developed* understanding and 'inward' appreciation of such matters requires extended study, exposure to a wide range of relevant experiences, grappling with conventions of representation that are initially unfamiliar, etc. None of this has stood in the way of the National Curriculum prescribing History study units (for quite young children) on aspects of mediaeval England, or a focus on the techniques of French Impressionism in National Curriculum Art. Moreover, this has been justified in the terms of the vital educational importance of inducting children into their cultural heritage: the 'high culture' of their nation and of Western Europe. Perhaps regrettably – but also inevitably – there is a sense in which schoolchildren are *always* too immature to apprehend such matters in anything like their full complexity. (So, for that matter are many adults!) But then, education in schools is often necessarily an exercise in legitimate simplification. How else did any of us come to understand any area of complex human activity? Once again, the conclusion has to be that Hargreaves has provided no distinctive reason why RE should be removed from the curriculum nor a convincing account of why the subject should not be taught to younger children.

(c) This brings us to Hargreaves' final argument – his characterization (or more accurately character assassination) of contemporary RE as 'a multi-faith pick 'n mix tour of religions' which risks trivializing each separate faith's claims to truth. Once more, there is an element of validity in this criticism, at least in some instances – but not of an order that would justify the conclusion that RE should no longer be part of a common curriculum for all children. In our multi-cultural and multi-ethnic society, there are two major justifications for teaching children about religions (plural) rather than simply about Christianity. One is that a major *general* focus of liberal education should be to promote an appreciation of the nature of human understanding – and that this must include certain aspects of religious thought and experience. As Charles Bailey has put it: 'to gain some sense of man's quest for religious understanding is to gain an understanding of man's attempt to understand himself' (Bailey, 1984, p. 117). Clearly, this objective requires some attempt to develop an appreciation of certain *general* features of religious thinking and experience; for example, an exploration of the kinds of fundamental questions with which religion is concerned, the nature of the distinctive concepts that figure in religious discourse, the place of religions in human history, conflicts between theological and scientific modes of understanding, etc. This would seem to require, if not the systematic study of a number of discrete religious traditions, then at least a knowledge of examples drawn from a diversity of kinds of religion – including, perhaps, those of pre-literate societies. In a multicultural society like modern Britain, a second important justification for religious education has to do with combating ethnocentric modes of thinking and promoting a respect for the achievements of cultures outside the Western European orbit. And although it is essential here not to fall into the trap of virtually *identifying* cultural difference with religious difference (as certain well-meaning but tokenistic approaches to multicultural education in schools have certainly risked doing), it would be no less fallacious to ignore the significance of religions in the development and flowering of many non-Western cultures.

To conclude on a more consensual note. Hargreaves rightly argues that non-denominational schools (and even the formally secular schools which he advocates) would have a duty to help their students to appreciate that for many religious people, *moral* behaviour, even if it is capable of independent justification, is also likely to be regarded as religiously sanctioned and grounded (op. cit., p. 36). Similarly, Bailey suggests that much is to be gained by encouraging young people to understand – but to understand clearly – the nature of the connections which often exist between religion and morality:

> Both religion and morality can... be inquired into as great human practices. Indeed, for most people, without religious and/or moral considerations there would be no overriding framework of consideration from which to approach inquiries into social, political or economic matters. This is further to emphasize the point that the divisions between these practices are not logical but idiomatic, divisions of significant focus of attention.

He continues, however, with the following significant clarification:

> I do not mean to suggest by linking religion and morality together that they are *necessarily* linked. A person can clearly be moral (and immoral) in ways other than religious ways, and according to principles not dictated by religion. That they *can* be so separated, whilst for some people *not* so separated, is one of the things that pupils must come to see. A liberal education does not set out to make pupils religious, but neither does it set out to prevent them so becoming. It does and should set out to bring pupils to some understanding of religion as a great influence in historical and contemporary affairs. (op. cit., p. 123)

CONCLUSION

This chapter has been something of a ground-clearing exercise. First, it has sought to identify a number of obstacles to clear analyses of the real tasks which schools face in the sphere of moral and civic education – the most important of these obstacles being the persistent attempts that have been made to conflate 'the moral' with both religion and 'the spiritual'. Secondly, it has suggested that owing to the diversity of overlapping and contradictory meanings which attach to it, the category of 'the spiritual' has little utility in clarifying appropriate aims and objectives for moral education – though clarification of the various meanings attaching to spirituality remains a central task for religious education. Finally, it has been argued that the important task of developing better approaches to moral education and citizenship education should not be pursued at the expense of the teaching of religious education. In the next two chapters, an attempt is made to analyse in more detail some of the key issues which need to be addressed if we are to achieve greater clarity of purpose in these important areas of the curriculum.

NOTES

1 My use of the term 'programmatic' here follows that of Israel Scheffler (Scheffler, 1960). In his usage, the term 'stipulative' definition refers to a definition offered for the sake of

argument and/or economy – and in order to facilitate communication or discussion. 'Programmatic' definitions, on the other hand, are those linked to some implied programme of action, and 'according to Scheffler, should be inspected not for their effects in enabling economy of utterance, nor for their relevance to prior usage, but rather for the moral and practical questions raised by the programme of action which they imply' (Lambourn, 1996, p. 155).

2   Among these disastrous consequences were the effects of 'over-population' evident especially in London. Arnold's work as one of Her Majesty's Inspectors of schools made him acutely aware of the living conditions of the children of the urban poor – and he did not hesitate to draw upon this experience:

> I remember only the other day, a good man looking with me upon a multitude of children who were gathered before us in one of the most miserable regions of London – children eaten up with disease, half-sized, half-fed, half-clothed, neglected by their parents, without health, without home, without hope... (Arnold, 1869, p. 152)

3   In this respect (as well as in others which will be discussed later), Arnold is very much part of the tradition of that long line of Tory and conservative cultural analysts which can be traced back through 'men of letters' like Coleridge, Wordsworth, Southey to eighteenth-century writers like the legal theorist William Blackstone (see Mathieson and Bernbaum, 1988; see also Chapter 1 of this book).

4   Arnold is acutely though cheerfully conscious that he is engaged in a battle on several fronts – with a range of adversaries which included *The Times*, the *Daily News*, etc. as well as his 'liberal friends' (utilitarians and others). The following catches a characteristic tone in *Culture and Anarchy* – a text that is far from solemn: 'And here I think I see my enemies waiting for me with a hungry joy in their eyes. But I shall elude them!' (ibid., p. 43).

5   The phrase 'reason and the will of God' occurs on the following pages of the John Murray popular edition of *Culture and Anarchy* (9th reprint, July 1961): p. 6; p. 21; p. 30; p. 49 (twice); p. 69; p. 92; p. 153.

6   The limitations, or at least highly contestable implications of Arnold's conception of culture 'in practice', as it were, are evident in some of the conclusions to which he was led on popular issues of the day. He was, for example, a supporter of the vigorous suppression of mass popular protest, for fear that it would precipitate a descent into ungovernable anarchy. And in spite of his very marked sympathy for the plight of the urban poor and his critique of free-market liberalism as one of the causes of this situation, his 'answer' to the problem of population increase among the Populace was a strikingly Malthusian and voluntaristic suggestion that the poor should be educated to understand that no *man* has a moral right to produce more children than he can afford to bring up decently:

> [T]o bring people into the world, when one cannot afford to keep them and to keep oneself decently and not too precariously, or to bring more of them into the world than one can afford...is just as wrong, just as contrary to reason and the will of God, as for a man to have horses, or carriages, or pictures, when he cannot afford them, or to have more of them than he can afford. (ibid., p. 153)

7   The Annual Report of HM Chief Inspector of Schools for the school year 1994–95 acknowledged that:

> A significant number of secondary schools fail to meet the legal requirements of collective worship. Most non-compliance is *attributed* by schools to a lack of suitable accommodation. However, some schools are ingenious in overcoming such difficulties ...[However], where teachers are reluctant to lead collective worship these attempts break down, even if well-prepared material is provided. (OFSTED, 1996, para. 214; my italics)

8   Admittedly, the subsequent inclusion of this part of the preamble was neither controversial nor contested.

9   'There are 47 openly declared humanists...in both houses of parliament, but not one of them is a member of the Conservative Party. A Tory MP has admitted to being gay, but

none will confess to being godless... The 26 MPs willing to advertise their irreligiousness through membership of the Parliamentary Humanist Group are all Labour, although private estimates suggest that six Liberal Democrats do not believe in God either. There are also 21 unbelieving peers, again mostly Labour... After 33 years, the Parliamentary Humanist Group cannot call itself an All-Party Group because no Tory will join...' (Routledge, 1996, p. 6).

10   The dilemmas which this increasing diversity of 'spiritual' beliefs and practices in contemporary society poses for the 'established' religious authorities are considerable. This was very clearly illustrated by the recent publication of a report commissioned by the Church of England and the Council of Churches in Britain and entitled *The Search for Faith and Witness*. According to the Religious Affairs Editor of the *Guardian*, the report warns that:

> people are increasingly turning to New Age spiritualities and superstition in an eclectic 'pick and mix' approach to religion which could lead to the collapse of our civilisation... The Bishop of Rochester warned that the drift away from orthodox Christianity could lead to social disintegration with individuals floundering in a spiritual vacuum: 'the drifting of belief without belonging to any institution is bound to get more and more eclectic... People's need to believe remains strong but they're relying on all sorts of dubious things and exotic phenomena'... (Bunting, 1996, p. 9)

A core problem for the supporters of 'orthodox' beliefs in such a time is, of course, precisely the undermining of *tradition* as a source of authority in contemporary society. In a 'market place of spiritualities', an authoritative basis for identifying 'genuine' as against 'false' spirituality becomes increasingly difficult to locate – let alone enforce!

11   The government requirement that OFSTED school inspections 'must evaluate and report on the school's provision for the spiritual, moral, social and cultural development of all pupils' (OFSTED, 1995) has been the stimulus for renewed and lively public debate about the meaning of 'the spiritual'. A notable recent contribution is the book *Education, Spirituality and the Whole Child* (Best, 1996) – a collection of papers originally delivered at a conference held at Froebel College, London, in 1994. This text reflects a wide range of views about the interpretation and utility of 'the spiritual' and spirituality in education. However, as the book's editor points out, some contributors invested the spiritual with a clearly religious connotation while others argued for more inclusive interpretations:

> The spiritual is conventionally thought of as to do with *religion*. Some contributors have approached spirituality from positions of personal faith, or from the convictions of those committed to education within church schools. Here, spiritual *leadership* is seen as crucial. Others argue for a concept of spirituality and spiritual maturity which is universal and not premised upon theism. (ibid., p. 344)

12   C.f. Ralf Dahrendorf's well-known argument that the intensity of social conflict tends to be positively associated with the superimposition of different social bases of division between social groups (Dahrendorf, 1959).

13   There is evidence, of its nature limited, that in some instances at least, the issue of separate religious schools may be bitterly contested *within* certain 'communities'. Discussing aspects of the education of Muslim girls in Bradford, for example, Saeeda Khanum has warned:

> [V]ery few have acknowledged the 'hidden agenda' behind the demands of religious fundamentalists: an attempt to stifle dissent and exert absolute control over the lives of women in the community. It is no accident, nor is it an act tinged with racism, that Muslim religious schools are referred to not as 'Islamic denominational schools' but as 'separate' or 'segregated' by those who have a particular idea of the kind of community they want to foster – both those who want the schools and those who oppose them. (Khanum, 1995, p. 287)

Chapter 4

Moral Education and Civic Education

CIVIC EDUCATION AS SOCIAL CEMENT

> The problem in Britain as a pluralistic society is how to find some social cement to ensure that people with different moral, religious and ethical values as well as social, cultural and linguistic traditions can live together in a degree of harmony; and to discover the contribution that the education system should play [sic] in generating social cohesion. (Hargreaves, 1994, p. 31)

Having relegated Religious Education to the margins of the curriculum in 'secular schools', not least because of its presumed inadequacy as an effective vehicle for moral education in an increasingly secular society, David Hargreaves goes on to propose a common curriculum of *civic* education as a way of helping to create and generate social cohesion:

> To help create social cohesion, to develop a moral cement that will withstand the strains of being pluralistic, schools should take the lead in teaching what Sacks calls 'the first and public language of citizenship': here is the shared or common core of a civic, moral and religious education. (ibid., p. 37)

This, it seems to me, is the right proposal but not quite for the right reasons. Both civic and moral education have long been neglected in British schools. However, the prime reason why it is indeed important to develop more adequate versions of both these areas of education is not to do with the role they might play in generating social cohesion; it is that both are *educational entitlements* of all young people in modern liberal democracies.

We have several times already argued that social order and stability in modern pluralistic, democratic societies does not depend primarily upon shared *values* – and indeed that, ironically enough, some of the principal sources of the stability in such societies actually derive from a conspicuously unequal – and arguably unjust – distribution of wealth, power and status, which is recurrently reinforced by persistent inequalities of opportunity. *Compliance*, rather than a conformity resulting from an extensive sharing of genuinely common values, explains much of the integration which these societies exhibit. Established routines, as well as a certain taken-for-granted acceptance of the 'inevitability' of these unjust social arrangements, account for a good deal more of this stability. Almost all theories of 'crisis' significantly underestimate the very considerable strength and durability of these non-normative bases of social integration – whether these be neo-conservative laments over the loss of traditional beliefs and values, or the claims of certain American liberal theorists that without effective civic education 'the attenuation of the civic spirit...will create pathologies with which liberal institutions...simply cannot cope' (Galston, 1989, p. 92).

Furthermore, in the UK at any rate, civic education has, historically, been poorly developed. Curricular provision in the area has been patchy and inconsistent, and at no time has civic education been more than a relatively marginal and optional addition to the mainstream curriculum. Nor can it be convincingly argued that, in the past, other areas of the curriculum did the job instead. As we have seen, religious education has been criticized (with good reason) by David Hargreaves precisely because of the *failure* of attempts by politicians and government agencies to use it as a vehicle for inculcating their preferred set of 'moral' values. Similarly, Nicholas Tate's vision of confident narratives of nationhood as the core of school history lessons in the early part of this century does not, according to Patrick Brindle's recent research, entirely stand up to examination. It may indeed have been the case, as John Ahier has shown, that the history textbooks of the period provided pupils with an invitation to make certain kinds of nationalistic identifications – identifications which were in fact often constructed in contra-distinction to clearly racist and patronizing portraits of the ethnic 'others' of 'our empire and colonies' (a feature which Dr Tate does *not* emphasize – see Ahier, 1987). But, as Brindle has argued, there is evidence which suggests that a significant gap existed between these textual narrations and the realities of classrooms – especially elementary school classrooms:

> Oral testimony from retired teachers indicates further shortcomings in Tate's analysis, primarily that of resources. While grammar schools had little problem providing their pupils with an ample supply of textbooks, many elementary schools, and especially those in cash-strapped rural LEAs, simply could not afford to purchase many school textbooks at all. It was the elementary sector that provided the overwhelming majority of the population with its only experience of education. For many teachers, improvisation was as necessary in History as in all subjects...Dr Tate...must not assume that the content of the textbook represents how history was taught in the past. (Brindle, 1996)

We should, perhaps, also take note of the views of certain kinds of liberal theorists in the USA, to the effect that what they see as the *wrong kind* of civic education – for example, the kind which encourages young people to examine critically the values and beliefs of their parents and local community – might be worse than no civic education at all. Such theorists have argued this because they believe that these kinds of education run the risk of alienating certain religiously conservative communities who do not share the modernist, secular assumptions of the majority of their fellow citizens. Such a critical, assumption-testing form of civic education, they warn, might undermine the real but limited political consensus which, according to this form of liberal analysis, is the indispensable basis of civic co-operation in societies which exhibit serious value pluralism (see Galston, op. cit.). Civic education *per se*, in other words, is no guaranteed or universal route to building social consensus: much may depend on the character of the society concerned as well as on the form(s) of civic education proposed.

AN ENTITLEMENT TO CIVIC AND MORAL EDUCATION?

Liberal political theory has provided many of the most interesting recent discussions of the dilemmas which cultural and value pluralism poses both for modern democratic societies and for the individual members of these societies. This is not surprising. After all, the origins of liberalism and of liberal theory are inseparable from conflicts over deeply held religious beliefs – associated historically to the rise of Protestantism. The very word 'Protestant' carries with it the idea of dissent from beliefs held by others within the same society. At the core of liberalism, most commentators agree, lies a strong valuation of individual *freedom* and the right of individuals to choose their own conception of the good life. Two other essential beliefs are closely linked to this: a principle of *toleration* of the right of others to choose *their* own version of the good life (including versions with which we may ourselves profoundly disagree) so long as they are not injurious to others; and secondly, a set of beliefs about the role of *government* – notably the duty of government to establish a framework of law which enshrines and protects these liberties while government itself remains impartial between parties who disagree about what is good in life: 'liberalism is a political theory of limited government, providing institutional guarantees of personal liberty' (Rosenblum, 1989, p. 5). Thus, as Stephen Macedo has succinctly put it: 'the permanent fact of pluralism is at the heart of the liberal political problem' (Macedo, 1990, p. 257). Now, for a number of reasons, the most important of which is the collapse of communist regimes across much of the world and the associated decline of Marxist theorizing, there has in recent years been what Rosenblum has called 'a proliferation of types of liberalism', in a context in which 'liberalism has emerged as *the* political theory, whose resources are most called upon, most severely tested and extended, and most aggressively explained and justified' (Rosenblum, op. cit., p. 4). This has intensified the range and vigour of debate between increasingly divergent theoretical positions all of which may, nevertheless, still be broadly described as liberal. Among the main dimensions of disagreement are divisions between more politically conservative and more egalitarian versions of liberalism, and also between those who differ about the extent to which liberal governments have (or do not have) a duty to promote individual *autonomy* among their citizens, especially within educational institutions.

In the United Kingdom, the idea that a main aim of public education should be the promotion of rational autonomy, including a disposition to critically question received attitudes and beliefs, has for some time enjoyed the status of an educational orthodoxy which few have had the confidence to question – at least publicly. This has been so ever since the early work of educational philosophers such as Richard Peters and Paul Hirst gained widespread public legitimacy in the 1960s (for a convenient summary see Hirst and Peters, 1970). In a broad sense, this aim is inscribed within most child-centred approaches to education, and even vocational education has quite frequently *represented* itself as concerned with promoting rational autonomy in young people.

Hence, in Britain in recent years, this basic conception of the aims of education has rarely been seriously challenged – except, of course, by a whole range of Marxist writers whose complaint was not about the aim itself but that schools in late capitalist societies could not hope to 'deliver' it, because they were condemned to serve the needs of an oppressive social totality of which they were merely a subordinate and functionally dependent part (see, to cite only the most influential examples, Althusser, 1971; Bowles and Gintis, 1972). Even the more recent neo-conservative criticisms of our education system have typically sought to claim that their advocacy of a stronger emphasis on instilling traditional beliefs and values is not incompatible with developing rational autonomy (see, for example, the discussion of Roger Scruton's conception of 'high culture' in Chapter 1 of this book). Of course, the actual *practice* of many schools and teachers may have been markedly at variance with this ideal; furthermore, what is actually at stake in seeking to bring about such autonomy may have often been poorly understood (see, for example, Charles Bailey's discussion of 'The methods of liberal education', Bailey, 1984, ch. 8). Nevertheless, public challenges to this goal as an educational *ideal* have been in the main muted or absent.

This is, however, *not* the case in the USA, where a significantly wider range of views about the aims of education has been taken seriously in public debate – not least as part of the debates within liberal political philosophy. As mentioned above, a prominent liberal theorist who adopts what might be called a strongly conservative position on this issue of promoting autonomy as part of civic education is William Galston. In a paper entitled 'Civic education in the liberal state' (Galston, 1989) he considers the kind of civic education which a liberal state is justified in prescribing for all children. He argues strongly against those who claim that a liberal democratic state is justified in going against the wishes of certain groups of parents in introducing forms of civic education which encourage children to become *critically reflective* about the different ways of life within their society, including the beliefs of their parents and local communities: 'the civic standpoint does not warrant the conclusion that the state must (or may) structure public education to foster in children sceptical reflection on ways of life inherited from parents and local communities' (ibid., p. 99). He argues that civic education *does* require that future citizens understand and accept the obligation to coexist peacefully with those whose beliefs they do not share, that they should support their political community, and that citizens should be equipped with 'at least the minimal conditions of public (political) judgement' – as, for example, in evaluating political leaders and their policies. But, for him, good citizenship in these respects is 'perfectly compatible with *unswerving* belief in the correctness of one's own way of life' (ibid., p. 99, my italics) and the state is not justified in encouraging scepticism about such unswerving beliefs. Liberal freedom, he argues, must include the freedom to live 'unexamined as well as examined lives' (ibid., p. 100) and he adds the very significant corollary that this is '*a right whose effective exercise may require parental bulwarks against the corrosive influence of modernist scepticism*' (ibid., p. 100, my italics). One of the great merits of Galston's discussion is that he faces this issue of the relative rights of parents and children in this matter head on: 'But doesn't liberal freedom mean that children have the right to be exposed to a wide range of possible ways of life? If parents thwart this right ... doesn't the state have a right – indeed, a duty – to step in? The answer is no on both counts' (ibid., p. 100).

Galston's justification for this stance is connected with his view that the intrusion of the state into the *private* affairs of adult individuals should be kept to a minimum: the limits of such legitimate intrusion, in this area, are that the state has a duty to prevent parents impeding 'the normal physical, intellectual, and emotional development of their children' as well as their children's acquisition of 'basic civic competence and loyalty': but 'what cannot be justified on this basis cannot be justified at all'. He adds, challengingly: *'this is how liberal democracies must draw the line between parental and public authority over the education of their children'* (ibid., p. 100, my italics).

But of course there is no *must* about it! And indeed, this debate is itself a most interesting illustration of the dilemmas of liberalism. What divides Galston from other liberal theorists who disagree with him is how much weight to place on a number of different principles about which, in general terms, all liberals broadly agree: for example, that 'liberals resist paternalism and minimize interference with people's choices' (Macedo, p. 262). Liberalism *per se* cannot provide a court of appeal which can resolve the disagreement. From his wider discussion, it seems clear that one consideration which inclines Galston to 'draw the line' in the way he does – in favour of parents having an unequivocal right to protect their children from modernist scepticism if they judge this to be desirable – is that the fact of living within a wider liberal society makes it anyway 'virtually impossible for parents to seal their children off (completely) from knowledge of other ways of life' (ibid., p. 101). Macedo, who appears to strongly *support* the active promotion of autonomy as part of liberal education within a liberal society, nevertheless goes along with Galston insofar as he accepts that there *is* a price to be paid in this respect:

> within open diverse, critical, experimental, uncertain and ever-changing liberal societies... certain things of value may be lost... Stronger forms of community, deeper, unquestioning, untroubled forms of allegiance (to family, church, clan, or class) might embody genuine forms of the good life lost to societies that flourish in a liberal way. (Macedo, p. 279)

He also recognizes that in societies organized according to such principles, there will be casualties: 'what some people experience as an adventure, others, ... will find unbearably burdensome' (ibid., p. 280).

How justified, then, are we if we argue that all children in modern, democratic, pluralistic societies are *entitled* to a form of education one of whose main aims is the promotion of a form of rational autonomy that involves the development of a disposition to question, to search for justification and seek relevant evidence? It will be argued here that we *are* justified in making such a claim. Anything like a full justification is, clearly, a complex and challenging matter, and such an argument cannot be developed here.[1] All that will be attempted is to indicate a number of supporting considerations.

At the heart of Galston's case is a view of the relationship between the public sphere and the private sphere: for him, the state is only justified in what he symptomatically terms 'interfering' in the private sphere, within very strict limits. The public sphere is the arena where a widespread social consensus can be established across all those who otherwise differ on their views of the good life; the private sphere is the arena where different individuals and groups are free to give their allegiance their own fuller and in some respects incompatible 'comprehensive' conceptions of the good life. Other liberal theorists, however, contend that the boundary between these two spheres is, in liberal societies, significantly more permeable than writers of Galston's persuasion are prepared to admit. Macedo, for example, develops an argument of this kind with considerable energy and flair (Macedo, 1990). He argues that liberalism requires commitments from all citizens (if unequally) to public reasonableness and public justification. Public justification is a key means of seeking to resolve the conflicts of belief that divide people in pluralistic societies. According to Macedo (and severely truncating here his complex argument) such justification involves going beyond neutrality in the public sphere: 'political justification concedes *something* to reasonable disagreement' between people with conflicting conceptions of the good life, 'but it does not abandon substantive liberal values, and it cannot help but shape people's lives broadly and deeply and relentlessly over time' (ibid., p. 52):

> [S]hared liberal values need not themselves be strong enough to override all competing ones so long as the weight, as it were, of liberal and supporting (or pro-liberal) values is enough to outweigh all competing (or anti-liberal) values and interests. Nevertheless, the success and stability of liberal politics depends on people's private beliefs and commitments becoming importantly liberalized – becoming, that is, supportive of liberal politics. (ibid., p. 54)

This imposes obligations on all liberal citizens:

> Liberalism elevates impartial standards of respect for all persons; it implies that people should be capable of reflecting on the whole range of their particular commitments...for the sake of interposing impersonal standards of justice and honouring the equal rights of others. Critical self-reflection is not required if our personal commitments are already liberal – but what guarantees that? The reflective capacity of liberal citizens, alert to possible conflicts between personal commitments and liberal rights, should be a central mechanism for preserving and advancing the cause of justice in a well-ordered society. (ibid., p. 56)

And, he concludes, a liberal society could not count as well ordered unless it were composed of people who could employ reason to distance themselves from their own personal commitments in order to examine how far any of these commitments might be in conflict with the requirements of liberal justice. And all this has important consequences for the relationship between the public and private spheres, where matters which are publicly controversial cannot but involve argument and negotiation which draws in people's private beliefs and convictions. Later in his argument, Macedo considers suggestions that in practice, more adherents might be recruited for liberalism if candid, open, public debate about controversial issues were *avoided* in favour of more unconscious forms of liberal socialization. Open justification and debate might well, he points out, be politically provocative and have the effect of diminishing public support for liberal ways of resolving disagreements. However, and consistently with his earlier line of argument, he expresses major reservations about supporting this kind of 'false consciousness', except in very special circumstances:

> Compromising on the full disclosure of what liberalism stands for, shying away from open and candid public justification, entails high costs. First of all, while public justification is a form of respect for persons, failing to be candid is a form of disrespect. Only when arguments are advanced and defended openly does the search for widely accessible reasons express respect for the reasonableness of common citizens. (ibid., p. 67)

Now in all of this, Macedo is, of course, talking about *adult* citizens – not about children. Moreover, he accepts that even many adults will only ever be capable of a limited form of 'reasonableness' rather than a fuller form of genuine autonomy. Nevertheless, the position he advances seems to have fairly clear implications for education in modern liberal societies. Although children are clearly *not* rational and autonomous beings, nevertheless, as Bailey reminds us, 'what they equally clearly *are* ... is *potentially* rational and autonomous' (Bailey, op. cit., p. 44) – or at least, a significant fraction of them are this and we cannot tell in advance who these will be. If, therefore, we have a well-founded belief that schooling could be organized in ways which would effectively develop this potential, then there is a strong case for doing so for *all* children in modern, democratic, liberal societies – and for doing so even in the case of those children whose parents and local or religious communities might prefer to protect them from the necessarily critical, questioning, evidential, rationalist pedagogy schools of this kind would employ. Such children cannot, as they grow to young adulthood in modern pluralistic societies, be effectively shielded from a whole range of controversial matters which cross-cut the private and the public domains, in the sense that such issues are both matters of ongoing public debate (and often legislation) and also matters about which the deeply held convictions of these children's own parents may differ markedly from the equally sincerely and deeply held convictions of others. For parents to raise their children to see such matters as absolutes rather than as legitimately contested by reasonable people is to do a disservice to these children in the long run, and it may also, in some instances, prove disabling in their individual lives. It is important that young people learn to see others who do not share their beliefs as nevertheless deserving of respect because they are rational beings like themselves – rather than regarding them as beyond the moral pale and/or as 'not worth arguing with'.

Of course, one must acknowledge here that all this does involve the liberal state in departing from a stance of impartiality in an area where what some parents want for their children is being denied, even though what they want is not indubitably and directly *harmful* to those children. In other words, it does involve the liberal state in differentially supporting certain kinds of conception of the good life against certain others. This is revealed very clearly, for example, in legal cases in the USA in which courts have had to adjudicate on controversies about 'creation science' versus evolutionary theory in schools. Macedo notes that in one such federal judgement, which overturned a state decision mandating *balanced* treatment for creation science and evolutionary theory, certain of the judges involved sought to 'paper over the cracks' by seeking to minimize the partisan nature of the federal court's decision. Other judges, however, 'came clean' in this respect, recognizing that the judgement unequivocally involved the state according differential support to a humanistic and scientific world-view against a certain type of religious world-view:

> Justice Brennan's opinion ... deployed the usual liberal arguments about keeping religion out of the public sphere without really acknowledging, as Justice Scalia points out in dissent, that this (decision) in effect promotes a scientific, man-centred, world-view which is a direct alternative to other world-views, such as ones offered by religion. (Macedo, op. cit., p. 67)

A range of further considerations may be adduced which also, in my view, point to the desirability of promoting rational autonomy as an educational aim for all young people in contemporary 'advanced' societies. The most important of these considerations relates closely to our earlier discussion of 'reflexive modernization' in Chapter 2. The kind of society in which the young people of the twenty-first century will be growing up is very likely to be one in which the pressures of *individualization* will go on intensifying. Individualization, in the sense meant here, is (somewhat paradoxically) precisely *not* something which will be optional for most individuals. Rather, as Ulrich Beck and Elisabeth Beck-Gernsheim have put it:

> Individualization is a *social* condition which is not arrived at by the free choice of individuals... Individualization is a *compulsion*, albeit a paradoxical one, to create, to stage-manage, not only one's own biography but the bonds and networks surrounding it, and to do this... at successive stages of life... (Beck and Beck-Gernsheim, 1996, p. 27, my italics)

Being a social condition, it has social causes – which were briefly outlined earlier (in Chapter 2): the accumulation of reflexively organized knowledge, globalization, and changes in the labour market. Two of these are directly related to education. Take the *labour market changes* first. As Ulrich Beck has suggested, the way the labour market is structured in late modern societies intensifies individualization in three ways:

(a) *Education* and educational *credentials* are increasingly significant as the key means of access to an increasing proportion of the jobs on offer in the societies of late modernity. This is only in part because the actual functional requirements of the kinds of work available involve a need for higher levels of education and skills. Real changes in the skill requirements of jobs combine with perceived advantages of staying longer in education, resulting in the now well-known phenomenon of 'credential inflation'. For any given level of job, increasingly higher levels of certification tend to be demanded. As a consequence, individual young people have to engage in risky calculations about their futures – for example, in some cases this involves balancing the cost of student loans and overdrafts against the uncertain prospect of gaining a reasonably secure and well-paid job at the end of a degree course. (In other cases, students are financially supported by their families throughout their courses and bear no such risks.)

(b) *Mobility* has always been demanded by certain kinds of higher level occupations in industrialized societies – for example many management positions in large organizations. But as with education, contemporary changes in the labour market are pressurizing a wider range of employees to become mobile – geographically mobile, mobile between employers, mobile even between different types of occupation as the expectation of a 'job for life' becomes increasingly unrealistic, etc. For some, upward (or more rarely) downward *social* mobility is a further consequence of occupational placement – with the risk of becoming both physically and culturally cut off from one's roots. This too is not new; but its scope is probably increasing.

(c) *Competition* to obtain and keep jobs, and for promotion, is also intensifying, as Ulrich Beck explains:

> Competition rests upon the interchangeability of qualifications and thereby compels people to advertise the individuality and uniqueness of their work and their own accomplishments. The growing pressure of competition leads to an individualization among equals, i.e. precisely in areas of interaction and conduct which are characterized by a shared

background (similar education, similar experience, similar knowledge). Especially where such a shared background exists, community is dissolved in the acid bath of competition. (Beck, 1992, p. 94)

Increasingly such competition also has, as was pointed out in Chapter 2, a *gendered* dimension as growing numbers of individually ambitious and well-qualified women enter the labour market in competition with men and with one another, and with expectations of pursuing a career.

Education is, of course, also centrally implicated in the phenomenon of the accumulation of reflexively organized knowledge. Again, this is partly related to the higher proportion of occupations in advanced societies which really do require ever higher levels of education, training and expertise. It is not accidental, for example, that undergraduate courses in physics and engineering in the UK have recently been extended from three to four years, at a time when pressures on public expenditure are leading to cuts in overall budgets for higher education. But the extension of the educational life which is such an evident feature of affluent societies has many other causes, including: the shrinking of jobs for unskilled teenagers (and their virtual exclusion from the labour market except as part of 'training schemes'), rising affluence, the *perceived* connections between education and occupations, etc. The overall effect is that higher proportions of young people are 'better educated' and for longer. As Ulrich Beck notes, this involves greater exposure to 'universalistic forms of learning and teaching, as well as universalistic forms of knowledge and language' (ibid., p. 93).

Two consequences of all this change are particularly significant as far as the aim of promoting rational autonomy is concerned. First, these changes are deeply corrosive of *tradition*. Individuals are increasingly likely to become removed – not only physically but culturally, from such localized, community ways of life as still remain – including cases where allegiances to the new globally dispersed 'communities of taste' are actively sought. A great deal of the educational knowledge acquired through schools and higher education will necessarily be reflexively ordered: i.e. it will not merely have an inbuilt critical, assumption-testing character (as for example in all basic scientific enquiry); but it will also (as the source of what Giddens calls 'expert systems') 'leak' into everyday life and consciousness, as the basis on which ordinary people make sense of their own situations and plan their futures. In the face of this, traditional forms of authority and domination lose their purchase. Moreover, and very significantly, the political assumptions of *liberalism*, for example in terms of the requirement for public debate and reasoned justification, operate to reinforce this undermining of tradition and to weaken the boundaries between the public and the private. As Macedo has noted:

> To accept the liberal settlement is to accept institutions, ideas, and practices whose influence over our lives and our children's lives will be broad, deep, and relentless: family life, religious life, and all paradigmatically private associations take on the colour of liberal values. In marriage, as Galston points out, the rule is no longer 'till death do us part' but rather, 'till distaste drives us apart'. Nuns criticize their bishops and even the Pope; authorities of all kinds come into question. (Macedo, op. cit., p. 62)

Not only this, however, but the strength of the close-knit social bonds which helped to attach people to traditional beliefs and ways of life is also undermined: those social networks which Peter Berger so tellingly calls 'plausibility structures' lose precisely their power to sustain the plausibility of traditional world-views (Berger, 1967).

The second major consequence of the processes we have been describing is that individuals are forced, to a degree which is without precedent, to take responsibility for their own lives and futures – and to do so in a context of growing uncertainty and risk. This point has been elaborated already in Chapter 2 and we shall not rehearse the argument again, except to emphasize that although there are real gains here in terms of freedom (albeit balanced by losses in terms of security), nevertheless, these are 'precarious freedoms' for many of those involved (Beck and Beck-Gernsheim, 1996). How does all this relate to the aims of education in societies which are experiencing changes of this far-reaching kind? What it chiefly suggests is that the requirement to make active *choices* – between competing comprehensive value systems, alternative life-styles, different occupational possibilities, etc. – will be *inescapable* for more and more individuals of both sexes and throughout their lives. This in turn suggests that living the wholly unexamined life will be less and less possible for anyone at all in these societies. In such circumstances, provided that schooling can be developed so as to offer properly thought-through and effective forms of personal, moral and civic education, then it is likely to be schools which are the agencies best placed to prepare young people for an uncertain future of this kind.[2] These considerations, combined with the justifications developed from our earlier consideration of liberal theory, do indeed suggest that there is a *strong educational entitlement*, based in part on the rights of children and of young people to receive an education which seeks seriously to help them to develop their potential for rational autonomy.

THE CHARACTER OF CIVIC AND MORAL EDUCATION

As the discussion so far has indicated, David Hargreaves was right to argue that if schools *are* to concern themselves with moral and civic education, then it makes a great deal of sense to see the two areas as closely interlinked (Hargreaves, 1994). Of course, many aspects of *moral* education can and should be carried on with little or no reference to matters of politics and citizenship. But, on the other hand, there are few matters concerning citizenship (whether broadly or narrowly understood) which do not bring in a consideration of values and of value-related concepts. Civic education is centrally concerned with the relationship between the 'public' and the 'private', and we have already seen that this is a complex and contested area. One main reason why it is contested has precisely to do with *values*. It is very important, both politically and educationally, to try to define what we might count as 'public' values, and also to clarify what it is that distinguishes them from 'private' values. The educational philosopher Terence H. McLaughlin has recently devoted a good deal of attention to considering this issue and to analysing what the educational implications might be:

> [T]he broad *theory of liberalism* draws a distinction between public and private values . . . Public values are those which, in virtue of their fundamentality or inescapability, are *seen as* binding on all persons. Frequently embodied in law, and expressed in terms of rights, they include such matters as basic social morality and, in democratic societies, a range of fundamental democratic principles such as freedom of speech. Public values in such societies also include ideals such as personal autonomy and the maximisation of the freedom of individuals to pursue their fuller conception of the good within a framework of justice through the distribution of 'primary goods' (basic rights, liberties and opportu-

nities). The liberal project is to specify a range of public values, free from significantly controversial assumptions and judgements, which can generate principles for the conduct of relations between people who disagree (on other matters). (McLaughlin, 1995b, p. 27, my italics)[3]

Now, it is very important indeed to be clear about what is and is not being claimed here. In the passage above, I have italicized the terms '*theory of liberalism*' and '*seen as binding on all persons*' in order to highlight the point that this is not a description of empirical reality. As I have argued several times already, we do not actually know to what extent different individuals and groups within liberal, democratic societies *really* subscribe to these values and accept them as morally binding. It is, for example, easy to see that in a country like Spain, not long free from the embrace of Fascism, significant sections of the society would like severely to restrict democratic freedoms if they could get away with it. Similarly, one may take leave to doubt the sincerity and depth of moral commitment to civil liberties on the part of, say, British companies who sell the means of repression and torture to illiberal regimes – for use in areas such as East Timor or Kurdistan. Such doubts might also apply to governments and political parties who acquiesce in such arms sales in the name of defending British jobs.[4] We should be very clear, therefore, that a key sense in which 'public' values are public is not that they are really universally held, but that few individuals and organizations in democratic societies are prepared openly to admit that they do *not* subscribe to them. This is not quite as depressing as it sounds! For one thing, it carries the implication that it is difficult for anyone to publicly contest the legitimacy of schools in these societies seeking to transmit such values as the core of civic and moral education. Shared 'public' morality may to some extent be a kind of 'virtual' morality – but even if it is partly a fiction, it is the kind of fiction which schools do well to perpetuate. In this way, what might be called a minimal 'national conscience' can be formed and sustained – albeit unevenly.[5] Moreover – and lest all this seem altogether too cynical – it is also important to recognize that the liberal value-consensus does really have significant (if qualified) social reality – not least because it is embedded in (and therefore protected by) certain legal and constitutional guarantees (inadequate as these too may be in the UK). The dissemination of these 'public' values, therefore, does have an important part to play in maintaining social order and social cohesion in liberal, democratic societies. But it is only *part* of a more complex and, in total, less consensual set of mechanisms.

McLaughlin goes on to argue that, within the framework of liberal theory, the role of the school in civic education, or at any rate the role of what he calls the 'common school', is reasonably clear as far as 'public' values are concerned: 'the common school has an obligation to "transmit" the basic or non-negotiable norms which articulate the framework of liberal democratic society' (McLaughlin, 1995a, p. 247). Furthermore, this process of transmission involves fostering not only understanding but *commitment* on the part of pupils. This is educationally legitimate in such societies, not least because it is precisely these 'public' values which help to justify rational autonomy as a key education aim. This, in turn, has implications for the way in which even these broadly consensual values should be dealt with by schools. It is not legitimate – and indeed it would be contradictory – simply to inculcate them as part of an unreflective process of political socialization. Rather, it is essential that they are taught in what Bailey calls an 'evidential' manner: i.e. with reference to counter-arguments, to reasoned justification, and with an awareness that the scope of the 'public' sphere is one of the things which is itself controversial (Bailey, 1984, pp. 137–42).[6]

When it comes to so-called 'private' values, the arguments about the school's role become more complex. First, however, it is important once again to be clear about what is *not* meant by 'private'. McLaughlin usefully clarifies this:

> [T]his description needs to be understood carefully. There is, for example, no non-social 'private' domain. Religious communities, for example, have a 'public' side, as do the lives of families and other associational groups...Nor do such groupings lack views about 'public' matters and the complexity of the language of the 'public' and the 'private' is increased by the further question of the intricate relationship between the two domains. (McLaughlin, 1995b, p. 28)

The key sense in which values associated with the 'private' domain *are* private is that they lie outside the shared (and relatively non-controversial) consensus of the public sphere. 'Private' values have to do with issues which are significantly controversial. That is to say, they are matters of some importance, about which equally well-educated, equally intelligent, and equally morally serious people disagree – sometimes profoundly. Obvious examples include many aspects of religious belief and many matters connected with sexuality and sexual behaviour. Slightly less obviously, many *political* matters are also part of this so-called 'private' domain – despite the fact that by virtue of being directly political, they are, in another sense of the word, quite clearly public. Moreover, it is not only many of the specific policies of different political parties that lie outside the 'public' consensus of liberal theory; so too do many aspects of the more general divergences between political ideologies. Indeed, as we shall argue in the next chapter, beyond a certain minimal definition, the concept of *citizenship* itself is fundamentally contested.

What stance should schools adopt when dealing with these complex areas in which value divergence and controversiality are the most salient features? First, there can be no justification for concealing, minimizing or denying the fact and the extent of controversiality surrounding many of these areas in modern, liberal societies. As we have seen, this is one of the most serious weaknesses of those who campaign for a return to the supposedly shared values of 'our' common heritage. The main point about the distinction within liberal theory between the public and private spheres is that the zone outside the 'public' consensus is one of *publicly tolerated and (in that sense) legitimate disagreement*. Schools clearly have a key role to play in helping young people to understand not only *that* this is so but also *why* it is so. This will in itself involve a complex task – not only of moral but of social education. Highlighting the importance of toleration in this way could be misunderstood. It does not imply either that the liberal position overall is value free or that it involves a stance of moral abdication. Again, McLaughlin makes the essential points with characteristic economy and clarity:

> The common school in relation to moral education . . . seeks the substantive commitment of its pupils to the public or fundamental values. They include basic social morality, ideals (such as individual autonomy), methodological principles (relating to the way in which public disputes are settled), and moral and political values (such as respect for persons and toleration). In view of the close connection of many of these values with the domain of the political (they include 'civic virtue'), this task should be conducted in close harmony with a significant form of political education – in particular, education for citizenship. In relation

to these public values the school seeks more than simply understanding and critical assessment on the part of pupils, and there is little room for pluralism and neutrality. For this reason, it is wrong to regard common schools of this kind as lacking a moral foundation, not least because the public values involved are not merely procedural; properly understood they require the formation of substantial commitments and virtues. On the other hand, in relation to the diversity of the private domain, the school seeks exploration, understanding, debate and critically reflective decision by individuals. This does not necessarily require the strategy of 'teacher neutrality', which is only one of a number of alternatives which can be employed. (McLaughlin, 1995b, p. 30)

If schools take seriously these notions of toleration and respect for persons, they are likely to want to help their students to appreciate that the mere fact of public toleration of certain acts – in the sense, say, that they are not illegal – does not mean that that is the end of the matter, morally speaking. The kind of exploration of morality and moral judgement which schools should engage in, in societies characterized by a significant degree of value pluralism, also needs to highlight the fact that the limits of the current public consensus are not coterminous with the boundaries of morality (or morali*ties*). McLaughlin discusses the implications of this point at some length (see McLaughlin, 1995a, pp. 248–50). One of the points he makes concerns 'respect' for the views of other individuals and groups with whom, in a pluralistic society, we may ourselves disagree. It is important that schools develop the moral sensibility of young people so as to help them appreciate why, say, within certain morally serious comprehensive frameworks of belief, the practice of artificial contraception, let alone abortion, may be held to be immoral (except in certain very special circumstances). As McLaughlin points out, 'the school has a principled responsibility to avoid giving illicit salience to "public" matters . . . for example, the school should not promote a secular view of life as a whole' (ibid., p. 248). This point is particularly important *educationally* in view of the wider contextual pressures of a modernizing and secularizing kind which, according to writers like Macedo, are an inbuilt part of modern liberalism. McLaughlin puts it like this:

Pupils must be provided with proper understanding of what is involved in giving 'respect' to differing views. Democratic mutual respect for reasonable differences of moral view requires more than a grudging attitude of 'live and let live'; . . . reasonable differences are to be judged as in some sense within the moral pale, and this enriches respect, and indeed toleration, with principle. (ibid., p. 248)

However, he immediately adds a crucial clarifying comment:

But such respect and toleration does not necessarily require that disagreement and disapproval concerning the substantive value differences can be dissolved. Our disagreements and disapprovals, often arising from our differing 'comprehensive' theories of the good, persist and should not be smoothed away . . . The common school must therefore achieve the right kind of openness to diversity on the part of pupils and avoid blurring the distinction in their minds between according differing views 'civic respect' and giving them unqualified approval, perhaps on a relativistic basis. (ibid., pp. 248–9)

THE NATIONAL FORUM FOR VALUES IN EDUCATION AND COMMUNITY

Some mention has already been made in Chapter 2 of the setting up, under the auspices of the School Curriculum and Assessment Authority, of a National Forum for Values in Education and the Community. The Forum, which began its work in March 1996, consisted of 150 invited members, chosen to represent a wide range of viewpoints and interests. The membership, drawn from a range of groups who work with young people, included: lawyers, representatives of the police service and magistrates, youth workers, teachers, teacher-trainers, parents, business people, trade unionists, religious leaders of various faiths and denominations, environmentalists, etc. The Forum's brief was to identify a 'non-negotiable core of moral values' which all state schools might reasonably be expected to endorse and transmit.

At the time when the Forum was established, no one could quite have foreseen the extraordinary circumstances which were to surround the publication of its conclusions in October 1996. The content of the report was extensively leaked a week ahead of the planned publication date – notably by the *Express on Sunday* – and a right-wing campaign of criticism and vilification was orchestrated so successfully that the Secretary of State for Education and Employment, Gillian Shephard, found it necessary to announce, before the report ever saw the light of day, that certain parts of it would have to be rewritten: 'I will not accept the report without proper reference to family values. There must clearly be a section reinforcing the traditional family' (*Express on Sunday*, 27 October 1996, p. 1). This press campaign was precipitated by the failure of 'five traditionalists on the Forum', led by a parent representative, Guy Hordern, to have an 'explicit statement on support for marriage' included in the SCAA document (*Daily Mail*, 31 October 1996, p. 12). The pre-emptive intervention by the Secretary of State becomes easier to understand once one appreciates that these events occurred in the context of a remarkable fortnight during which a succession of issues concerning the moral state of the nation and the nation's schools hit the headlines. As a result, the public was treated to the unedifying spectacle of politicians of all parties elbowing one another aside in increasingly frenetic attempts to be seen to be occupying the 'moral high ground'. These issues included:

- the aftermath of the Dunblane tragedy and political divisions arising from the 'Snowdrop Campaign' to ban the sale of all handguns in the UK;
- the conclusion of the trial of the killer of headteacher Philip Lawrence and the publication by his widow Frances Lawrence of a personal 'manifesto for the nation' which contained proposals ranging from a ban on the sale of combat knives to suggestions that all schools should embrace 'the "three Es" – effort, earnestness and excellence';
- the publication by the Roman Catholic Bishops' Conference of a document on social principles and common values which was widely interpreted as encouraging voters to support the Labour Party in the 1997 General Election;
- a subsequent attack upon the leader of the Labour Party, Tony Blair, by the head of the Roman Catholic Church in Scotland over his 'failure' to unambiguously declare his opposition to abortion;
- a very public difference of opinion between John Major and Gillian Shephard over the possible reintroduction of corporal punishment in schools, which was almost immediately followed up by a campaign by right-wing Conservative MPs to persuade the government to allow a 'free vote on the return of caning' (*Daily Telegraph*, 31 October 1996, p. 1);
- the cases of Manton Junior School in Worksop and The Ridings School in

Halifax in which teachers resorted (or threatened to resort) to industrial action as a means of drawing attention to problems of teaching disruptive pupils within mainstream classrooms – events which were interpreted elsewhere as clear evidence of the 'breakdown of discipline in our schools'.

In this atmosphere of moral panic, hype, and over-reaction, the planned launch date of the National Forum's consultative report was brought forward by two days. The result was that the launch coincided with the announcement in Parliament of the government's latest Education Bill which contained, *inter alia,* highly controversial proposals to permit Grant Maintained schools to select more of their pupils on the basis of academic ability. This change of date, combined with the continuing furore over the caning proposals, had the effect of significantly over-shadowing the impact of the document itself – as distinct from negative comment about it. This may or may not have been a deliberate ploy to defuse an issue that had become yet another source of political embarrassment to a government under pressure. According to the *Express*, 'SCAA was *ordered* to bring forward publication of the report' (*Express*, 31 October 1996, p. 20, my italics). However this may be, it was notable that sections of the right-wing press quickly distanced themselves not only from the document but also from its sponsor – Nicholas Tate.

The *Express* went for a direct attack – in the course of continuing its campaign to get the SCAA Statement changed:

> Dr Nick Tate indicated that he would not bow to pressure over his document making no mention of the value of marriage while stressing the importance of the family. His refusal to commit himself to supporting the institution is a clear snub to Education Secretary Gillian Shephard. Mrs Shephard said that it was 'ludicrous' that the blueprint made no mention of marriage – as revealed in the Express on Sunday. (*Express*, 31 October 1996, p. 20)

In somewhat more sympathetic vein, a *Daily Mail* leader began:

> There can be few more thankless tasks than to tease an agreed set of values from 150 diverse representatives of shifting views in an unsure age. So there should be some sympathy for the Schools [sic] Curriculum and Assessment Authority as its chief executive, Nick Tate, faces the critical flak. Nevertheless, the sins of omission from its draft moral code cannot be excused. Not only, in their blurred benevolence do the authors of this evasive document fail to focus on the intrinsic worth of marriage. They also cannot bring themselves to mention parents... (*Daily Mail*, 31 October 1996, p. 8)

On the same page as this leading article, the *Daily Mail* ran a piece by the well-known right-wing journalist Paul Johnson which sharply criticized not only the content of the SCAA statement but also, and just as significantly, the manner in which it was generated. It is worth quoting from this article at some length because it illustrates very clearly why, in a society in which certain kinds of moral divisions coincide with *political* fault lines, it is likely to prove chronically difficult to generate a *genuinely* consensual and educationally relevant public statement about morality:

> First the Government – and a Conservative Government, ye gods – turned to a quango called the School Curriculum and Assessment Authority. That, of course, far from being an answer to the moral decline in our schools, is part of the problem – but no matter. This quango in turn set up another quango, called the National Forum for Values in Education and the Community. The composition of this second quango is of hair-raising imbecility... an enormously complicated body of 150 people was assembled, equipped

with secretariat, staff and high-tech back-up, and told to come up with a formula which would make moral-sounding noises but offend nobody. Everyone had to be represented – Christians, Jews, Hindus, Buddhists, Muslims and atheists. (I am not making this up: one member of the committee was from the British Humanist Association.)...There were 'researchers' and 'consultants' galore, people from the National Council of Hindu Temples and the Muslim News, a spokesman for the Kite Club, Mr Dilip Kadodwala of the National Association of SACREs – whatever they may be [sic] – and, not least, a representative from the Royal Society for the Protection of Birds.

The concept of this giant talking-shop, its composition, and its procedures...sound as if they had emerged from a rather tired satire factory. What it came up with was entirely predictable: a compendium of high-minded waffle; a digest of the fashionable pseudo-beliefs of the Nineties; a rag-bag of the politically correct, dos-and-don'ts currently taught at Fabian summer schools. (Johnson, 1996)

This same strategy of associating 'suspect' institutional mechanisms with 'worthless' outcomes was also employed, albeit rather more succinctly, by the *Express*:

[T]he forum has 150 members who could have been selected with a pin from directories of academia, religious groups and media...The idea that you can get anything worthwhile from 150 disparate individuals is laughable. No wonder what emerges shows all the weary hallmarks of hours of difference-splitting...

Frankly, it is hardly worth the paper it is written on, and the Government would be better advised, on this evidence, to forget the whole idea. (*Express*, 31 October 1996, p. 10)

There are rich ironies here. The most obvious is to find Nicholas Tate positioned as the *target* of neo-conservative attacks! A more serious point is that it is precisely Conservative traditionalists who have most loudly and persistently proclaimed that society needs to be held together by shared values. Yet in this instance, it turns out that the only values which they are actually prepared to support are their own. When confronted with a quite broadly representative body which comes up with ideas they do *not* like, they fall back upon populist denunciation and discursive appeals to some *presumed* consensus which all 'ordinary' and 'right-thinking' people simply 'know' is right. Alternative ideas are portrayed as typical of the 'dangerous nonsense' peddled by 'liberals', the 'educational establishment' and the like:

[F]or fear of offending the permissive liberal consensus, the national curriculum proposals avoid mentioning marriage. Neither, for the same reason, do they refer to the Ten Commandments or authority. What we have, by contrast, is typical of what we are likely to get from the educational bureaucracy...

A national curriculum for morality is potentially harmful if, as seems all too likely, it endorses suspect or subversive values. Even if it simply comes out with platitudes, it would be highly unlikely to lay down firm moral principles in a way that had any bite. We should here and now firmly close the door on any such idea. The education establishment cannot be trusted. (*Express on Sunday*, 27 October 1996, p. 26)

Now, as Rob Moore has recently pointed out, the way interventions of this kind 'work' is by laying claim to a distinctive kind of *discursive authority*. It is, symptomatically, of a kind which sets aside normal criteria of evidence, cogency, reasonableness, etc. and relies instead upon a 'restricted code' which operates on quite different principles:

there is another form of discursive authority...that operates by the *presumption* of agreement. Here there is a tacit assumption of shared understandings. We could call this the 'you *know* what I mean' principle (in contrast to 'do you see what I mean?'). Although we have common phrases to indicate this presumption... it is often marked non-verbally, by a significant pause or gesture, (raising our eyes to heaven, a shrug). The authority claimed by this aspect of discourse is essentially that of intimacy or of *consanguinity* – the assumption/assertion that we are all 'akin' and share understandings on certain matters. (Moore, 1996, p. 33)

In such discourse the appeal to what Moore calls 'consanguinity' often also means that racism is often just underneath the surface – as in the following fragment from the *Express on Sunday* article just quoted: 'Accepting diversity' (one of the SCAA statement's principles) 'is educational code for the relativism and multi-culturalism which is tearing our social fabric apart.'

We shall now move on from considering the reception given to the SCAA statement, to an appraisal of its actual *content*. It is as well to remind ourselves that the document, published at the beginning of November, was a *consultation* paper – with SCAA seeking responses by the end of the year – in a context where the forum was scheduled to be reconvened early in January 1997, with a view to producing a final version in February. Gillian Shephard, employing finely judged and soothing 'needs talk', tried to set a tone which suggested that this process of consultation could and should lead to reconciliation:

This is a consultative document and I think, if we look at it calmly, we will realise it needs to be changed. (*Observer*, 27 October 1996, p. 1)

In another interview she commented:

I am sure that the consultation will help to establish agreement on a statement of core values. (*Express*, 31 October 1996, p. 20)

Nicholas Tate, speaking at the launch of the statement, also sought to strike a conciliatory note.

The Secretary of State has made known her views. We look forward to getting the views of the community. We are trying to get the views of as large a number of people as possible. We will review the situation in the light of the response to our consultation exercise. (*Express*, ibid.)

At the same time, however, he was commendably firm in his backing for the Forum's work. In a letter dated 28 October 1996, sent out to all Forum members, he spelled out where he stood in relation to the torrent of adverse press criticism:

You may have seen some adverse comments in the press over the weekend regarding the report of the Forum. Let me assure you that the consultation on the basis of your recommendations is going ahead as planned and that I have spared no pains in offering a robust defence of your work. (Tate, 1996d)

What then of the *content*? As can be seen from Table 4.1, the Forum's conclusions in the consultation paper are set out in the following form:

- four broad areas are identified: society, relationships, self, and environment;
- within each of these, a 'statement of values' is offered, accompanied by a series of 'principles for action'.

Let us focus first on certain characteristics of the values statements. Well ahead of the report's publication, Dr Tate had already anticipated one line of critical response:

Table 4.1

SCAA National Forum for Values in Education and the Community: Statement for Consultation

The forum divides the subject into four areas: society, relationships, self and environment. In each case a statement of values is accompanied by a number of 'principles for action'.

SOCIETY

We value truth, human rights, the law, justice and collective endeavour for the common good of society. In particular, we value families as sources of love and support for all their members and as the basis of a society in which people care for others.

On the basis of these values, we as a society should:

- understand our responsibilities as citizens;
- be ready to challenge values or actions which may be harmful to individuals or communities;
- support families in raising children and caring for dependants;
- help people to know about the law and legal processes;
- obey the law and encourage others to do so;
- accept diversity and respect people's right to religious and cultural differences;
- provide opportunities to all;
- support people who cannot sustain a dignified life-style by themselves;

- promote participation in our democracy;
- contribute to, as well as benefit fairly from, economic and cultural resources;
- make truth and integrity priorities in public life.

RELATIONSHIPS

We value others for themselves, not for what they have or what they can do for us, and we value these relationships as fundamental to our development and the good of the community.

On the basis of these values, within our relationships we should:

- respect the dignity of all people;
- tell others they are valued;
- earn loyalty, trust and confidence;
- work co-operatively with others;
- be mutually supportive;
- respect the beliefs, life, privacy and property of others;
- try to resolve disputes peacefully.

SELF

We value each person as a unique being of intrinsic worth, with potential for spiritual, moral, intellectual and physical development and change.

On the basis of these values, we as individuals should:

- try to understand our own character, strengths and weaknesses;
- develop a sense of self-worth;
- try to discover meaning and purpose in life and how life ought to be lived;
- try to live up to a shared moral code;
- make responsible use of our rights and privileges;
- strive for knowledge and wisdom throughout life;
- take responsibility for our own lives within our capacities.

ENVIRONMENT

We value the natural world as a source of wonder and inspiration, and accept our duty to maintain a sustainable environment for the future. On the basis of these values we should:

- preserve a balance and diversity in nature wherever possible;
- justify development in terms of a sustainable environment;
- repair habitats devastated by human development wherever possible;
- preserve areas of beauty wherever possible;
- understand the place of human beings within the world.

'I expect that when the report is published we may be criticised for the very general nature of the moral code on which the forum has agreed' (Spencer and Whitehead, 1996). In one sense, the values statements do indeed have this character. Many of the things which 'we value' are specified in highly general terms: truth, justice, the law, families, other people as beings of intrinsic worth, etc. Now, as far as certain of these elements are concerned, this seems eminently reasonable and right. Valuing *truth* is not seriously optional for educational institutions – on logical as well as moral grounds. Of an almost similar degree of fundamentality, many people would accept, is the principle of respect for persons (see, for example, Peters, 1966), whilst principles such as justice and freedom (essential to most accounts of human rights) also have a central place in any serious approach to moral education. Of course, as we have argued at length above, moral education also needs to address the many and complex questions concerned with the *application* of these principles to particular issues, instances where certain principles may conflict with one another, and the like. But the authors of the SCAA Statement would almost certainly not disagree with this.

Certain of the *other* elements included in the values statements, however, are *not* quite of this fundamental kind. The statement about families is a case in point. First, it not entirely clear why families are something which we should value 'in particular'. Secondly, in this case there may be a more serious problem about the level of generality. The family is not a fundamental moral principle; it is a social institution – and one which, in modern societies, is increasingly difficult to define in consensual terms. This is no doubt one reason why the original version of the Forum's statement spoke of 'families' – in the plural and without specifying the scope of the term. But that approach actually highlights the problem. As the neo-conservative backlash against this original version of the SCAA statement so clearly illustrates, we do *not* all attach value to all those institutions which might be included within an elastic definition of family. More than that: certain forms of 'family' are quite clearly anathema to certain sections of society – and in at least one instance, this is legally codified: Section 28 of the Local Government Act 1988 'prohibits local authorities...from promoting the teaching in any maintained school of the acceptability of homosexuality as *a pretended family relationship*' (DES, 1994a, p. 19, my italics). Elsewhere, however, and in the very month in which the SCAA Statement was published in the UK, the United States Supreme Court upheld an appeal which had the effect of legally validating marriages of gay and lesbian couples in the state of Hawaii.

Now, it is entirely understandable that for 'political' reasons, members of the Forum may well have felt under a considerable degree of constraint to include in their Statement some kind of endorsement of family values, particularly when a small but determined minority within the Forum itself was urging explicit and even exclusive support for the traditional two-parent family.[7] Nevertheless, this decision to include in the original version of the document a statement which did *not* command universal support demonstrates only too clearly how limited is the scope for achieving value consensus once one moves away from the level of abstract moral principles towards considering substantive social issues. A subsequent attempt, in December 1996, to achieve consensus around a 'revised version' of the original statement once again failed to completely satisfy Guy Hordern, the leader of the objectors within the Forum. This 'compromise' formulation stated:

> We value families as sources of love and support for all their members, and as a basis of a society in which people care for others. On the basis of these values, we as a society should support marriage as the traditional form of family while recognizing that the love and commitment required for a secure and happy childhood can be found in families of other kinds. (quoted in *Daily Telegraph*, 20 December 1996, p. 4)

This version was said to be the product both of a 're-examination by SCAA of discussions within the Forum' as well as of extensive national consultation with schools, religious bodies and others (ibid.). Guy Hordern welcomed the change insofar as the word 'marriage' was now incorporated into the statement but remained concerned that 'SCAA is proposing that marriage be supported only as the "traditional" form of family, instead of as the "ideal" form of family in which to bring up children' (quoted in ibid.). He added 'that the proposal drew no distinction between marriage and cohabitation or between heterosexual and homosexual relationships' (*Guardian*, 20 December 1996, p. 4). Some people *outside* the forum, however, are likely to find the revised statement significantly harder to support than the original version; this is likely to include the very large numbers of (mainly younger) people who have quite deliberately chosen to live in stable, committed but *unmarried* relationships.

It is important to point out, however, that the contentiousness of what the statement has to say about the family (whether in the original or the revised version) actually goes well beyond this dispute between traditionalists and those favouring a more 'inclusive' interpretation. Consider, for example, the claim that 'we value families as sources of love and support for all their members *and as the basis of a society in which people care for others*' (my italics). Is this supposed to be a quasi-empirical claim about families and their social effects? If so, it is not implausible to argue that there is at least as much evidence *against* the claim as for it. Arguably, it is precisely the self-centred egoism of increasingly privatized families which has become one of the most powerful influences *undermining* collectivist values within the wider society. One only has to call to mind Mrs Thatcher's famous assertion that 'there is no such thing as society; there are only individuals and their families' (cited in Bilton *et al.*, 1996, p. 498), or John Major's 1992 vision of family wealth 'cascading down the generations', to appreciate the point. And of course, there is nothing novel about this insight. Thomas Hardy in *Jude the Obscure* put his finger on just this tension between the potential exclusiveness of familial interests and a more inclusive sense of social obligation:

> What does it matter, when you come to think of it, whether a child is yours by blood or not? All the little ones of our time are collectively the children of all the adults of our time and entitled to our general care. That excessive regard of parents for their own children, and their dislike of other people's, is like class feeling, patriotism, and save-your-own-soulism, a mean exclusiveness at bottom. (Hardy, 1895)

By putting this speech into the mouth of the socially marginalized Jude, Hardy was, of course, drawing attention to the gulf which actually existed between this generous and inclusive vision and the values which really motivated many of his fellow citizens.

The generalized and socially decontextualized character of many of the Statement's 'principles for action' raises similar problems. If they are really to operate as principles for *action*, there would seem to be a need for there to be an achievable consensus on how these principles might be translated *into* action. Once again, this seems unlikely, especially with regard to those sections of the document dealing with social issues – e.g. Society and the Environment. Take, for example, the following two principles: 'provide opportunities for all' and 'make truth and integrity priorities in public life'. Now of course almost no one, and certainly no politician, would declare themselves opposed to these principles in general terms. But once we move from the level of public rhetoric to that of real policy and political realities, we encounter various combinations of chronic disagreement and political evasiveness. The highly publicized divisions within the Labour Party over the issue of Grant Maintained schools are symptomatic of this situation as far as the issue of equality of educational opportunity is concerned. Moreover, the unenviable choices faced by the Blairs and by Harriet Harman and Jack Dromey highlight the acute tensions surrounding the *competing* claims of family responsibilities (to secure a good education for one's own children) and wider social responsibilities (to secure good education for all children). Similarly, we are all in principle in favour of truth and integrity in public life – but there is much less consensus about what this should mean in practical terms. There is not even agreement any longer about whether the House of Commons is capable of effective self-regulation in these respects! Even if we turn to the sections of the Statement concerned with principles governing individual conduct and interpersonal relationships, similar problems are encountered. The essential point was well made by Frances Gumley-Mason contributing her 'Thought for the Day' to the Radio 4 *Today* programme on 7 November 1996, shortly after the publication of the SCAA statement. She pointed out that in schools we are often exhorted to tell children that they each matter as individuals, that they are uniquely valued, that they are not just statistics. But what 'we' actually then *do* is to sum up their contributions to school precisely *as* sets of reductive statistics! – indicating where they came in national tests compared to other children, where their school was placed in local and national league-tables, etc. The public message this sends often contradicts the assurances which schools and teachers themselves sincerely try to provide.

It would be a mistake, however, to conclude that the Statement taken as a whole is simply so generalized as to be merely a collection of platitudes. For all his calculated bluster, Paul Johnson (1966) identified something real when he claimed that the report was imbued with political correctness and was a product of 'Fabian summer schools'. One does not have to be a right-wing journalist to discern in certain sections of the statement a broadly 'social democratic' orientation. Not withstanding its lack of specificity, the document does seem to lean towards a particular view of citizenship – one broadly indebted to the ideas of T. H. Marshall and which therefore builds an element of *social* citizenship into the very notion of what it is to be a citizen (Marshall, 1950). This political orientation is of course not overt; nevertheless the SCAA statement seems to endorse this conception of citizenship in several ways. First, there is the stress on certain substantive issues: collective duties, support for those who cannot sustain a dignified lifestyle by themselves, equal opportunity, enabling people to benefit fairly from economic and cultural resources, etc. Secondly, there is the overall ordering of categories and priorities: the fact that of the four main areas addressed, one is Society and another is Environment. Finally, there are the omissions: there is nothing explicit on the values of enterprise, competition, wealth creation, self-sufficiency, the prime importance of taking responsibility for those one has oneself brought into the world – in other words, what Oliver Letwin has called 'the robust virtues' (Letwin, 1992).

The key issue here, in relation to the status and purposes of the Statement, is not which orientation one personally supports. It is that the document, despite its collective authorship, cannot convincingly claim to be politically neutral, nor is it politically innocent. One can only speculate on the question of whether some of its authors (i.e. members of the Forum) shaped it with one eye on the possibility of a Labour victory in the 1997 election. But however this may be, *educationally* it is not helpful to try to found moral and civic education in the nation's schools on a statement that is open to the accusation of political partiality. It is both more honest and in the long run more productive for all concerned to face up to the very limited nature of the ideas about which most people really can agree even as ideals – in other words to acknowledge the limited extent of the consensus on *public values* (to use the terminology of the previous discussion). If we were to do this, we could then perhaps accept that one key role of moral and civic education in societies like our own is to help people to understand, in a context which emphasizes the value of tolerance, why it is that we disagree about so much and why so many issues in our society are now controversial. This uncomfortable conclusion may not be one that recommends itself to many people – on any side of the debate. It is, nevertheless, the one which seems to me most justifiable. Further reasons why this is so are explored in Chapter 5 – which considers the specifically political dimensions of citizenship education.

NOTES

1   For properly systematic and philosophically informed discussions of autonomy as an aim of liberal education, see, *inter alia*: Bailey (1984) (which includes a critical examination of the work of Philip Phenix, Paul Hirst and John White in this area), Gutman (1987) and (1989), and (from a more child-centred perspective) Bonnett (1994).
2   A really serious approach to the task we are outlining – particularly in societies in which 30 to 60 per cent of 18-year-olds continue in full or part-time education – would also need to involve institutions of further *and* higher education. In this respect, some of the proposals in the forthcoming Dearing Report on higher education, which suggest that its role should be broadened to encompass more than narrowly academic or vocational objectives, point in the right direction – even if some of the more specific proposals leave a great deal to be desired.
3   This example is occasioned by a recent legal case in which four Christian women were acquitted by a majority verdict of 10 to 2, on a charge of criminal damage relating to their having caused £1.5m worth of damage to one of 24 Hawk jet 'trainers' destined for export to Indonesia. This case raises complex issues about when it may or may not be justifiable to break the law, but the most pertinent point for our present purposes is that a clear majority of the jurors accepted the women's argument that they had 'used reasonable force to prevent a crime'. This has been a frequently used defence in analogous trials involving peace movement activists. However, in this case there was a very direct link between the damage caused to a specific aircraft and the defence claim that aircraft was destined to be an instrument of political repression. (See Andrea Needham's article in the *Independent on Sunday* [Needham, 1996, p. 21].)
4   In a series of recent papers, McLaughlin has developed a much more philosophically informed and nuanced analysis of these issues than I have been able to provide here. (See, for example, McLaughlin, 1992, 1995a, 1995b.) My whole discussion of these issues, and of liberalism more generally, is heavily indebted to his work.
5   At some stage in their education, young people (or at least the more perceptive among them) are likely to come to appreciate that there *is* something fictitious about our shared public values. Helping them to understand these complexities, and the reasons for them, is a difficult but significant task for schools and others in society.

6   Bailey's term 'evidential teaching' applies not only to subject areas like the natural sciences where hypotheses derived from competing theories are tested empirically. As he emphasizes:

> Our evidential teacher . . . will have a sharper realization of the varying status of evidential claims across different kinds of knowledge and understanding, knowing that the justification of beliefs in some areas like religion, morality and politics is far less clear and agreed than in areas like science and mathematics, and (will) vary teaching strategies accordingly. In assessing and examining, a teacher concerned in this way will distrust the values of testing factual recall and strive to find other ways of getting at the more complex structures of the pupil's understanding. (Bailey, 1984, p. 141)

7   The five dissenting members of the forum argued for:

> a stronger statement on the nature of the family as follows:

> The most important relationships throughout life are those experienced within the immediate and extended family. Children should be nurtured and developed within a stable, moral and loving home environment with preferably both mother and father present in a happy marriage relationship. Marriage and parenting successfully undertaken are very creative of good values in adults and children.

> The majority of the Forum, whilst not necessarily disagreeing with a stronger statement, considered that the consensus did not go beyond the statement proposed. However, SCAA wished to review the situation in the light of wider consultation. Respondents have an opportunity to give their views on this issue in the questionnaire. (SCAA, 1996, 96/43)

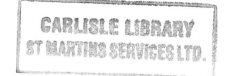

Chapter 5

Citizenship Education: Problems and Possibilities

INTRODUCTION

In the summer of 1995, the headteacher of a comprehensive school was invited to talk to an audience of over 400 secondary Postgraduate Certificate of Education students who were nearing the end of their course of initial teacher training. The subject of the talk was Education for Citizenship. Outlining the process of whole-school curriculum review and development within his own school, the headteacher remarked, somewhat wryly:

> Of the five cross-curricular 'themes' of the National Curriculum, we have taken on four more or less full-frontal. As for the other one – when someone tells us what education for citizenship is, I'm sure that will trigger a response.

This plea for enlightenment may, at first sight, seem surprising. After all, the National Curriculum Council's 'Curriculum Guidance' documents included Education for Citizenship alongside similar guidance on each of the other four cross-curricular 'themes' (National Curriculum Council, 1990a), and since then no less than three specialist organizations have been active in developing curriculum materials and disseminating good practice in this area: the Citizenship Foundation based at the University of London Institute of Education, the Centre for Citizenship Studies in Education based at Leicester University, and the Institute for Citizenship established in 1990, with Bernard Weatherill the then Speaker of the House of Commons as its first president (see Abrams, 1993). On further analysis, however, the perplexity expressed by this particular headteacher and his staff becomes more readily comprehensible. Among the most important reasons why teachers may still, *and with good reason*, feel uncertain about the nature and aims of education for citizenship are the following:

- the seriously inadequate nature of the guidance offered to them from official sources, notably *Curriculum Guidance 8: Education for Citizenship* (hereafter *CG8*) but also the most recent OFSTED handbook on the inspection of schools (OFSTED, 1995);

- the contested, indeed *essentially contested* nature of the concept of citizenship itself (Gallie, 1955);
- the fact that discussion of what I shall deliberately and neutrally term 'citizenship education' has been mainly focused upon the idea of 'educating *for* citizenship' rather than, for example, educating *about* citizenship.

Each of these issues will be examined in turn.

OFFICIAL GUIDANCE ABOUT EDUCATION FOR CITIZENSHIP, WITH PARTICULAR REFERENCE TO *CURRICULUM GUIDANCE 8: EDUCATION FOR CITIZENSHIP*

There is evidence that from its inception, the cross-curricular 'theme' of Education for Citizenship was an area of particular political as well as educational sensitivity. Duncan Graham, the first chairman and chief executive of the National Curriculum Council, has chronicled the 'ministerial panic and interference' which surrounded the writing and publication of this particular Curriculum Guidance booklet (Graham, 1993, p. 105). One source of pressure on the NCC to *include* Citizenship as one of the five 'themes' in the first place was the fact of the existence of the all-party House of Commons Commission on Citizenship, which had been set up in December 1988 (sometimes known as the Speaker's Commission on Citizenship). And indeed, the Commission's final report, *Encouraging Citizenship*, was published in the same year as *CG8* itself (Commission on Citizenship, 1990). Duncan Graham notes that 'the government viewed the recently announced Speaker's Commission on Citizenship as being dangerously left wing' – and insofar as *Encouraging Citizenship* takes T. H. Marshall's 'classic' definition of citizenship as its point of departure (ibid., p. 4), such suspicions were perhaps not wholly unjustified, at least as seen from a broadly New Right standpoint. Graham's account goes on, however, to document instances of direct political interference, for example on the part of David Waddington, the then Home Secretary, and his department's civil servants:

> Waddington took the view that it was up to the council to tell teachers in every school what they should teach. Specifically, teachers should concentrate on the evils of car thefts and the need to co-operate with the police ... The Home Office saw the citizenship booklet as a propaganda medium rather than an exercise in educating young people to participate and discriminate before making their own judgements. (Graham, 1993, p. 105)

Despite evidence which Graham also provides of robust independence on the part of DES officials in the face of such pressures, his account lends plausibility to the view that the final form taken by *CG8* may, in various respects, have been the result of a series of compromises between undeclared but fundamentally opposed conceptions of the purposes such a document should serve *and* of the nature of citizenship itself.

The Introduction to *CG8* goes out of its way to emphasize that the booklet 'is *intended as a framework for curriculum debate* and is certainly not a blueprint or set of lesson plans' (National Curriculum Council, 1990a, p. 1, my emphasis). It is, however, precisely *as* a contribution to serious debate about its chosen topic that the document must be judged as so conspicuously deficient. Interestingly, John Ahier, in a recent analysis of two of the other booklets in the Curriculum Guidance series, *CG4: Education for Economic and Industrial Understanding* (National Curriculum Council, 1990b) and *CG7: Environmental Education* (National Curriculum Council, 1990c), has identified deficiencies of essentially the same kind as *CG8* displays (Ahier, 1995). All these documents are presumably addressed by the NCC to an audience of fellow professionals (they were not, after all, intended for pupils). Nevertheless, as Ahier points out, there is a persistent failure to introduce readers to the most important level of debate concerning areas of this kind: that they are not grounded in either public or academic consensus but are, rather, areas of lively disagreement:

> Just as there are vital disagreements within the academic subjects which inform these themes, these public concerns are not defined in a consensual way either. There are very definite divisions between the groups who construct these debates. For example, behind what might be described as the environmental lobby lie a number of serious disagreements on theory, philosophy, tactics, strategy and political perspective. Similarly, the pressures to include industrial understanding in schools arose from a variety of conflicting expressions of the needs of industry and explanations of Britain's industrial decline...Unfortunately the documents...identify no major differences of informed opinion about economic or environmental matters, no 'schools of thought', no theoretical or ideological conflicts. The documents' 'coyness' about what one might call organized oppositions means they can suggest no ways in which teachers within a democratic society should deal with such disagreements and differences. (ibid., pp. 140–1)

As Ahier goes on to argue, weaknesses of this kind are particularly regrettable within curriculum areas whose essential justification for being part of a national curriculum at all resides in the fact of their being of more than merely academic concern. Within the insulations established by the strong boundaries of traditional school subjects, differing perspectives or ideologies can be presented as interesting (but safely academic) 'interpretations'. However, the *raison d'être* of *cross*-curricular constructs such as Environmental Education or Education for Citizenship is their direct relevance to everyday life – in its public as well as private dimensions. Within such cross-curricular domains, competing points of view may 'connect with a whole range of understandings' and are 'likely to have close connections with how we live our personal lives, how we vote, and so on' (ibid., p. 141). Ahier concludes: 'If...cross-curricular themes are curricular constructions which are built on, or reflect major public concerns, then it is important to determine the extent to which the guidance offered reflects the range of positions expressed within those concerns' (ibid., p. 147).

Let us now examine *Education for Citizenship* in the light of this question. We have already noted that in view of the circumstances surrounding its production, we should not be surprised to find that *CG8* is a somewhat contradictory document. For example, one salient piece of phraseology, recurring like a mantra throughout the text, reiterates the centrality of 'the duties, responsibilities and rights of the citizen in a democratic society based on the rule of law'. This is in one sense a 'classic' formulation. It also happens, however, to echo uncannily certain of the speeches which Sir Keith Joseph delivered to teachers during his time as Education Secretary – speeches in which the dominant message was the 'need' for teachers to give greater prominence to the virtues of the free market, economic individualism, and the kind of minimalist State which (in Joseph's view) best guaranteed the economic liberties of enterprising individuals. Thus, for example, in a speech delivered in 1985 to the Geographical Association:

They (geography teachers) can help pupils to consider the different priorities and strategies which different governments have chosen and to examine how far there is tension between encouraging a more even distribution of wealth and of opportunities on the one hand and supporting changes which foster innovation and the creation of wealth on the other. Pupils can be helped to consider the application of democratic values and the rule of law and the consequences of their absence. (Joseph, 1985)

Or, a year earlier, to the Historical Association:

I maintain . . . that it is that commonality (of shared values) that defines us as a society. It is mercifully the case that almost all the people in this country subscribe, in general terms, to the value of liberty for the individual under the law, and believe that liberty is least insecure in a parliamentary democracy . . . History, properly taught, justifies its place in the school curriculum by what it does to prepare all pupils for the responsibilities of citizenship . . . (Joseph, 1984)

Such formulations, at one level unexceptionable, at another representing a very particular New Right agenda, illustrate the considerable difficulty involved in characterizing citizenship in a neutral, non-tendentious way. Some readers may feel that I am here reading altogether too much political and even party-political significance into innocent terminology. If they do, however, they would do well to reflect that Duncan Graham was only too conscious of considerations of this sort when he came to read through the final draft of the report of the working party which drew up *Education for Citizenship*:

MacGregor (Secretary of State for Education in 1990) became very concerned about what the citizenship document would say and . . . I showed him a draft to reassure him. *He did not change anything, but I had before I sent it to him.* The team who had written it had put rights before duties and *I turned it round to duties before rights.* Presentation is all. (Graham, 1993, p. 105, my italics)

What is at stake in such a change, of course, is more than a cosmetic question of 'presentation'. Underlying such a re-ordering of words – particularly of terminology which, in its variant forms, recurs so insistently throughout the document – is a political (and politically influenced) privileging of one interpretation of citizenship over another. A more strongly Conservative conception is foregrounded: one which stresses the duties of subjects, the legitimacy of existing constitutional arrangements, obedience to the law, and duty to respect the agencies of law enforcement.

Notwithstanding this evidence of caution, it cannot be said that the guidance document as a whole is blind to the *controversial* character of some of the subject matter with which it deals. Nevertheless, although controversy *is* acknowledged in *CG8*, it tends (as in both *CG4* and *CG7*) to be recognized only as attaching to particular *issues* (cf. Ahier, 1995, p. 141): 'Education for citizenship involves discussing controversial issues upon which there is no clear consensus . . . It is essential that such issues are presented in a balanced way, which recognizes all the views' (National Curriculum Council, 1990a, p. 14). What is never clearly spelt out is that the central concept of citizenship *itself* is controversial and contested. Not only that, there is not even an attempt to *define* the term with any clarity. The 'Foreword' offers a thoroughly circular characterization of its subject matter – whilst at the same time asserting that citizenship is an indispensable part of every child's education:

Education for citizenship is essential for every pupil. It helps each of them to understand the duties, responsibilities and rights of every citizen and promotes concern for the values by which a civilised society is identified – justice, democracy, respect for the rule of law. (ibid., p. 2)

This 'coyness' about definition is clearly not an accidental omission. The Report of the Commission on Citizenship, published a few months earlier than *CG8,* defined its terms clearly (if contentiously) – pinning its colours to the mast of 'the definition, framework and approach to be found in the work of T. H. Marshall', including Marshall's '*social* element' of citizenship – and roundly asserting that the inclusion of this social element 'seems to reflect the British approach to citizenship' (House of Commons Commission on Citizenship, 1990, p. 4). Although such a definition was hardly intellectually satisfactory as an introduction to this contested concept, particularly in Mrs Thatcher's Britain, it *was* at least a definition. We shall explore further the contested nature of the concept of citizenship in the second part of this chapter. For the present, it is more pertinent to examine how, having failed seriously to examine the concept with which it is centrally concerned, *CG8* actually fills out what it sees as the central content of education for citizenship.

As we have seen, the document is far from displaying a completely self-consistent approach to its topic. Nevertheless, certain emphases are clear enough. One of these, as noted above, is the repeated dwelling on the theme of duties, responsibilities and rights (and in that order!) within a framework of the rule of law and parliamentary democracy – though as we have also seen this was not the ordering intended by the original authors. However, even here, sometimes it is the element of *rights*, including human rights and the importance of enlarging and defending such rights, which is given prominence (see section 6: 'The citizen and the law' for example), whilst elsewhere in the document, the stress seems to fall more on *duties and conformity*. In view of this unevenness, Keith Crawford's recent neo-Marxian interpretation of the document as consistently rooted in a 'functionalist paradigm' and as a product of 'the political concerns of the New Right in the 1980s' seems more than a little reductive – particularly since Crawford himself detects in places the influence of the broadly social democratic approach to citizenship represented by writers like T. H. Marshall and A. H. Halsey (Crawford, 1995, pp. 131–2).

Nevertheless, Crawford's analysis is far from wholly implausible. *CG8*'s overall approach does seek to construct citizenship primarily around an inadequate and overly consensual conception of citizenship as a sphere of action of *individuals* who may elect to participate in a series of overlapping and harmoniously integrated *communities*. The reasons for making this conception so central appear to be partly pedagogic: children and young people can then be seen as developing their understanding and skills of citizenship (in the broadest sense) through opportunities to participate in a widening range of such 'communities'. Thus the first of *CG8*'s 'knowledge objectives' is '*the nature of community*' and it is indicated that children should develop knowledge and understanding of 'the variety of communities to which people simultaneously belong: family, school, local, national, European and worldwide' (op. cit., p. 3). This emphasis is further reinforced by the recommendation in the Introduction, that *community involvement* should be central to developing and implementing a whole school approach to education for citizenship:

Education for Citizenship . . . emphasizes the place of the school in the community and the important role of parents, governors, members of the community, religious groups, voluntary bodies, local and national government, local services, industry, commerce and many others. They must share in policy development and implementation. (ibid., p. 1)

At one level, all this is again relatively innocuous. But various unsatisfactory consequences follow from it. In the first place, the notion of 'citizenship' becomes so expanded that it loses focus and specificity. *CG8* contains within its list of '*essential* content components' no less than eight major topics, which include 'the family', 'work, employment and leisure' and 'community', in addition to more specifically political/ civic components like 'democracy in action' and 'the citizen and the law'. Secondly, this emphasis on voluntary participation within the 'community' could so easily and so innocently reinforce very particular party-political conceptions of 'active citizenship', for example, the version which was being energetically promoted by the Conservative Party in the run-up to the 1989 General Election at precisely the time the *CG8* working party was preparing the document. Within this conception, the active citizen is one who (tacitly at least) supports the New Right agenda of severely cutting back on public expenditure and public provision of welfare in favour of a mixture of privatized and voluntary provision, and who accepts a personal obligation to contribute time and energy to such voluntary activity. Douglas Hurd, writing in 1988, brought out very directly the connection between the policies of Thatcherite Conservatism and this version of active citizenship – which he explicitly contrasted with what he termed 'Fabian socialism':

> The Conservative Party is moving forward from its justified concern with the motor of wealth creation towards a redefinition of how the individual citizen, business or voluntary group can use resources and leisure to help the community... The English tradition of voluntary service is, of course, not new... What *is* new is the rediscovery that schemes based on this tradition are often more flexible and more effective than bureaucratic plans drawn up on the Fabian principle... A social policy founded upon ideals of responsible and active citizenship is compatible with free market economic policies... (Hurd, 1988)

Another way of looking at this vision of 'active citizenship' is somewhat less flattering. As Colin Wringe has recently put it: 'when active young citizens take the responsibility for picking up the pieces left by the market economy, those who benefit from that economy need not be constrained to do so' (Wringe, 1992, p. 35).

What is really significant in all this, as far as *CG8* is concerned, is that by offering only a thoroughly *de-politicized* approach to 'community', the 'guidance' offered gives teachers and pupils no basis for adequately contextualizing or conceptualizing, let alone debating, the merits and de-merits of the variety of conceptions of 'active citizenship' which different political groupings may be concerned to promote.

A third problem arising from the prominence given to 'individuals' and 'communities' as the key *subjects* within the arena of citizenship is that other crucially significant kinds of 'subject' are pushed into the background. For example, among the most important innovations of the uninterrupted period of Conservative rule from 1979 to 1997 was the creation of what some have called 'the quango state' – a state in which 'nearly two thirds of all civil servants are employed by new executive agencies that are accountable to no one' (Gray, 1995); correspondingly, the powers of local government have been systematically curtailed. One view of the cumulative effects of this on the freedoms of individual citizens is that, in John Gray's words, 'the individual citizen is virtually helpless against the impenetrable apparatus of the quango state' (ibid.). What is pertinent for the present discussion is not whether Gray is correct or not in such an assessment – but that unless discussion of citizenship provides young people with some means of analysing such *institutional* changes *and* of assessing their constitutional significance, it is hardly worth attempting. Once again, this neglect of what one might call the 'institutional dimension' is not unique to *CG8*. As Ahier points out, *CG4*'s account of the economy and the 'world of work' similarly neglects powerfully significant institutional 'actors':

> [I]mportant economic actors, whether they be identified as owners, managers, profes-sionals, or various forms of economic enterprise such as companies or corporations, are generally missing. The whole economic world of *Education for Economic and Industrial Understanding* is built on the individual, rational, economic calculator. Thus companies are 'workplaces' where individuals, protected by the law (Key Stage 3, Section 17) do different tasks ... (op. cit., p. 151)

The final version of the Dearing Report (Dearing, 1994) and the Revised National Curriculum documents which followed it were notably *silent* not only about education for citizenship but about the cross-curricular 'dimensions' and 'themes' more generally. It is, therefore, in some small degree reassuring that the most recent school inspection handbooks from OFSTED (OFSTED, 1995) do include at least some reference to what might be called the 'social subjects' within the curriculum. However, as far as citizenship education is concerned, the OFSTED guidance to inspectors is both very limited in its scope and expressed in a form likely to reinforce the most anodyne and 'community' focused approaches to its subject matter. Page 90 of the handbook for secondary schools requires inspection teams to investigate and report on the following question: '*does the school encourage pupils to relate effectively to others, take responsibility, participate fully in the community and develop an understanding of citizenship?*' (OFSTED, 1995, p. 90). However, this not only conjoins citizenship explicitly with the theme of social responsibility ('social development hinges on an acceptance of group rules and an ability to set oneself in a wider context') but also, insofar as 'citizenship' is elaborated upon at all, what is stressed is the *school* community as a context for the exercise of such responsibility: 'account should be taken of opportunities for pupils to take on responsibility, demonstrate initiative and contribute to the life of the school as a community' – adding (as if these things were particularly pertinent for less academic pupils) 'vocational courses at KS4 and post-16 can play a significant part in this development' (ibid., p. 90). How inspectors are supposed to assess the adequacy of pupils' *understanding* of citizenship is left to them – or to chance!

CITIZENSHIP: AN ESSENTIALLY CONTESTED CONCEPT

The idea of 'essentially contested concepts', which has now become part of the established terminology of various social science disciplines, was first introduced by W. B. Gallie, who defined the term in the following way: essentially contested concepts are ideas 'which inevitably involve endless disputes about their proper use on the part of users' (Gallie, 1955, p. 169).

It will be argued here that citizenship is pre-eminently a concept of this kind and that this being the case, the idea of educating *for* citizenship is, in a society which is both formally democratic and politically and culturally pluralistic, somewhat problematical. In a brief chapter such as this, considerations of space preclude anything approaching a comprehensive discussion of citizenship as a concept. Rather than attempting any kind of 'overview', the strategy we shall adopt is that of contrasting just two approaches to citizenship – each of which has been prominent in recent public debates in this country: first, a view of citizenship based primarily upon the ideas of T. H. Marshall, and second, citizenship as represented in recent Conservative Party policy initiatives and associated discourses.

We have already seen that the authors of *Encouraging Citizenship* (Commission on Citizenship, 1990) chose to frame their analysis within the terms set by T. H. Marshall's highly influential conceptualization of citizenship as 'involving three elements, civil, political and social, which he argued were developed in successive centuries: civil rights in the eighteenth, political in the nineteenth and social in the twentieth' (ibid., p. 5). The novel element in Marshall's analysis when it was first proposed was the *social* element. As Barry Hindess has pointed out, for Marshall, this social element was indispensable to what he saw as the capacity of citizenship in modern 'welfare' societies, to generate 'a direct sense of community membership based on loyalty to a civilisation which is a common possession' (ibid., pp. 40–1). The extension of social security and the public provision of services such as health care and education were 'not primarily a means of equalising incomes' but chiefly a means of conferring a much enhanced equality of *status* – status precisely *as* citizens – which would mean, *inter alia*, that the social significance of differences of money income would be increasingly confined to the sphere of consumption (Hindess, 1987, pp. 37–8). The extension of welfare also meant that *all* citizens could enjoy a minimum level of safeguarding against risk, illness and insecurity – and therefore, the capacity to participate more fully in society and to exercise more effectively their civil and political rights.

Hindess has also shown very clearly that Marshall's own position on the extension of welfare was actually *less* radically egalitarian than that of some other contemporary analysts of welfare provision such as Richard Titmuss. Although Marshall certainly believed that, at the level of principle, there was a fundamental conflict between the extension of this social component of citizenship (which was based upon *moral principles*) and the *amoral* operation of the capitalist market economy, he also regarded 'the present phase of development of democratic citizenship' as the product of a compromise between these conflicting principles, and (what is most distinctive about his position) *he evaluated this compromise positively* (Hindess, op. cit., ch. 3). For Marshall, the capacity of social citizenship to function as the key source of social integration depended precisely upon this compromise – and upon its *being* a compromise – one which involved the preservation of two distinct spheres: the welfare state and the 'mixed' (but therefore primarily capitalist) economy. Marshall himself put it like this: 'the hyphenated society (of democratic-welfare-capitalism) can survive only if it is recognized that both the welfare sector and the mixed economy are contributing to the creation of welfare' (Marshall, 1950, p. 131). In this respect, his position was impeccably social democratic. Titmuss, on the other hand, adopted a more radically egalitarian stance – one which saw the market as continually threatening to undermine welfare, and for this reason, he argued 'that the moral values enshrined in social policy ought to predominate' (Hindess, 1987, p. 40).

Among the recent contributors to debates about citizenship who have, in a broad sense, adopted Marshall's tri-partite approach are not only the members of the Speaker's Commission on Citizenship but also Derek Heater in his scholarly examination of *Citizenship: The Civic Ideal in World History, Politics and Education* (Heater, 1990). The conception of citizenship which *Encouraging Citizenship* (Commission on Citizenship, 1990) seeks to promote preserves Marshall's social element and indeed strengthens it by introducing the term 'social *entitlements*': 'The Commission considers that it is the duty of government to enable people to have an equal opportunity to participate in citizenship. The duty includes the provision of a floor of social entitlements' (ibid., p. 21). Their more detailed discussion makes clear their antipathy to what they see as the political curtailment of various of these 'entitlements' in recent years – in such areas, for example, as 'the exercise of legal citizenship rights in the sphere of the welfare state' (ibid., p. 22). They also emphasize that in their view, voluntary provision of care is far from being an acceptable alternative to state provision and that, indeed, the duties of caring may themselves constitute 'a very considerable restriction on citizenship' (ibid., p. 21).

Heater's book, as he is among the first to acknowledge, contains a highly ambitious attempt to define *and advocate* 'an ideal of perfect citizenship' which, he suggests, should ultimately serve as a reference point having *global* application:

> the case for defining an ideal of perfect citizenship for the world is even more cogent: the whole social and political tone of the life of mankind depends on the construction of such an ideal and the will of states and individuals to strive towards its realisation. (Heater, 1990, p. 314)

This 'holistic' conception of citizenship is grounded, like Marshall's, in a grand narrative of the successive development of 'legal/civil', 'political' and 'social' elements of citizenship. Along with these, Heater identifies two further essential components: dispositions to exercise the *virtues* of citizenship, and an *identity* component, with citizenship identity being distinguished 'by its potential to moderate the divisiveness of other identity feelings – gender, religion, race, class' – and even those of nation where citizenship attaches to supra-national entities and allegiances (Gilbert, 1995, p. 21). What Heater particularly shares with Marshall, therefore, is the belief that, in modern democratic polities, a form of citizenship which embraces the social element plays a vital role in the maintenance of social integration. Finally, both Heater and the authors of *Encouraging Citizenship* argue that '*education* for citizenship is not an optional extra but an integral part of the concept: . . . one may be born a little citizen in status, but one must learn about the rights and duties, the attitudes and skills this status entails' (Heater, 1990, p. 319).

A common interpretation of Marshall is that his theory of citizenship posited an 'evolutionary' view, in which the emergence of the 'social element' was seen as the outcome of certain immanent or tendential characteristics of the later stages of capitalist development (Giddens, 1982). However, as Bryan Turner has argued, such criticisms are, to say the least, open to question. Marshall, he argues, saw only too clearly 'the contingent importance of wartime conditions on the development of social policy' (Turner, 1990, pp. 192–3) while, as Hindess has shown, although Marshall did see post-war British society as exhibiting an uneasy compromise between the 'moral' principles of social citizenship and 'amoral' market-based class relations, he was perfectly clear that this balance might prove impossible to maintain *and* that it might tilt in either direction (Hindess, 1987, pp. 35–6). Heater's analysis at first sight also appears to be evolutionary and there can be no doubt about his desire to *promote* the particular conception of citizenship he espouses. However, here too, it would be a mistake see him as believing that there is anything *inevitable* about a continuing progression towards his ideal of citizenship. If anything, the reverse is the case: he devotes an entire chapter to discussing 'barriers to a holistic concept' (Heater, 1990, pp. 282–312).

It is worth quoting at some length a passage from the beginning of this chapter, which is impressive for the honesty with which it faces up to contemporary challenges to citizenship as Heater wishes it to be conceived, but which also displays some of the basic problems with his overall stance:

> Citizenship as a useful political concept is in danger of being torn asunder and any hope of a coherent civic education left in tatters as a consequence. By a bitter twist of historical fate, the concept which evolved to provide a sense of identity and community, is on the verge of becoming a source of communal dissension. As more and more diverse interests identify particular elements for their doctrinal and practical needs, so the component parts of the citizenship idea are being made to do service for the whole. And under the strain of these centripetal forces, citizenship as a total ideal may be threatened with disintegration. Maybe the attempt we are making . . . to bundle so much meaning into the term is to unrealistically overload its capacity. (ibid., p. 282)

It is interesting and symptomatic that the final sentence of this passage identifies the problem as one of overloading the concept with *too much* meaning. Arguably, however, the real problem is not – or not mainly – a quantitative one. It has, rather, to do with the *kinds* of meaning which Heater (and Marshall before him) install into their view of citizenship – and with the fact that competing conceptions, *which are no less conceptions of citizenship than theirs*, tie together a different bundle of elements. *Pace* the views of the Speaker's Commission, there *is* no single and consensual '*British* approach to citizenship' and it is questionable whether there ever was. What has happened is that competing conceptions are now being advocated much more vigorously and with much greater confidence than in the thirty years of the post-war 'long boom'.

Contemporary Conservatism in the UK has been in process of elaborating, albeit in a somewhat piecemeal fashion, one such alternative conception (or perhaps more than one – insofar as internal tensions between neo-liberal and neo-conservative standpoints can be clearly discerned). The idea of the Citizen's Charter is of no little interest here. At one level, it is tempting to dismiss this notion as a rather transparent and unconvincing attempt to link the grey premiership of John Major with a 'big idea'. An alternative and more interesting way of seeing it is as an innovation which seeks to replace *real* citizenship with consumer rights – and which therefore diminishes *true* citizenship. Tempting, and for some of us comforting, as this might sound, it is actually unhelpful. Unquestionably certain kinds of 'rights', including certain kinds of social 'rights', *have* been diminished as a result of recent Conservative policy initiatives. But it is also true that, under the banner of the Citizen's Charter, a range of specific and significant rights have been *extended* to ordinary people – and by virtue of their status *as* citizens, not simply as consumers. The various rights recently published under the banner of the Parent's Charter (DFE, 1994b), for example, include a range of enhanced rights and powers attaching to those citizens who are parents of children attending state schools. These include: increases in parental representation on the governing bodies of schools, the right to call for and participate in ballots on Grant Maintained status, the capacity of school governing bodies to manage their own budgets, the right of each parent to receive at least an annual report on their child's progress, informing them of results in relevant national tests, the right of access to the published reports of OFSTED inspection teams, etc. Of course there has been significant controversy about these changes, and of course there are arguments that they have involved corresponding reductions of other rights of citizenship – for example, there are important questions to be asked about the rival merits of certain forms of representation and accountability being devolved to the level of individual schools rather than being retained by local education authorities. But these are precisely aspects of debates *between* competing views of citizenship. And representatives of the Conservative Party have hardly been reticent in advocating their preferred conception of citizenship as not only different from but superior to social democratic versions:

> As (the Conservative Party) expands the scope for voluntary acts of citizenship, the left is still stuck with the bureaucratic definition of citizenship as something to which we are compelled by the state... Underpinning our social policy are the traditions – the diffusion of power, civic obligation, and voluntary service – which are central to Conservative philosophy and rooted in British (particularly English) history... So the shift of government policy is to shift power outwards, away from the corporatist battalions to the small platoons. Thus parents will get a bigger say in education; council tenants will get more control over the management of their estates... What is new is the rediscovery that schemes based on this tradition are often more flexible and more effective than the bureaucratic plans drawn up on the Fabian principle. (Hurd, 1988)

EDUCATION FOR CITIZENSHIP?

> Finally, the teacher cannot possibly be expected to prepare young people for adult life as citizens without a *complete and agreed* understanding of what that status entails. (Heater, 1990, p. 316; my italics)

Heater's view of the relationship that should obtain between education and citizenship is thoroughly consistent with the overall argument of his book. The relationship should be one of developing in a nation's future citizens not only an understanding of citizenship but also a set of dispositions, commitments and skills, attaching to the 'holistic' ideal of citizenship which he believes democratic societies should promote. These are focused upon the fostering of the requisite *virtues* of citizenship which, along with knowledge and understanding, will hopefully contribute to the individual developing a well-founded sense of *identity* as a citizen. Education for citizenship as Heater conceives it is, of course, very far from being uncritical. Future citizens need, for example, to understand the potentialities for conflict which exist both within pluralistic societies and also between nation states and supra-national organizations. Nevertheless, for Heater, the major goal of educators remains the promotion of the 'holistic' ideal: 'educationalists... must preserve a vision of the ideal of citizenship; and they must judge the most appropriate pedagogical methods for leading their pupils to the best approximation of that ideal they are likely to achieve in the prevailing circumstances' (ibid., p. 339). Clearly, however, this conception of citizenship education is problematical. In a society in which *rival* conceptions of citizenship can claim significant intellectual and political support, it is far from clear that it is either educationally desirable or pragmatically possible to achieve anything like 'complete and agreed understanding' around a conception of citizenship which is as fully specified and extensive as that which Heater puts forward.

Another writer who has recently addressed these problems is the educational philosopher Terence H. McLaughlin (McLaughlin, 1992). In a very tightly argued analysis of the issues, McLaughlin draws a carefully defined distinction between 'maximalist' and 'minimalist' versions of education for citizenship and he points out that *both*, as well as the various underlying conceptions of citizenship with which each may be connected, are controversial.[1] He is considerably more sensitive than Heater to the *complexity* of the *educational* dilemmas which this state of affairs poses:

> It is the absence of agreement about . . . 'public virtues' and the common good, which gives rise to the various disputes about 'citizenship' and 'education for citizenship' which have been alluded to. With regard to the educational task, this lack of agreement constitutes a challenge to those seeking to justify a 'maximalist' approach, to specify the concrete shape it should take . . . and to provide confident answers to questions such as whether education for citizenship can transmit a particular way of life. (ibid., p. 243)

McLaughlin goes on to suggest (and the suggestion is wholly consistent with his earlier arguments) that if a society is, through its schools, to educate *for* citizenship in a significant way, what is needed at the practical level is a wide ranging and informed national debate, to establish 'as far as possible a degree of agreement, about the "public virtues" and the "common good" and about how "citizenship" and "education for citizenship" are to be understood' (ibid., p. 244). This is, at least in principle, one possible way forward – and it has certainly not so far been seriously embarked upon, as was demonstrated by our analysis of the inadequacies of the official 'guidance' that has been offered about education for citizenship.

However, in the light of the intensely partisan lobbying and political interference which surrounded the development of not only *Curriculum Guidance 8* but the National Curriculum as a whole (for example, Black, 1992; Cox, 1991; Cox, 1995; Graham, 1993), one may be forgiven for doubting whether, in contemporary Britain, the political conditions exist in which such a debate could even be *launched*, let alone carried through to the sort of consensual conclusion which could then inform educational policy decisions. As Ahier has noted: 'in a more confident democracy, acknowledging disagreements within the discourses from which a national school curriculum is developed, should cause no difficulty' (Ahier, 1995, p. 140). Regrettably, we do not seem to live in that kind of democracy.

In practice, therefore, schools seem likely to remain caught in a dilemma:

(a) the cross-curricular 'themes', including Education for Citizenship, still exist as part of the National Curriculum – at least to the extent that the Dearing Review did not explicitly discontinue them – and various elements alluding to citizenship are included within the OFSTED inspection handbooks;
(b) official guidance offered so far is seriously defective;
(c) no open and serious national debate linked to education is in prospect.

In such a situation, schools which wish to take this area at all seriously will inevitably have to seek their own solutions. One approach which may recommend itself would be to aspire mainly to educate *about* citizenship rather than *for* citizenship.[2] Such a task would be primarily cognitive: it would not extend to fostering any particular set of attitudes, dispositions or 'virtues' – other than those associated with the aims of liberal education generally. The focus would be, rather, upon extending young people's knowledge and understanding of political ideas, institutions and issues – and where appropriate, enhancing pupils' awareness of the contested nature of some of the most central concepts within the political realm, not least, of course, the concept of 'citizenship' itself.[3] In one respect at least, the wider context for pursuing such an approach is encouraging. The general level of public interest in issues connected with citizenship has been significantly heightened in recent years by a variety of developments – for example: the ongoing debates about Britain's role in the European Community, pressures in Scotland for devolution or even 'independence within Europe', the tarnished reputation of the 'royals' and a greater willingness to think about alternatives to monarchy, growing concern about excessive centralization of power within a set of national constitutional arrangements which provide few safeguards against elective dictatorship, etc. The situation in *schools*, however, seems at least in some respects less promising. The competitive climate generated by local management of schools, devolved budgets, league tables, publication of OFSTED inspection reports, etc. is likely to encourage many headteachers and governing bodies to 'play safe' and avoid tackling issues which are (or are likely to be perceived as) 'political' and controversial. Nor are teachers well placed to develop effective political education. Experienced teachers struggle constantly to juggle competing demands upon their time and areas such as the cross-curricular 'themes' are hardly a priority for in-service funding. Similarly, reforms of initial teacher-training are progressively eroding all but the most directly instrumental and competency-oriented aspects of the preparation of new teachers. How much easier and safer, in such circumstances, for schools to settle for fostering soft-centred and unanalysed forms of 'citizenship' education centred upon voluntary participation in small-scale 'community' endeavour!

To conclude on a note of qualified (and perhaps uncharacteristic) optimism. It may happen that the new New Labour government will give its backing to a serious initiative in the area of citizenship education in the nation's schools. If so, one can only hope that the *intellectual* foundations of such an enterprise will not be neglected.

NOTES

1   McLaughlin's distinction between 'maximalist' and 'minimalist' interpretations – of citizenship and of education for citizenship – is, as I have indicated, very carefully defined. He warns explicitly that 'it should not be assumed that these "maximalist" interpretations are necessarily hostile to conservative thought and policy' and he carefully explains that:

> The interpretation, as I have sketched it, merely insists that questions relating to substantial identity, to virtues of general focus, to significant participation and to the problem of social disadvantage be seen as *relevant* to citizenship, *not that they are given any particular answer.* (McLaughlin, 1992, p. 237, my italics)

One recent author who seems to partially misread McLaughlin on this point is Karen Evans, in an otherwise very interesting discussion of competence and citizenship (Evans, 1995). Evans, reasonably enough, identifies the Speaker's Commission Report as offering a 'maximalist' interpretation but she (all too briefly) counterposes this to a claim that 'at the other pole, minimal interpretations are reflected in government policies which are attempting to redefine citizenship in terms of individual consumer rights' (ibid., p. 16). As the discussion in the second section of this chapter has tried to show, recent Conservative re-definitions of citizenship are significantly more complex (and therefore more challenging) than this. A *simplified* maximalist/minimalist dichotomy cannot do justice to this complexity.

2 The tri-partite typology, 'education *about,* education *for,* and education *in/through*', is one which has been widely employed in relation to cross-curricular issues in recent years. Originally proposed by Blyth, it has been extensively employed in relation to areas such as education for industrial and economic understanding (Blyth, 1984; Mercer, 1983), environmental education (Huckle, 1983), etc.

3 Schools could, indeed, do very much worse than revisit some of the ideas and approaches developed in the late 1970s by the Programme for Political Education (Crick and Porter, 1978), centred on the idea of 'political literacy'. In particular, the heart of that approach still has much to recommend it: it was organized around a Brunerian 'spiral curriculum' of core political concepts, deliberately specified at an abstract level (for example: 'power', 'representation', 'rights', 'welfare') – though, oddly enough, not 'citizenship' itself.

Chapter 6

Enterprise Culture and the New Managerialism: Institutional and Curricular Implications

THE MEANINGS OF CULTURE

At several points in this book, we have seen that the term 'culture' may be used with a range of different meanings and for a variety of purposes, and that failure to distinguish these differing usages can create misunderstanding and confusion. In order to clarify certain issues raised in this chapter, it will be useful to make a distinction – admittedly pretty rough and ready – between three uses of 'culture', which I shall call, respectively: descriptive, evaluative and programmatic.

Descriptive uses of culture

Social and cultural anthropologists, ever since these disciplines emerged in the nineteenth century, have taken the study of culture and its relationship to social structure as their central focus. They aspired to define the object of their studies in an essentially descriptive and inclusive way – i.e. in a way which sought to avoid making value judgements about the worth of different elements of any particular culture, or the relative superiority/inferiority of different cultures. E. B. Tylor's classic definition is perhaps the best known and most influential attempt to characterize culture in this way:

> [C]ulture...is that complex whole which includes knowledge, belief, art, morals, law, custom, and any other capabilities and habits acquired by man as a member of society. (Tylor, 1871)

Ideally at least, this anthropological conception of culture is value-neutral: the purpose of studying 'other cultures' (or the anthropologist's own culture for that matter) is to describe, interpret and explain, rather than to judge or evaluate. Subsequent debates within anthropology have, of course, questioned the degree to which Western ethnographers ever can (or could) occupy such a standpoint of objectivity or neutrality. Recently, influenced by postmodernist ideas and a growing sensitivity about the part played by anthropology within Western imperialism, there has been a radical questioning by some anthropologists of the grounds on which they can claim to offer any authoritative ethnographic interpretations at all. This can create a relativism in which different 'accounts' are juxtaposed. James Clifford, for example, has written: 'indigenous statements make sense on terms different from those of the arranging ethnographer... This suggests an alternate textual strategy of plural authorship which accords to (indigenous) collaborators not merely the status of independent enunciators, but of writers' (Clifford and Marcus, 1986, quoted in Gellner, 1992a, p. 28). Whilst acknowledging that there are real problems here, particularly where cross-cultural or inter-cultural comparisons are at stake, I shall contend that it remains legitimate, at least for certain purposes, to employ the term 'culture' in a sense which at least *aspires* to be descriptive and non-evaluative. This is worthwhile, if only to distinguish such primarily descriptive usages from other ways of using the term whose very point is to inscribe value-judgements and/or to establish hierarchies, both within and between cultures.

Evaluative uses of culture

The paradigm instance of an evaluative use of culture is the idea of 'high culture'. Here, after all, comparative evaluation is of the essence: certain aspects of a culture are accorded the status of being of greater worth, more enduring significance, etc. than others. And, as Scruton suggests with regard to high culture, within these judgements 'aesthetic values are paramount' (Scruton, 1987, p. 127). On some interpretations, the judgements involved have to do with *intrinsic* value. Viewed more sociologically, for example in the work of the French sociologist Pierre Bourdieu, those elements of a culture which come to be thought of as 'high' may more accurately be regarded as areas upon which a certain *cultural legitimacy* has been conferred. From this standpoint, 'judgements of taste' do not simply correspond with the intrinsically superior and inferior quality of cultural objects. Rather, such evaluations are *socially* conferred through the agency of a network of institutions which have achieved a status which gives their verdicts an authoritative, even unquestionable, character. According to Bourdieu, this fact is often misrecognized. Differences between those who 'are' cultured and those who 'are not' are often thought of as resulting from intrinsic, given, differences. This misrecognition applies not only to the objects of 'culture' but also to those individuals and groups who appear to be the possessors of 'natural' gifts of good taste, discrimination, etc. (Bourdieu, 1986). Whatever position one adopts within debates of this kind, however, it remains the case that the *evaluative* character of judgements about high culture is inescapable.

Programmatic uses of culture

Programmatic definitions of culture are usually evaluative too – but they have another and more important characteristic. This is that they seek to be *persuasive* – to win adherents to some new (or sometimes revived) conception of culture. As we have seen, Matthew Arnold's use of the term in *Culture and Anarchy* had this character (Arnold, 1869). He was *recommending* his own very particular conception of culture to his fellow countrymen (not entirely excluding women!) as offering the best chance of overcoming the social divisions which afflicted Britain in the mid-Victorian period. 'Culture' had a programmatic role to play. It was to be the foundation of a Christian, enlightened, ethical consensus which would help remedy the divisive effects of free-market liberalism whilst, at the same time, helping to prevent society succumbing to nascent socialism. Programmatic uses of culture are normally, therefore, *moralistic*. At their core, there tends to be some particular set of *values* which are to form the core of a new sense of identity and purpose. Because of this, they are also likely to be more than a little controversial – since the values they champion are, at the least, unlikely to be fully shared by all sections of society. The overall agenda of Thatcherite and subsequent Conservativism in the UK actually yoked together *two* distinct, indeed contradictory, cultural visions of this kind. On the one hand, there was the project of cultural restoration: this is programmatic in that its agenda is one of active re-creation of a core of common values which supposedly existed in the past. On the other hand, there were the free-market visions, most vividly embodied in the notion of *enterprise culture*. Many commentators have drawn attention to the contradictory character of the *overall* Thatcherite vision which resulted (though its political effectiveness has also won grudging admiration). Ken Jones, for example, described it as 'Janus-headed' (Jones, 1989) and James Donald summed up the whole programme as one of 'backward-looking modernization' (Donald, 1992, p. 126).[1]

ENTERPRISE CULTURE AND CONSUMER CULTURE

It is interesting to compare the notions of *enterprise culture* and *consumer culture* in terms of the foregoing discussion. The former is clearly programmatic – and enterprise culture remains a core component of New Right ideology, even if the first flush of its active promotion as part of the Conservative assault on collectivist social democratic values is now over. Consumer culture is more difficult to categorize. The term suggests that a set of shared values is involved, and indeed this is hard to deny: most significantly a preoccupation with the consumption of economic goods as a key element in a widely shared conception of the good life. It is, moreover, generally recognized that 'consumer culture' is invasive – in the sense that it is subversive of other value-systems, and also because its effects are invasive of the *environment*. Furthermore, consumer culture is 'carried' by powerful mechanisms of persuasion such as advertising, whose latent message, beneath the specific products featured, is: 'consume', 'consume', 'consume'. These aspects are vividly illustrated in a short passage from John le Carré's recent novel *Our Game*. The setting is the 'new Moscow' – capital of post-Communist, free-market Russia:

> And everywhere, as evening gathered, the beacons of the true conquerors were flashing out their gospel: 'buy us, eat us, drink us, wear us, drive us, smoke us, die of us. We are what you get instead of slavery.' (le Carré, 1995, p. 347)

As this passage also suggests, the preoccupation with consumption is perhaps the most truly general and successful 'shared value' of our times – and is increasingly global in its reach. Yet consumer culture is not programmatic in the sense that enterprise culture very clearly *is*. Whereas enterprise culture is a *gospel* – as the associated language of mission statements and corporate vision so strongly suggests – consumer culture is (merely!) a way of life, albeit a way of life which is of central concern to more and more people. What most decisively demonstrates its non-programmatic nature is that what it leads to is increasing diversity of life-styles and values – even though these are 'framed' by the shared preoccupation with consumption itself. Differences in *what* is consumed and in the *manner* of consumption are, after all, the proto-typical markers of social and sub-cultural difference: between 'the vulgar' and 'the discriminating', between the generations, within the generations, etc. Rising affluence increases this proliferation of diversities – as, say, the notion of niche-marketing illustrates.

Enterprise culture, on the other hand, sets out actively to win adherents (or if persuasion fails, to coerce them) to embrace an old-new faith, complete with prophets both ancient (like Samuel Smiles) and modern (like Margaret Thatcher herself). More seriously, it is helpful to see enterprise culture not as a simple or unified development but as having at least three partially separate strands:

- an energizing *vision*
- a modality of *control*
- a legitimation of inequality.

Each of these dimensions and their interrelationships will be discussed in turn, and where appropriate, educationally relevant aspects of each will be examined.

ENTERPRISE CULTURE AS VALUES AND VISION

The concept of enterprise culture emerged and became influential in the 1970s and 1980s in both the UK and the USA. As Paul Morris has pointed out with reference to the UK, enterprise culture has been 'a *dynamic* concept, having a series of meanings and generating a series of different policies' (Morris, 1991, p. 21). Morris has traced the genesis and influence of a number of distinct versions of 'enterprise culture' which had a significant impact on Conservative Party thinking and policy formation during the 1980s. For example, he outlines aspects of the work of Professor Brian Griffiths who, for a time in the early 1980s, headed the Policy Unit at 10 Downing Street. Griffiths' thinking about enterprise appears to have attracted Mrs Thatcher, partly because it offered a 'middle way' between the more purely Hayekian ideas espoused by Sir Keith Joseph – such as the notion of 'spontaneous order' – and elements of neo-conservative thinking emphasizing the importance of tradition, family responsibility, and most importantly and distinctively, the role of *Christianity* in moderating the amoral tendencies of unregulated free markets. As Morris puts it, for Griffiths, 'particular cultural values are necessary for operation of the market, and these have been eroded . . . these values are to be fostered by Christian education and the inculcation of Christian values and virtues' (ibid., pp. 27–8). This is, however, a stern Christianity which legitimizes significant social inequality. For example, Griffiths' view of the role which the principle of *justice* plays in the market is primarily concerned with the maintenance of the non-coercive operation of the economy (as contrasted with socialist forms of regulation). This in turn 'results in "a certain kind and degree of inequality in the distribution of income and wealth" which is "essential" if the market economy is to function' (Morris, ibid., p. 27).

Of more direct relevance in terms of its impact on Conservative *educational* policies is the thinking about 'enterprise culture' associated with David Young, later Lord Young, who was from 1984 appointed as a minister without portfolio and ran the Enterprise Unit in the Cabinet Office. David Young was, *inter alia,* the architect of TVEI (the Technical and Vocational Education Initiative) which, it will be remembered, was introduced in 1982 from the Department of *Employment* and under the auspices of the Manpower Services Commission (MSC) (whose Chairman was Young himself). This mode of implementation can be seen as typically 'enterprising' in that it was deliberately calculated to by-pass the 'educational establishment' of DES ministers and civil servants, and the LEAs. It enabled an agency from outside the 'educational sub-government' (Kogan, 1978) to intervene directly into the heart of the secondary school curriculum and to impose its own criteria for curriculum development. The initiative, at the time of its introduction, was actually backed by the threat that should LEAs and schools *not* respond positively, the MSC was 'ready to set up its own separate schools to provide technical and vocational courses for youngsters from 14 to 18' (*Times Educational Supplement,* 19 November 1992, p. 1). In the event, of course, the attraction of the additional funding on offer was more than sufficient, despite opposition from the National Executive of the Labour Party (*Times Educational Supplement*, 15 June 1984), to encourage schools and LEAs to bid into the scheme in large numbers. The enterprising spirit behind this initiative was thus characterized by an impatient disregard of opposing views and a willingness to override them if necessary through the use of centralized power and funding mechanisms. In these respects (and others), the MSC can be seen as the prototype of the task-specific and non-accountable quango which has subsequently become such a crucial institutional mechanism for effecting 'reform' in education – and elsewhere.

David Young was, however, not merely a practitioner but a *theorist* of 'enterprise'. As Morris demonstrates, his ideas were developed in a series of speeches and articles written in the mid-1980s and were a key source for Conservative Party promotion of 'enterprise culture' around that time. In David Young's view, it was important to draw a distinction between enterprise itself and enterprise *culture*. For him, enterprise was an attribute of individuals – 'manifest in all "men"', or rather, in all children', and it included: independence, risk-taking, innovation, energy, hard work, etc. (Morris, op. cit., p. 31). Enterprise *culture,* in Young's usage, is a property of certain *societies.* Moreover, he asserted, Britain had never had such a culture. In developing these ideas, he drew on a version of the familiar Corelli Barnett/Wiener thesis to explain this unfortunate absence (Barnett, 1986; Wiener, 1981). The entrepreneurial *spirit* displayed by outstanding individual industrialists in late eighteenth- and early nineteenth-century Britain had been neutered – partly as a result of cultural and social assimilation of businessmen into the landed gentry and partly by the anti-industrial biases of the education system. Subsequently, the flowering of enterprise had been further inhibited by collectivist 'class' ideologies and by welfarism represented by the trade unions and socialism – all seen as symptoms of the 'British Disease'. The professions were a further bastion of anti-enterprise attitudes: not only were they 'producer' monopolies protective of their own vested interests; but also, their patrician values sustained anachronistic and disabling attitudes of disdain towards the real economy and the business of wealth creation. The necessary remedies followed from the diagnosis: the long-standing biases of the educational system needed to be challenged so that the values of enterprise could be unashamedly articulated and actively promoted both within schools and in higher education. This required amongst other things, Young claimed, 'the promotion of changes in language so that words like profit and wealth are used positively and not as apologetic asides' (Morris, ibid., p. 31).

The promotion of enterprise as part of educational curricula in the UK is hardly new. Its earliest and still most common manifestation – in the form of mini-enterprise schemes in schools – originated in the 1960s with the 'Young Enterprise' organization (see Maier, 1982). Similarly, the mid-1970s saw the creation of numerous lobby groups whose mission was to bridge the perceived gulf between educational culture and business culture. These included organizations such as the CBI-sponsored Understanding British Industry and the Schools Council Industry Project. More recently, in addition to TVEI and its successors, there has been, within higher education, the Enterprise in Higher Education initiative (EHE) which was introduced by the MSC in 1987. As with TVEI, this involved setting up a series of five-year pilot schemes. The rather grandiose objective of the initiative was to reshape the attitudes and values of individual students – and eventually of *all* students – within higher education institutions. At the launch of the project, Norman Fowler (then Secretary of State for Employment) suggested that enterprising students would be capable of: 'generating and taking ideas and putting them to work; taking decisions and taking responsibility; taking considered risks; welcoming change and helping to shape it; and creating wealth...' (cited in Heelas, 1991, p. 73).

This is not the place to attempt any summary or evaluation of these various initiatives. Instead, I want to focus critically on two major issues. The first concerns the underlying *legitimation* for these interventions, i.e. the endlessly repeated claim that they are necessary to counteract the anti-industry and anti-enterprise biases inherent in English culture – including educational culture. The second relates to the distinction which (as we have seen) David Young himself made, between enterprise as a general quality of *individuals* and enterprise culture as a property of certain *societies*. Both these areas have centrally to do with questions of values and their supposed effects.

Assertion rather than considered argument was the outstanding characteristic of claims made at the beginning of the Thatcher era about the value of enterprise and the need to bring about a change of culture within educational institutions and in the curricula of schools. For example: 'It is enterprise which lies at the base of our ability to create wealth and we need to create a mood in society which values enterprise as it deserves to be valued' (Pope, 1979, quoted in Maier, 1992, p. 85). And in relation to education:

> There is no shortage of organizations and conferences to promote these changes. What are lacking are the *incentives*...to bring school and teacher culture closer to business and industrial culture.
>
> The key to prosperity is a *qualitative* change in the education system, particularly in the culture of its teachers. (Nisbet, 1982, p. 83)

Behind these confident assertions lay an equally confident *diagnosis* which held that the fundamental cause of British economic uncompetitiveness was also cultural. This was why effecting a culture change in education was such an urgent task. The diagnosis in question is, of course, that outlined above and associated with the names of a succession of amateur and professional cultural historians from C. P. Snow to Correlli Barnett and Martin Wiener. The key tenets of the analysis are well known and need not be repeated. What *is* important is to emphasize the quite remarkable degree of plausibility which has accrued to this actually highly contestable thesis. The historian David Edgerton is guilty of only a little over-statement when he characterizes the situation in the following way:

> This 'declinism' has painted a composite picture which shows British science and technology as weak in comparison to most comparable countries; which shows British higher education dominated by the arts, and latterly the social sciences; which shows British government and big companies dominated by arts graduates; which shows British business to be very reluctant to invest in research and development (R & D); and so on, *ad nauseam*. This picture is more than something we merely know: it is part of the very fabric of British intellectual life. It is a fact beyond dispute that Britain is an anti-scientific, anti-technological and anti-industrial culture. (Edgerton, 1996b, p. 29)

The almost unquestionable status this thesis has achieved is all the more remarkable because, as Edgerton (who is but the most recent of a long line of critics) has demonstrated, it is based on erroneous assumptions, tendentious arguments, and weak or sometimes virtually non-existent evidence. Among the most significant of the many weaknesses identified by these critics are the following:

(a) Social elites in nineteenth-century England were very much more diversified – socially, culturally and regionally – than the thesis of assimilation of the industrial bourgeoisie into an aristocratic culture of gentrified values allows for (see, for example, Wolff and Seed, 1988). Moreover, as John Ahier has pointed out, Martin Wiener's work

> uses concepts like 'accommodation', 'adaptation', and 'absorption' (pp. 9–10) to describe the relationship between the cultures of the aristocracy and the bourgeoisie, thus presuming that there were at a crucial point in the nineteenth century two quite distinct and essential sets of values and ways of life ... Such approaches require both the simplistic reduction of a group's culture to a set of values and a belief that one group's apparently predominant values were set and generated internally before contact with the other. (Ahier, 1991, pp. 125–6)

(b) Seed and Wolff also criticize Wiener's over-reliance on *secondary* historical source material when describing the dominant characteristics of English culture in the nineteenth century. The apparent social reality of a pervasive anti-industrialism is established largely from the writings of contemporary cultural critics – ranging from Pugin through Arnold to Morris – and from somewhat selective interpretations of the writings of certain famous novelists, notably Charles Dickens.[2] Reference to *primary* source materials suggests a much more complex and uneven picture. For example, as Gunn has argued, the role of the Victorian public schools cannot be reduced to the moulding of a unified, anti-industrial elite. Rather, these schools served the distinctive and *diverse* needs of 'a class society that was at once agricultural, industrial, commercial and above all imperial' (Gunn, 1988, pp. 35–6).

(c) Another strand of the 'declinism' argument is the claim that the dominant anti-industrial culture disastrously weakened the quality and quantity of British science, technology, and research and development over a long period. Here again, recent critics have shown that such assertions are not, for the most part, supported by the available evidence. Edgerton, for example, concludes his recent survey of these aspects of the 'declinism' argument with the following comment:

> Until the 1960s Britain was the second richest large industrial economy in the world. And it had science and technology to match. This was true both of the education of scientists and engineers, especially after 1945, and of innovation. From 1870 to the late 1960s its innovative record was better than or comparable to that of Germany, its main rival other than the United States. (Edgerton, 1996a, p. 67)

He adds that among the most important proponents of the techno-declinist arguments were scientists and engineers themselves, and that they often failed to distinguish between science and technology in general, and innovation. He concludes, with heavy irony, that far from it being the case that scientists and technologists have had a *marginal* influence in British intellectual and educational life, 'the pervasiveness of the techno-declinist position is evidence of the high esteem in which scientists and engineers are held' (ibid., p. 69).

The basic claim, therefore, that Britain has been a failing industrial power for a century and more, and that this failure is principally due to an undermining of the *entrepreneurial spirit* by pervasive anti-industrial attitudes transmitted by the nation's schools and universities, turns out to be a mistaken answer to a false question! This declinist thesis has been assiduously promoted – sometimes innocently, sometimes for self-interested reasons – by industrialists, the science and engineering lobbies, supporters of vocational education, New Right ideologues of various sorts, and, not least, the declinist historians themselves. This is not to deny that there have of course been persistent currents of anti-industrialism within liberal education. The writings of the literary critic F. R. Leavis may serve as a sufficiently representative example – from his famous critique in the 1930s of the deadening 'mass civilization' supposedly engendered by industrialism (Leavis, 1930), to his late writings on the idea of a university, whose essential mission was to combat what he called 'the blind assumptions of technologico-Benthamism' (Leavis, 1972, p. 205). However, as numerous commentators have pointed out, anti-commercialism and anti-industrialism of this kind is a general characteristic of a certain sort of liberal education and of literary and artistic culture – and has been so since at least the beginnings of the Romantic Movement. It is not at all peculiar to Britain. Moreover, as Edgerton so clearly demonstrates, it is simply not the case that these anti-industrial currents have been a dominant let alone hegemonic influence within British education taken as a whole.[3] Science, including engineering and technology, has long had a strong and prestigious place – in public and grammar schools, and in universities, as well as within the wider intellectual culture.[4]

The argument that energetic interventions into education are necessary in order to *counteract* the deep-rooted anti-industry biases peculiar to British schools and universities was and is, therefore, very largely without foundation, as is the related claim that such interventions are essential if we are to reverse national industrial decline. It would, however, be very naive to imagine that this inconvenient truth is likely to deter further pressures for just such interventions! As David Reeder noted, such campaigns have been a recurrent feature of the British educational scene (Reeder, 1979), while Edgerton has noted, conversely, that 'declinist' writers themselves have tended to claim a quite unjustified originality for their 'findings' and have been surprisingly unaware of the continuity of their arguments – so that there has been a recurrent 'disinvention of tradition' (Edgerton, 1996a, p. 7). John Ahier, writing in 1988, has offered what is still the most illuminating explanation of why these ideas remain so enduringly attractive – and not only to those on the right of the political spectrum:

> At a time when the economy seems so open, so easily influenced by the strength of the American dollar, so penetrated by manufactured imports, and so dependent on decisions by multi-national companies based both in the UK and elsewhere, the appeal of a thesis which keeps explanations of economic failure and success within national boundaries is reassuring to many. Plus, when the explanation requires a revised national culture, enshrined, perhaps, in a national curriculum and prompted by the spread of enterprise initiatives, then it is truly comforting.
>
> All the institutions of British capitalism are kept intact, along with their traditional interrelations. Continuity is ensured for long-held conceptions of the British national interest and status as a world power, and the only change envisaged is within people's attitudes and beliefs. In important respects, national unity is secured; 'our problems' are 'our own fault' and the cure is 'within ourselves'. Educators are given a role for the future, but only just so long as they adopt and promote the values of enterprise, initiative and competitive individualism. (Ahier, 1988, pp. 134–5)

And this observation brings us to the heart of what has been recurrently problematic and controversial about successive attempts to promote '*education* for enterprise' in British schools. Even *if* the 'declinist' thesis were correct, that fact would not make it legitimate for educational institutions to engage in what would, in effect, be counter-indoctrination in favour of 'enterprise culture'. It is no part of the role of schools committed to the overall aim of promoting rational autonomy, to unduly influence their pupils either in favour of (or against) such a clearly political value position. Discussing the Enterprise in Higher Education initiative, Charles Bailey has highlighted the recurrent element of double-speak which has characterized a great deal of recent educational writing about enterprise – the tendency to deliberately conflate two senses of the term: on the one hand, enterprise simply in the sense of *being enterprising* and on the other hand, 'enterprise *culture*':

> The ambiguity ... is now manifest: an enterprising disposition becomes associated, if not conflated, with 'enterprises' which are certain kinds of favoured socio-political forms. Not only that, but such institutions are assumed to be now so unquestionably universal, so unquestionably superior in terms of efficiency and social morality, that initiation into their attitudes and practices can be a necessary part of liberal education ...
>
> It is not the understanding of enterprise in any generalized dispositional sense that is sought by certain of those who wish schools to educate *for* enterprise but a limited understanding of the enterprise society ... In addition to this selective understanding of the free market economy, advocates of enterprise education appear to want pupils to come to adopt and value such a world view. This seems pure indoctrination – what the academic Marxists (if one dare now mention them) would have correctly called the reproduction of the dominant ideology. (Bailey, 1992, p. 102)

Such programmatic conceptions of enterprise culture can have no legitimate place as part of the curriculum in schools of liberal education. Yet support from most sections of the business community for more open, critical, and questioning forms of industrial and economic education has been conspicuous by its absence. Similarly, 'official' guidance documents such as the National Curriculum Council's booklet *Education for Economic and Industrial Understanding* (National Curriculum Council, 1990c) have generally fought shy of acknowledging the controversial character of many of the issues which would arise in any *impartial* study of the national economy or 'the world of work' (see Ahier, 1995, and Chapter 5 of this book). Within the framework of a National Curriculum which is defined primarily in terms of traditional school subjects, the prospects for a more open and intellectually liberating form of economic and industrial education seem as limited as do those for similarly open and critical forms of citizenship education.

ENTERPRISE CULTURE AS COERCION AND CONTROL

This pessimistic conclusion is reinforced when one turns to consider the impact on educational institutions of enterprise culture in the guise of the restructuring of relationships of control within and across educational *workplaces*. It is now a commonplace that within schools, colleges and universities (in common with very many other public sector institutions) a far-reaching 'managerial revolution' has been effected – one which has certainly brought business culture much closer to educational culture – by the simple expedient of *imposing* the former on the latter! This way of putting it, of course, greatly over-simplifies what has actually been a long, complex and contested process – and one which is by no means concluded. Nevertheless, critics, as well as spokespersons of the New Right themselves, have frequently described what has happened in terms of a conscious *project* of culture change. For example, Oliver Letwin, an ardent exponent of the new doctrine, has described the Thatcher years as involving a crusade to reform institutions so as to promote what he calls 'the vigorous virtues' of 'uprightness, self-sufficiency, energy, independent mindedness, adventurousness, loyalty and robustness' over the 'softer virtues' which include 'caring, sympathy, humility and gentleness' (Letwin, 1992, p. 35, quoted in Esland, 1996, p. 26). Within the state sector, this was seen as involving unavoidable *confrontation*: such a culture change could not happen without defeating those forces which were seen as centres of resistance to the new vision. Letwin puts it with brutal candour: 'In each case, what was being "taken on" was an establishment which was thought of as a "cosy cartel", a source of complacency, a centre of defeatism, an obstacle to vigour, an instigator of dependency, a cause of poverty or powerlessness' (ibid., p. 41).

Critics of the New Right have described the whole phenomenon in similar though, of course, much less adulatory terms – for example, as 'an explicitly formulated new right culture change project directed against public sector professionals' (Moore, 1994, p. 2). Several of these critics have also laid great stress on the moralistic *certainty* with which this whole endeavour was prosecuted. Geoff Esland, for example, has commented that 'the fundamentalist zeal with which this crusade was undertaken gave rise to a political style in which contempt and derision were visited upon any organization or individual who dared to put forward policies derived from a different value position' (Esland, op. cit., p. 27). Stephen Ball, similarly, has described the New Right onslaught (amplified by right-wing sections of the media) as a 'discourse of derision' (Ball, 1990).

Because these developments were the product of 'conviction politics', especially in the UK and the USA, it is certainly tempting to draw attention to the role of *discourse* and a sense of the programmatic cultural mission driving the overall process. And there certainly *is* abundant evidence that, repeatedly, dissenting voices have been silenced, ignored, marginalized, etc. It is, for example, symptomatic that a whole line of officials who occupied very senior positions within 'the educational sub-government' during the Thatcher and Major administrations became successively disenchanted with the ever rightward drift of policy as well as with the fact that their own views (once 'flavour of the month' or at least 'within the pale') came to be subsequently slighted or disparaged. It is only necessary to mention names like Duncan Graham (Graham, 1993), Brian Cox (Cox, 1991 and 1995), Paul Black (Black, 1993), Eric Bolton (Bolton, 1994), Colin Richards (Richards, 1996), etc. to confirm the point. The following comment by Eric Bolton, former Chief Inspector of Schools, sums up the treatment that was too often accorded to even very moderate critics of government policy:

> One of the side-effects of conviction politics is the labelling of any critical voices as self-interested whinging: 'They would say that, wouldn't they?' It has been an effective tactic, ensuring that informed and reasonable critical voices have been shut out from debates even before they get started. (Bolton, 1994, quoted in Esland, op. cit.)

Nevertheless, there is a danger of exaggerating the 'steamroller' effect of these undeniably real tendencies, and a related risk of according too much weight to the role of discourse within the whole ensemble of changes that have occurred. An associated danger is that of implying that the Right was bereft of intellectually respectable arguments, and that social democracy and the professional establishment within the state sector could therefore only ever have been defeated by *force majeure*. Such an analysis would also suggest too great a degree of ideological homogeneity among state professionals – not a few of whom have turned out to be among the most committed *supporters* of various aspects of the 'new managerialism'.

An interesting set of arguments which provides an antidote to over-estimating the role of discursive forces in the whole set of processes which have radically transformed the control and management of state institutions, focuses upon the idea of *governmentality* – a rather forbidding term taken from the late work of Michel Foucault (Foucault, 1991). The core idea is that neo-liberalism may have effected an *enduring* transformation of the way in which state institutions are governed *and* in ways in which control is exercised within them. As Nikolas Rose has suggested, this set of changes may prove to be more potent *and* longer-lasting than the phenomena loosely labelled as 'Thatcherism' or 'Reaganism':

> Whilst the breathless celebrations or condemnations of Thatcherism have proved to be overblown, it is none the less possible, I suggest, to identify a more modest yet more durable transformation in rationalities and technologies of government. (Rose, 1993, p. 295)

It will not be possible to offer more than a much simplified outline of this approach – but at its heart is the insight that 'advanced liberalism' has brought into existence a set of interrelated developments which (in the UK at least) involve at least the following features:

- a new form of distanced ('distantiated') relationship between the political centre of decision-making and what is increasingly represented as the *non*-political level of *institutions*, such as universities, schools, hospitals, even prisons;

- the establishment of semi-autonomous forms of institutional governance and management: this has typically involved the creation of 'lay' boards of governors or trustees, and powerful senior management teams led by chief executives who report to these governing bodies; it also involves the incorporation of such institutions as legally independent entities in various respects, for example as the direct employers of much of their own labour force, as capable of entering into contracts with other agencies, etc.;

- these institutions vary greatly in scale: they include at one end of the spectrum bodies such as large universities, major NHS Trusts, etc. right through to small organizations such as opted-out schools and fund-holding GPs' practices;

- a prime responsibility of management in all such institutions, irrespective of size, is the requirement to manage efficiently within the cash-limited budgets set by governmental agencies; nationally, this operates as an essential mechanism for controlling public expenditure; however, there is also strong encouragement for such institutions to become independently entrepreneurial, especially by realizing the value of 'unproductive' assets such as land, by cutting costs (especially labour costs, e.g. through compulsory competitive tendering), and by engaging in various forms of income generation;

- the imposition of the disciplines of 'marketization' is a further means of inducing compliance with government policy by compelling institutions to operate within a competitive environment: the formula funding of schools in proportion to the number of pupils recruited is a well-known example;

- mechanisms of financial audit are also critical to the operation of this complex set of structures; there is a very real sense in which 'the balance sheet rules, OK';

- however, audit extends to much more than finance; the system (being still largely dependent on public money) does not operate in a real market, only in various kinds of quasi-market; consequently, it is seen as necessary to monitor and assess 'quality' and 'product' by measures additional to those which operate in real markets (such as sales, profitability, share price, etc.);

- direct assessment of quality and performance has therefore been instituted both by *external* agencies, e.g. OFSTED inspections of schools, which now include the direct grading of teacher competence, HEFCE and HEQC quality audits within higher education, etc. and also via *internal* mechanisms such as (in schools and teacher training institutions) career entry profiles, staff appraisal, management training for headteachers, etc.

Nikolas Rose has highlighted probably more clearly than anyone else, just what it is that is so genuinely innovative about all these changes ushered in by neo-liberalism:

> Neo-liberalism was potent because it did not merely articulate a range of familiar criticisms of welfare – its cost, its bureaucracy, its granting of discretionary authority to unaccountable administrators, its paternalism, its inequity, its crushing of autonomy – but managed to turn these criticisms governmental – that is to say, to render them technical . . .
> Neo-liberalism managed to reactivate the sceptical vigilance of classical liberalism and link it up with a series of techniques – none of them in itself particularly new or remarkable

– which could render them operable – techniques such as monetarization, marketization, enhancement of the powers of the consumer, financial accountability and audit. It is this capacity to create operable technical forms for exercising perpetual scrutiny over the authority of authority that made the formulae invented by neo-liberalism so versatile for all those other programmes and strategies that sought to govern in an advanced liberal way. (ibid., pp. 294–5)

Rose also notes that the implementation of these new techniques of control and scrutiny reflect a significant 'erosion of trust', particularly the trust which governments in the era of consensus politics were prepared to place in *professionals*. This, he suggests, partly reflects a more general public scepticism about experts of many kinds. Anthony Giddens has argued that this suspension of belief in the somewhat omnipotent claims of professionals and experts is a rather paradoxical consequence of reflexive modernization (see Chapter 2). In the sphere of health, for example, Giddens notes the proliferation of many forms of 'alternative' medicine and therapies, which flourish *despite* the ever-increasing success of science-based orthodox medicine in defeating major diseases such as cancer. In this climate of more generalized distrust of experts, policies which cut professionals 'down to size' and render them accountable have a significant public appeal, which professionals themselves would do well to try to understand. What the new mechanisms of audit, marketization, quality assessment, etc. do is to substitute formally demonstrable kinds of bureaucratic accountability for the trust which was once accorded to professionals to manage their own affairs and the institutions in which they worked.

Within teaching and teacher education, this is leading to a systematic effort, which appears to be increasingly successful, to redefine the core meaning of the term 'professional'. Emphasis is no longer placed on the *broad liberal education* of professionals and upon professional *autonomy* – that of the individual practitioner and of the collective occupational group – which were two of the hallmarks of traditional criteria of professional occupations. Instead, a concerted attempt is being made to define teacher professionalism in terms of specific, demonstrable *competencies* and *managed career progression*. What is highly significant is that the source of these new definitions is a set of government agencies – in this case, principally OFSTED and the latest educational quango the Teacher Training Agency (TTA). The following remarks by Anthea Millett, the first chief executive of the TTA, spell out the new thinking very clearly in the context of promoting the idea of a national curriculum for Initial Teacher Training:

Students need clarity to help them prepare for their role and to underpin their entitlement to high quality training. But it is also needed by the providers of initial teacher training, who need to know what content they are expected to deliver and what standards the Secretary of State, the Teacher Training Agency, and OFSTED expect them to meet . . .

Behind the national curriculum is an equally important issue – teaching as a profession. Teaching needs a professional structure, supported by national standards, and, where appropriate, qualifications. That is why, with the help of those from inside and outside education, and following our advice to Mrs Shephard (Secretary of State for Education and Employment) last summer, we have already begun work on drawing up national standards at four key points in the profession – newly qualified teacher, expert teacher, expert subject leader, and expert school leader.

We have also drawn attention to the need for a concerted effort by schools and local education authorities in induction, and are piloting career entry profiles. All these initiatives will underpin the professionalism of teaching, as well as our emphasis on making teaching a research-based profession. These developments can only be good for teaching, good in attracting people of high quality into teaching and therefore good for providers of initial teacher training. (Millett, 1996, p. 9)

The confident and repeated use of 'needs' talk, the appeal to the 'obvious' good sense of such ideas, etc. is symptomatic of the new style. Debate is not invited. This *is*, now, what it is to become a professional teacher or even headteacher.

Nevertheless, there is plenty of evidence that such thinking is persuasive – and not only because it has a coercive element – though that is important.

(a) For senior new-style professionals, the professional task is increasingly one of being an effective *manager* – of material resources and of 'human resources'. Although this can be viewed cynically, it is also a role conception which permits a range of satisfactions: genuine and extensive autonomy (albeit within a range of tight externally imposed constraints); clearly defined role expectations and clear criteria of success and failure; the respect that comes from being *recognized* as an efficient manager – by clients, employees, and external agencies; widening pay and status differentials between managers and managed, etc. As the concluding section of Anthea Millett's comments illustrates, it is even possible to incorporate aspects of more 'traditional' conceptions of professionalism within this framework. By making a bid to control a significant slice of funding for *research*, the TTA aims to create a self-contained instrumentally oriented 'research culture' which serves priorities identified by itself and government but which also offers a new source of status to those sometimes previously seen as (mere) 'practitioners'. It is similarly possible that elements of traditional professional dignity will be salvaged by the establishment of a General Teachers Council – as long as such a body is constitutionally 'contained' within the emerging frameworks of occupational control.

(b) For those officially described as 'trainees' undergoing initial teacher-training, access to alternative conceptions of what it might mean to be a professional has been sharply diminished (not least as a result of the marginalizing of 'theory') whilst, correspondingly, the new definitions are pervasively present. Trainees encounter these definitions at every turn: in the criteria by which their training courses are defined and evaluated; in the batteries of competency definitions which form the basis for the assessment of their individual progress; and in the structured framework for career induction, progression and promotion – which is, increasingly, the *only* framework for professional advancement.

(c) A further consequence of all this may be that, at least in some schools, growing numbers of younger teachers could be becoming increasingly impatient with certain 'disaffected' older members of staff – including some of those who are seen as seeking to cling on to 'obsolescent' notions of professionalism. A partial breakdown in communication and trust between different generations of teachers around these issues would not be surprising – particularly in view of the difficulties of articulating a clear and unifying conception of the role of teacher *unions* within the new dispensation. All of this may take place in a context in which the majority of teachers continue to feel considerable resentment about more 'bread and butter' issues such as excessive workloads, inadequate pay, excessive external scrutiny, etc.

(d) Recent work by Basil Bernstein has identified a further aspect of these changes – one which also has intriguing long-term implications. He suggests that what we are currently witnessing in education, especially at the level of schools, is something more complex but also more interesting than a simple intensification of the dominance of managerial discourses and practices within an agenda which is increasingly set by central government. With unrivalled sociological insight, Bernstein has begun to explore the implications of such changes for various new kinds of *identities* which teachers may be constrained to embrace. On the one hand, he suggests, they are likely to face a future which is increasingly 'pedagogized'. That is, they are increasingly likely to be seen to need 'continuous pedagogic re-formations' in order to be equipped to cope 'appropriately' with the changing demands facing schools (Bernstein, 1996, p. 72). The TTA's hierarchy of new National Professional Qualifications outlined by Anthea Millett (see above) exemplifies almost perfectly what Bernstein is talking about. Teachers have to be brought to accept their 'need' to be successively 'formed' and 're-formed' by vocationalist, skills-oriented forms of training which are deemed necessary to equip them to 'perform' in the ways that are needed by the overall system. These forms of 'professional' development will also provide them with the appropriate *credentials* for career progression. (Beneath this, of course, lurks the evident sanction that *without* submitting oneself to such training programmes, career progression may be difficult if not impossible.) Bernstein points out that structures of this kind are grounded in a kind of 'short-termism' which is oriented to the changing priorities dictated by market forces and/or new government agendas. In terms of identity, however, Bernstein points to certain sources of potential instability. In the first place, the underlying identity that training of this kind presupposes is centred in the notion of 'trainability'. But this also turns out (somewhat paradoxically) to be the *object* of such programmes: beneath their specific content their deep structure has to do with teaching people to be increasingly trainable – and, if possible, to develop in the recipients of such training an inner need to be successively *re*trained. Yet, as Bernstein points out, trainability, considered as a source of identity, is a strangely empty notion. It is also one which is oriented to a succession of (by definition) unpredictable *futures* (in Bernstein's own terminology, it is a 'prospective' identity). Secondly, however, and contradictorily, the introduction of a National Curriculum made up of a collection of traditional school subjects, each clearly demarcated from the other (what Bernstein terms a 'collection code'), is a source of pedagogic identities which are 'retrospective' and grounded in allegiance to academic disciplines:

> The culture of the *pedagogic* discourse of schools is retrospective, based on a past narrative of the dominance and significance of disciplines, whereas the management structure is *prospective*, pointing to the new entrepreneurialism and its instrumentalities. The State has therefore embedded a retrospective pedagogic culture in a prospective management culture. (ibid., p. 75)

Bernstein's provisional assessment of the likely outcome of these identity contradictions, however, offers little comfort to those who might wish that the more traditionally oriented identities will somehow win out:

> [T]he emphasis on the performance of students and the steps taken to increase and maintain performance, for the survival of the institution, is likely to facilitate a state-promoted instrumentality. The intrinsic value of knowledge may well be eroded even though the collection code of the curriculum appears to support such a value.

Thus the state, through greater centralizations and new forms of decentralization, has shifted pedagogic models and modes, management structures, and cultures of all educational institutions... The reproduction of state-recognized and state-rewarded forms is facilitated by (a range of factors) and, *of crucial importance, the dominance of new actors with new motivations.* (ibid., p. 75, my italics)

There are, then, good reasons for thinking that 'enterprise culture', in the guise of the new modalities of occupational control, is successfully taking root within schools and even within the much-criticized institutions of teacher-training. This should not occasion surprise – as both Rose and Bernstein have demonstrated, what is happening is something much more complex than any simple notion of 'cultural imposition' might suggest. We are witnessing a much more far-reaching set of changes – a transformation of the institutional relationships through which we are governed and our lives are regulated.

Both main political parties are likely to retain the essentials of these new structures as well as the various legitimating rationales. The 'new professionalism' and 'New Labour' are likely to prove profoundly compatible.

ENTERPRISE CULTURE AS LEGITIMATION OF WIDENING INEQUALITY

The notions of enterprise and enterprise culture have been pro-actively employed throughout the 1980s and 1990s as a basis for efforts to justify or at least legitimize policies designed to widen social inequality. At the heart of this process is an attempt to *moralize* economic individualism. And this has been attempted in a double sense: on the one hand by seeking to morally valorize activities which might otherwise seem to be motivated primarily by self-interest, most notably by elevating the activity of 'wealth creation' to the status of a cardinal social virtue; and on the other hand, by ascribing poverty to a moral defect – of both the poor themselves *and* of those 'welfare societies' misguided enough to 'entrap' their poorest citizens within a culture of dependency. 'Dependency culture' is thus the essential counterpart of 'enterprise culture': it is a concept which combines explanation with condemnation and which contains its own 'obvious' remedy: cut welfare spending in the name of self-reliance and family responsibility. Similarly, cut those taxes which directly penalize the 'productive' members of society, notably, *direct* taxation on earnings and wealth, and allow people (in the famous phrase popularized by Mrs Thatcher) 'to keep more of their own money'. On this basis, policies of 'principled inequality' can be vigorously proclaimed and, within the limits of what is politically possible (e.g. stopping short, so far, of fully privatizing the National Health Service), actively pursued.

Paul Morris has argued that the promotion of enterprise culture evolved through a series of phases which, somewhat paradoxically, developed by the late 1980s and early 1990s into a government-led project of 'cultural engineering' – this being strangely at odds with neo-liberal rhetoric about the necessity for rolling back the role of the state within a society founded on enterprise values[5] (Morris, 1991, p. 34). One key objective of this cultural engineering was to create a new 'common sense', which would increasingly take for granted both the 'obvious' rightness of rewarding rather than penalizing 'enterprise' and success, as well as the obvious good sense of discouraging dependency. Certain aspects of the institutional changes discussed in the previous section may be seen as powerfully contributing to the creation of common-sense understandings of this kind. For example, requirements on public sector institutions to 'contract out' various kinds of work on the basis of competitive tendering have generally had the effect of forcing down wage levels and worsening job security and working conditions – particularly of the lowest paid groups. In each institution where they are implemented, such changes can be very plausibly represented as 'unavoidable' accommodations to 'market realities' and to the (real) alternative of job losses throughout the organization. This is the public sector version of people 'pricing themselves back into jobs'. Similarly, a concomitant of the emphasis on 'management's right to manage', as well as of the undeniable real increases in managerial responsibilities and workloads which have accompanied it, has been increased pay differentials between senior management and other grades of salaried employees – right across public sector institutions.

These new forms of common sense not only permit the affluent and secure to enjoy the privileges of their position with a good conscience but also enable them to regard toughness on the poor as a form of public virtue. In this sense, the duality of enterprise/ dependency culture is a far more 'comfortable' one for certain sections of society than the dichotomy which Zigmunt Bauman (drawing upon the work of Pierre Bourdieu) sees as more truly characteristic of so-called consumer society. Bauman suggests that a more accurate picture is of a division between two nations: the 'seduced' and the 'repressed' – 'those free to follow their needs and those forced to comply with norms' (Bauman, 1987, pp. 168–9; Bourdieu, 1984). A growing fraction of public opinion appears prepared to listen with at least some degree of sympathy to those voices which blame the poor for their own misfortune – with the result that it becomes increasingly difficult to win support for social and economic policies based upon even modestly redistributive agendas. In Britain, the acute anxieties displayed by New Labour's leadership and 'spin doctors' in the face of any mention of arguments for higher direct taxes to pay for redistributive policies may be seen as one symptom of the drift of public opinion on such issues. In certain parts of the USA, the highly localized structure and financing of many welfare services has led not only to conspicuous geographical ghettoization of poverty but also to an increasing tendency for the affluent physically as well as mentally to segregate themselves and their families from the disadvantaged. The famous liberal American economist John Kenneth Galbraith has recently drawn attention to the way in which a relatively affluent majority has not only come to regard high levels of unemployment and tight-money policies as safeguards against the erosion of their assets by inflation, but also has shifted towards supporting policies 'involving a devastating deprivation of the unfortunate' (Galbraith, 1996). This has produced a decisive shift in the US in terms of the sayable and the unsayable:

> Once unemployment was considered flatly adverse, was all but universally condemned. Now low unemployment is seen as a serious threat to price stability and to investor confidence...We have come to accept that, along with central bankers, idle men and women are the basic defence against inflation. As matters now stand, financial markets would react well to an increase in joblessness, a consequent weakening of the job market and thus again the threat of inflation. *This can now quite openly be said.* (ibid., my italics)

It is, however, far from being the case that the values of enterprise culture have become *hegemonic* in the UK. There was and is plenty of evidence of widespread public reservation and unease – at least about the more radical versions of such doctrines. There is also evidence of deep public dissatisfaction with a whole range of perceived *excesses and abuses* which many associate with the twenty years or so in which 'enterprise values' have been proclaimed and promoted so blatantly.

(a) In the late 1980s, the leadership of the Conservative Party itself saw a need to take corrective action to try to undo the political damage resulting from the 'wrong kind' of celebration of enterprise values. A vigorous campaign was launched around the time of the 1989 Conservative Party Conference to promote 'active citizenship'. The context of this initiative was a perceived need actively to counter the widespread negative publicity which had been given to claims that 'Thatcherism' had engendered a climate of individual and corporate greed (exemplified in the figure of the 'loadsamoney yuppie'). Led by influential ministers, the 'active citizenship' campaign proclaimed that there were in fact natural continuities between enterprise values as exemplified by success in business, and the voluntary devotion of energy and time to community concerns. Kenneth Baker, for example, in a speech to the Bow Group in 1989, stated: 'there is another side to economic individualism; those who succeed have obligations over and beyond that of celebrating their own success' (*Daily Telegraph,* 28 April 1989). Around the same time, the Foreign Secretary, Douglas Hurd, delivered a series of speeches in which he sought to depict enterprise culture and active citizenship as complementary parts of a single set of values:

> The idea of active citizenship is a necessary complement to that of enterprise culture. Public service may once have been the duty of an elite but ... modern capitalism has democratized the ownership of property and we are now witnessing the democratization of responsible citizenship. (Hurd, 1989)

and

> Those qualities of enterprise and initiative which are essential for the generation of material wealth are also needed to build a family, a neighbourhood, or a nation which is able to draw on the respect, loyalty and affection of its members. (Hurd, 1988, p. 14)

(b) Such attempts to moralize 'enterprise culture' and to associate it with voluntary commitment to 'communitarian' values, however, have proved less than wholly convincing. At the time, i.e. in the mid-1980s, there was an all too evident discrepancy between the virtues *traditionally* associated with enterprise – thrift, frugality, industriousness, deferred gratification, etc. – and the institutional realities of the years of the 'Lawson Boom', a time of financial deregulation, the active encouragement of personal and corporate indebtedness, the celebration of conspicuous (even reckless) consumption, and so on. In more recent years, the wider public has, by and large, and with good reason, remained stubbornly sceptical about at least certain aspects of the virtues claimed for enterprise – and particularly about claims that there is any 'natural' continuity between commitment to wealth creation and commitment to the well-being of the wider community. For one thing, among the highest paid and most prominent of the leaders of the business community, there are too many who are judged to have displayed an all too conspicuous preoccupation with their own self-interest – as, for example, in the case of the share option schemes awarded to chief executives of the recently privatized public utilities. Furthermore, there is little evidence that the

Greenbury Committee, set up to curb excessive increases in the pay of top executives, has been effective. A TUC report published at the end of 1996 indicated that 'the gap between the pay of leading directors and their workers has grown by 4 per cent over the past year' and called for 'employee representatives to join companies' remuneration committees' (*Guardian*, 27 December 1996, p. 20). Three days earlier, the same newspaper carried a leading article drawing attention to a *Sunday Telegraph* survey which indicated that '1500 bankers and brokers in the City of London will share bonuses this Christmas of over £500,000 each – a total of £750 million' (ibid., p. 24). It seems, then, that many of those who control the remuneration of such senior executives remain oblivious of such public concern – or perhaps they are simply contemptuous of it.[6] The relationship between industrial and commercial 'fat-catism' and sections of the *political* class has been a further area where the general public has become increasingly disenchanted. The events surrounding the Scott Report (occasioned by the 'cash for questions' allegations), and especially the disavowals of responsibility by many of the politicians criticized in it, have probably heightened this sense of disenchantment.

(c) A third reason why extensive and whole-hearted subscription to enterprise values has not developed relates to the increasingly widespread sense of *insecurity* which growing numbers of people feel – especially insecurity about employment. This is by no means confined to the poor and casualized; even among the modestly affluent, many more people *feel* increasingly at risk, and this includes people who have much more to lose – for example the loss of a company pension or enforced premature retirement without adequate pension enhancement. Anxieties of this kind may be leading increasing numbers of people to doubt whether privatized provision and self-reliance is a secure enough form of provision when it comes to matters such as health care, pensions, education for their children, etc. In Will Hutton's '30:30:40' society, only the top 40 per cent ('the advantaged') can be reasonably confident that they could manage 'on their own'. Below them, the 30 per cent of 'the disadvantaged' have – on Hutton's analysis – now been joined by another 30 per cent: 'the newly insecure' (Hutton, 1995b, pp. 2–3).

Interestingly, the political philosopher John Gray has recently pointed to certain possible *cultural* consequences of the phenomenon of what he terms 'the casualization of the working lives of people who consider themselves middle class' (Gray, 1996). He points out that it was the expectation of a stable career which formed a key foundation of 'the bourgeois culture of work' and hence of those broader bourgeois values which provided the basis for stable family life, or for the conditions in which deferred gratification and prudent long-term planning could become a significant part of the motivational structure of middle-class individuals. 'A normal bourgeois life was one in which the phases of a career tracked the stages of the life-cycle' so that it was a career which 'gave many people their most enduring sense of themselves'. He speculates that the radical fracturing of these expectations among even the affluent could engender not so much a set of stable commitments to some coherent set of alternative values organized around 'enterprise' but rather 'a hitherto unrecognized class culture – that of the lumpen-bourgeoisie'. Gray does not specify their values – but he hints darkly at rising levels of anomie, short-termism and narrow self-interest, and 'an anxious, restless and speculative' mentality (ibid.).

(d) One of the justifications offered for an 'enterprise economy' is the claim that, in time, the overall levels of employment and economic growth, which an untrammelled free market will generate, will result in higher levels of prosperity *for all*. The pursuit of principled inequality is thus the surest route to comparative prosperity for all sections of society. There is, however, very little empirical evidence so far that the so-called 'trickle-down' effect has even begun to happen. According to the Report of the Commission on Social Justice, 'between 1979 and 1991/92, the poorest 10 per cent saw their incomes *fall* by 17 per cent'; while between 1989 and 1991 'the very highest-paid people in London and the South East increased their earnings by an average of £22,000 a year . . . while the bottom 50 per cent of earners took an average pay *cut* of more than £200 a year' (Commission on Social Justice, 1994, pp. 29–30).[7]

(e) Fifthly, there is the issue of sheer moral offence. To a significant fraction of the population – though how large a fraction is admittedly difficult to judge – there remains something fundamentally unacceptable *morally* about 'one nation' in which 'some people today get paid £1.50 an hour and others £1.50 a minute' (Atkinson, 1996, p. 15). Conspicuously excessive (and in some cases wholly undeserved) wealth – and increases in that wealth – are similarly obnoxious to many. The fact that it is no longer remotely plausible to regard the Church of England as 'the Conservative Party at prayer' is not unconnected with New Right Conservatism's support for policies calculated to widen social inequality. Although the Established Church is far from united in opposition to such policies – it is not even united about *being* the Established Church! – a significant proportion of its bishops past and present (including David Jenkins, Hugh Montefiore, David Sheppard and former Archbishop Robert Runcie) have, over the last two decades, been outspoken in their criticism on these issues, and there is little doubt that a significant proportion of the laity share their views to some extent.

(f) A final reason why enterprise culture may fail to become hegemonic has to do with a significant inbuilt ambiguity about what 'enterprise values' now really amount to – within 'late capitalist', consumer societies. As we have noted several times already, the 'Victorian values', with which enterprise is *traditionally* associated, included not only certain of Letwin's 'vigorous virtues' – such as self-sufficiency, independent-mindedness, and uprightness; but also values centring in self-discipline and even self-denial: thrift, deferred gratification, abstinence, etc. Whilst we may readily acknowledge that there has always been a significant element of *idealization* in such Samuel Smiles imagery, this portrait of the entrepreneurial classes of a previous age is far from wholly inaccurate or simply self-serving. What is most pertinent for our purposes, however, is that these qualities do not constitute a recognizable portrait of many of our *contemporary* representatives of enterprise.

On reflection, this should occasion little surprise. As the French sociologist Pierre Bourdieu has pointed out, the transition to contemporary, consumer-oriented capitalism could hardly have taken place without a process which he calls 'ethical retooling' – involving a rejection or at least an abandoning of certain of the older values associated with enterprise, and their replacement by a new and strikingly more hedonistic 'morality':

> The new bourgeoisie is the initiator of the ethical retooling required by the new economy from which it draws its power and profits, whose functioning depends as much on the

production of needs and consumers as on the production of goods. The new logic of the economy rejects the ascetic ethic of production and accumulation, based on abstinence, sobriety, saving and calculation, in favour of the hedonistic morality of consumption, based on credit, spending and enjoyment. This economy demands a social world which judges people by their capacity for consumption, their 'standard of living', their life-style, as much as by their capacity for production. (Bourdieu, 1984, p. 310)

Bourdieu analyses this change in terms of the working out of a conflict *within* the dominant class, in which the values and style of the 'new bourgeoisie' steadily displace those associated with traditionally dominant groups. This change is particularly evident, he suggests, in the less 'visible' ways in which power relationships – in workplaces and in society at large – are now expressed. There is, in particular, what he terms 'a euphemizing of all manifestations of social distance' (ibid., p. 311) in terms of a blurring of the old sharply visible hierarchies of dress, forms of speech, modes of institutional segregation, etc.:

And the whole opposition between the *vieux jeu* and the *nouveau jeu*, between the old-style authoritarian industrialist and the modern manager, tuned in to the latest techniques of business administration, public relations and group dynamics, can be read in the opposition between the pot-bellied, pompous *patron* and the slick, sun-tanned cadre, who is as 'casual' in his dress as in his manner, as 'relaxed' at cocktail parties as in his relations with those he calls his 'social partners'. (ibid., p. 311)

We may see here a Gallic version of the contrast between the heroic Thatcherite figure of the small business man (or woman) and the figure of the dynamic executive epitomized by another kind of Conservative hero – Maurice Saatchi, for example. Lord Saatchi's recent elevation to the peerage perhaps epitomizes a uniquely English element of *added* contradictoriness in these changing embodiments of 'enterprise culture'.[8]

CONCLUSION

There is, then, in our own times a deep and structural ambivalence about the *moral* grounding of enterprise culture – and this has persistently weakened its pretensions to provide an over-arching framework of justification for a new social order. But at other levels, the spread of attitudes and beliefs which are consistent with the value basis of enterprise culture has been steady and insidious. John Major's proposal in 1992 to abolish Inheritance Tax in the UK – popularized in his vision of 'wealth cascading down the generations' – illustrates how far things have shifted. Such a proposal is clearly quite inconsistent with a consistently *meritocratic* version of enterprise culture, in that it involves further enriching many who may not themselves have contributed significantly to wealth creation. Nevertheless, opposition to it has been muted – since even the fairly modestly affluent see benefits accruing to themselves and their families. To take another example, the values of enterprise culture have recently also taken over a large part of the building society movement in the UK, with more and more societies abandoning their mutual status and converting themselves into commercial banking operations. Although this development led to further complaints about 'fat catism' – 'there is only one reason for this stampede which is relentlessly sweeping building societies into the gutter: to enrich the directors with ridiculous salaries and share options' (Foot, 1996, p. 13) – nevertheless, hardly any building society shareholders voted to preserve mutuality, preferring instead to be 'bribed with their own money' (ibid.). The resulting changes are certainly cultural – emblematic of what Foot calls 'a huge cultural shift in British capitalism' – but they are also institutional, cementing the cultural changes and making the diminishing group of mutual societies which remain seem curious leftovers from a by-gone age.

John Kenneth Galbraith, in the article already cited, puts his finger on what is perhaps the *fundamental* reason why the affluent and now numerous elements of the populations of modern industrial economies see less and less reason to care about welfare and the poor:

> The attitudes...are present in all the fortunate lands. There are concerned and compassionate people who reject them along with the silent poor. Perhaps it is time to bring them out into the open – to seek the therapeutic value of clear speech. In the modern economy let us say simply that the rich do not want to pay for the poor; that unemployment is necessary and good; that recession can be tolerated, certainly by the many who do not suffer as compared with the smaller number who do. Even mild inflation affects the many as compared with unemployment, which affects the relatively few, and there is this fear that it will get out of hand...
>
> Perhaps two further truths might be added. Some people were meant to suffer. And whoever thought that economic life was meant to be fair? (Galbraith, op. cit.)

In such a world, the possibility of equality of opportunity in education recedes steadily. All major UK political parties are now preoccupied with an increasingly limited equal opportunities agenda – for example, an almost obsessive concern with school effectiveness, curriculum 'entitlement', raising standards, etc.[9] This, while worthwhile so far as it goes, is primarily a politically convenient way of distracting attention from a range of much more significant but also far more intractable sources of educational advantage and disadvantage – those linked to the diverging *material* conditions of existence of different sections of the population. It is also a way of, once again, blaming schools, teachers and educationalists for problems which are not of their making.[10]

NOTES

1 Jones, for example, opened the first chapter of his book *Right Turn* with the following words: 'Conservative education policy, Janus-headed, fuses the archaic and the modern, mixes nostalgia with technology, evokes community and promotes entrepreneurialism' (Jones, 1989, p. 1). Donald, rather similarly, comments: 'the paradox is that the strategy of modernization has been articulated in terms of a social imaginary that is profoundly conservative' (Donald, 1992, p. 126).

2 And even within his discussion of Dickens' work, Wiener offers one-sided and contentious interpretations. He does, admittedly, accept that there is much in Dickens which *celebrates* rather than denigrates industry – noting that on his death, Ruskin called Dickens 'a pure modernist – a leader of the *steam whistle* party par excellence' (Wiener, 1981, p. 33). However, he then seeks to argue that the writings of Dickens' *maturity* display a profound ambivalence about both industry itself and the whole industrial class: 'One critic has found *the essential development* of Dickens' social thinking in "a rejection of the self-made man, towards an affirmation of a gentlemanly ideal which has been purged of its associations with class and social ambition"' (Wiener, ibid., p. 35, my italics).

It is, however, just this desire to identify so-called 'essential developments' – especially where they support his overall thesis – which is at the heart of what is wrong with Wiener's approach. What he actually offers are interpretations which are reductive and unconvincing.

Panks in *Little Dorrit*, for example, is cited to illustrate Dickens' alleged increasing hostility to the creation of wealth as a social goal (ibid., p. 34). This, however, quite overlooks the celebration in the same novel of Mr Doyce, 'a smith and engineer...well known as a very ingenious man' who perfected an invention 'of great importance to his country and his fellow-creatures', as well as the pivotal role in the narrative of the small business partnership of Doyce and Clennam (Dickens, 1907, pp. 117–18). It also oversimplifies the satire of the Circumlocution Office – which certainly ridicules the accumulation of *unmerited* wealth (and the nepotism which often went with it) but which satirized this parasitic *section* of the dominant class precisely because it operated to frustrate the entrepreneurial energies of others. This is the whole point of the famous image of the 'Barnacled' ship-of-the-nation:

> [W]hat the Barnacles had to do, was to stick to the national ship as long as they could. That to trim the ship, lighten the ship, clear the ship, would be to knock them off; that they could but be knocked off once; and that if the ship went down with them yet sticking to it, that was the ship's look-out and not theirs. (Dickens, 1907, p. 119)

3   For all his eminence as a literary critic, it is worth remembering that Leavis was not even a dominant influence within his own faculty within the University of Cambridge, while the English Faculty itself was (and remains) small and of limited weight when compared with the large, well-funded and prestigious Cambridge faculties of engineering and the various natural sciences.

4   Edgerton's critique of one aspect of Correlli Barnett's work is pertinent here:

> Barnett has made much of the difference between British and German technical education before 1914. He compares Oxbridge and the civic universities with the German technical universities. But this comparison is misleading because it ignores the *traditional* German universities. Traditional universities in Britain embraced science and technology far more readily than their German counterparts. Cambridge had the largest school of engineering in Britain until the 1940s. (Those who link the classics to British decline should recall that German universities were citadels of the classics before 1945.) (Edgerton, 1996b)

5   Many commentators have drawn attention to this paradox and have argued that a key element in the success of 'Thatcherism' was precisely the capacity to bring together, under the auspices of a small but strong state, philosophically contradictory elements of neo-liberal and neo-conservative ideology, and to combine them into a programme which had clear *political* effectiveness and broad electoral appeal (see, for example, Gamble, 1983; Whitty, 1990).

6   For example, the columnist Paul Foot has commented critically on a series of decisions by the remuneration committee of Vickers to augment the pension entitlements of Sir Colin Chandler, Chairman of Vickers, who was 'severely criticised by Scott for his role in the notorious Hastie affair' in which Hastie, who was Chandler's successor as marketing director of British Aerospace, was 'seconded' to the Ministry of Defence Export Sales Organization where a substantial part of his job was to sell British Aerospace Hawk fighters to the Iraqi government. According to Foot, Scott 'described the conflict of interest here as "plain as a pikestaff" and denounced it roundly'; yet Vickers' remuneration committee agreed to increase Sir Colin's total remuneration package for 1995 to £667,788, 'a rise of just over £100,000 on the previous year' (Foot, 1996, p. 13).

7   It is, admittedly, difficult to be fully confident about the significance of findings related only to *incomes*. Other researchers have measured *expenditure*, and using this criterion, the Institute of Fiscal Studies found that between 1979 and 1992, while the income of the poorest tenth of the population fell by 18 per cent, their expenditure rose by 14 per cent (Institute of Fiscal Studies, 1995). Commenting on the report Andrew Dilnot, Director of the Institute, stressed that these findings did not in themselves invalidate the data on income distribution: 'it is another way of looking at living standards, but it does suggest the picture is more complex than previously thought'. Part of the explanation may lie in the fairly rapid change in the composition of the proportion of the population in the bottom 10 per cent of incomes: there may be significant movement in and out of the poorest section of society in any given year.

8 Very recently, Ralf Dahrendorf (the illustrious German sociologist who was at one time the Director of the London School of Economics) has offered the following penetrating assessment of the significance of Thatcherism:

> One interpretation of Thatcherism is that it set out to demolish the remnants of both working-class and upper-class Britain. Hence the attack on the unions, the symbols and the representatives of working-class life. Hence, above all, the unrelenting battle against traditional institutions, including the professions and the Civil Service, the BBC and the universities, one-nation Toryism and the great and the good. The success of the onslaught is there for everyone to see. BBC English of the 50s today sounds ridiculous. The aristocracy, including the monarchy, has joined its Continental counterparts as fodder for illustrated magazines. The universities have been destroyed by expansion without funding or structure changes. And everyone talks all the time about what was for long unspeakable – money, money, money. The notoriously weak profession of business now dominates all. (Dahrendorf, 1997)

9 It is symptomatic that even programmes of moral education can now be 'marketed' by reference to this preoccupation with raising standards and increasing school effectiveness. At a recent SCAA conference on the work of the National Forum on Values Education, Nicholas Tate saw fit to suggest that there might well be a causal connection between moral education and rising academic standards! Asked about the potential effect on schools of the SCAA statement of values (see Chapter 4 of this book), he pointed out that 'the four countries which came top in a recent international comparison of maths and science performance – Hong Kong, Japan, Korea and Singapore – all had moral education in the curriculum':

> Countries that have explicit moral education in their curriculum seem to be performing extremely well academically ... Schools not doing well are often those where a clear statement of values and attitudes is not being promoted. (quoted in the *Guardian*, 20 December 1996, p. 5)

Comment would be superfluous!

10 The election in 1997 of a New Labour government with an overwhelming parliamentary majority has so far produced no significant diminution in criticisms by politicians of teachers and teacher-trainers. New Labour has projected a whole series of strikingly contradictory messages and images as far as teachers are concerned. For example, a teacher recruitment campaign in cinemas and newspapers, featuring various 'celebrities' fondly remembering 'my favourite teacher', has coexisted with draconian policies of 'zero tolerance' and 'fast track dismissal procedures' for poor teachers, alongside a reiteration of the government's commitment to the so-called 'blame and shame' strategy of publicly identifying 'failing schools'. Similarly, in the field of initial teacher-training, a House of Commons Select Committee on Education has called for a stipulated minimum Advanced Level points score to be used in the selection of new entrants to the profession, whilst at the same time Alec Reed, chairman of Reed Executive, has been appointed by the Prime Minister to help solve the looming crisis in teacher supply! Simultaneously, initial teacher-training courses are being subjected to ever more prescriptive national criteria and an intensified inspection regime as the new National Curriculum for Initial Teacher Training is phased in. In yet another area, teachers are told that more pupils with special education needs must be 'mainstreamed' (but without significant additional resources) while the proportion of 'statemented' pupils should be reduced from 3 per cent of all pupils to 2 per cent.

So far, then, the evidence suggests that the dominant values of New Labour in office, at least as far as schools are concerned, might be summed up as '*modernize, advertise, enterprise*', whilst its main commitment in the area of economic policy is that of continuing New Right Conservatism's commitment to flexible labour markets.

Bibliography

Abrams, F. (1993) Rights, duties and the greater scheme. *Times Educational Supplement,* 16 July, p. 10.

Ahier, J. (1988) *Industry, Children and the Nation: An Analysis of National Identity in School Textbooks.* London: The Falmer Press.

Ahier, J. (1991) Explaining economic decline and teaching children about industry: some unintended consequences. In Moore, R. and Ozga, J. (eds) *Curriculum Policy.* Oxford: Pergamon/Open University, pp. 123–45.

Ahier, J. (1995) Hidden controversies in two cross-curricular themes. In Ahier, J. and Ross, A. (eds) *The Social Subjects Within the Curriculum: Children's Social Learning in the National Curriculum.* London: Falmer.

Althusser, L. (1971) Ideology and ideological state apparatuses. In *Lenin and Philosophy and Other Essays.* London: New Left Books, pp. 123–73.

Alves, C. (1991) Just a matter of words? The religious education debate in the House of Lords. *British Journal of Religious Education* 13(3).

Anderson, B. (1983) *Imagined Communities: Reflections on the Origin and Spread of Nationalism.* London: Verso.

Anderson, P. (1990) A culture in contraflow – I. *New Left Review* **180**, 41–78.

Arnold, M. (1869) *Culture and Anarchy: an essay in political and social criticism.* London: John Murray.

Atkinson, T. (1996) Why do Britain's have-nots have less? *Times Higher Education Supplement,* 12 April, p. 15.

Bailey, C. (1984) *Beyond the Present and the Particular: A Theory of Liberal Education.* London: Routledge and Kegan Paul.

Bailey, C. (1992) Enterprise and liberal education: some reservations. *Journal of Liberal Education* **26**(1), 99–106.

Ball, S. J. (1990) *Politics and Policy Making in Education: Explorations in Policy Sociology.* London: Routledge.

Barnett, C. (1978) Education and British industrial decline. *Journal of the National Association of Inspectors and Advisers* **9**, Autumn.

Barnett, C. (1986) *The Audit of War.* London: Macmillan.

Bauman, Z. (1987) *Legislators and Interpreters: On Modernity, Post-modernity and Intellectuals.* New York: Cornell University Press.

Beck, J. (1996a) Nation, curriculum and identity in conservative cultural analysis: a critical commentary. *Cambridge Journal of Education* **26**(2), 171–98.

Beck, J. (1996b) Citizenship education: problems and possibilities. *Curriculum Studies* **4**(3), 349–66.

Beck, U. (1992) *Risk Society: Towards a New Modernity*. London: Sage Publications.

Beck, U. (1994) The reinvention of politics: towards a theory of reflexive modernization. In Beck, U., Giddens, A. and Lash, S. *Reflexive Modernization: Politics, Tradition and Aesthetics in the Modern Social Order*. Cambridge: Polity Press.

Beck, U. and Beck-Gernsheim, E. (1995) *The Normal Chaos of Love*. Cambridge: Polity Press.

Beck, U. and Beck-Gernsheim, E. (1996) Individualization and 'precarious freedoms': perspectives and controversies of a subject-oriented sociology. In Heelas, P., Lash, S. and Morris, P. (eds) *Detraditionalization: Critical Reflections on Authority and Identity*. Oxford: Blackwell Publishers Ltd.

Beck, U., Giddens, A. and Lash, S. (1994) *Reflexive Modernization: Politics, Tradition and Aesthetics in the Modern Social Order*. Cambridge: Polity Press.

Benfield, C. (1996a) Simple lesson for the intellectuals who waffle on but fail to grasp the nettle. *Yorkshire Post*, 21 October, p. 9.

Benfield, C. (1996b) Neo-paganism 'a threat to society'. *Guardian*, 12 November, p. 9.

Berger, P. L. (1967) *The Social Reality of Religion*. London: Faber and Faber.

Bernstein, B. (1996) *Pedagogy, Symbolic Control and Identity: Theory, Research and Critique*. London: Taylor and Francis.

Best, R. (ed.) (1996) *Education, Spirituality and the Whole Child*. London: Cassell.

Bilton, T., Bonnett, K., Jones, P., Skinner, D., Stanworth, M. and Webster, A. (1996) *Introductory Sociology* (3rd edn). London: Macmillan.

Black, P. (1992) Prejudice, tradition and the death of a dream. *Times Educational Supplement*, 28 August, p. 12.

Black, P. (1993) The shifting scenery of the National Curriculum. In O'Hear, P. and White, J. (eds) *Assessing the National Curriculum*. London: Paul Chapman Publishing.

Blackstone, W. (1783) *Commentaries on the Laws of England*, vols I–IV (9th edn).

Blyth, A. (1984) Industry education: case studies from the North West. In Jamieson, I. (ed.) *We Make Kettles: Studying Industry in the Primary School*. London: Schools Council Programme 3/Longman.

Bolton, E. (1994) One last push. *Education Guardian*, 17 May.

Bonnett, M. (1994) *Children's Thinking: Promoting Understanding in the Primary School*. London: Cassell.

Bourdieu, P. (1984) *Distinction: A Social Critique of the Judgement of Taste*. London: Routledge and Kegan Paul.

Bowles, S. and Gintis, H. (1972) *Schooling in Capitalist America*. London: Routledge and Kegan Paul.

Bridges, D. (1986) Dealing with controversy in the curriculum: a philosophical perspective. In Wellington, J. J. (ed.) *Controversial Issues in the Curriculum*. Oxford: Basil Blackwell.

Brindle, P. (1996) The golden age that never was. *Times Educational Supplement*, p. 5.

British Humanist Association (1993) *The Human Spirit*. London: The British Humanist Association.

Bunting, M. (1996) Neo-paganism: a threat to society. *Guardian*, 12 November, p. 9.

Carvel, J. (1996) Teaching union seeks the abolition of OFSTED. *Guardian*, 4 April.

Castaneda, C. (1968) *The Teachings of Don Juan: A Yaqui Way of Knowledge*. Berkeley: University of California Press. (Penguin Books edition, 1970.)

Chitty, C. (1988) Two models of a National Curriculum: origins and interpretations. In Lawton, D. and Chitty, C. (eds) *The National Curriculum*. Bedford Way Papers 33. London: University of London Institute of Education.

Clifford, J. and Marcus, G. E. (1986) *Writing Culture: The Poetics and Politics of Ethnography*. Berkeley: University of California Press.

Coleridge, S. T. (1930) Lecture on *Romeo and Juliet*, December 9th, 1811. In T. Raysor (ed.) *Coleridge's Shakesperian Criticism*. London: Constable/Cambridge, MA: Harvard University Press.

Coles, R. (1986) *The Political Life of Children*. New York: The Atlantic Monthly Press.

Commission on Citizenship (1990) *Encouraging Citizenship*. London: HMSO.

Commission on Social Justice (1994) *Social Justice: Strategies for National Renewal*. The Report of the Commission on Social Justice, London: Vintage.

Cox, B. (1991) *Cox on Cox: An English Curriculum for the 1990s*. London: Hodder and Stoughton.

Cox, B. (1995) *Cox on the Battle for the English Curriculum*. London: Hodder and Stoughton.

Cox, C. B. and Dyson, A. E. (eds) (1969) *Fight for Education: A Black Paper*. London: The Critical Quarterly Society.

Crawford, K. (1995) Citizenship in the primary classroom. In Ahier, J. and Ross, A. (eds) *The Social Subjects Within the Curriculum: Children's Social Learning Within the National Curriculum*. London: The Falmer Press.

Crick, B. and Porter, A. (eds) (1978) *Political Education and Political Literacy*. London: Longman.

Dahrendorf, R. (1959) *Class and Class Conflict in Industrial Society*. London: Routledge and Kegan Paul.

Dahrendorf, R. (1997) Who won the class war? People just like them. *Observer*, 9 March, p. 27.

Daily Express (1996) How the rich got £15 bn. richer in just a year. 13 April.

Daily Telegraph (1995) Curriculum chief backs Britishness. 19 July.

Daily Telegraph (1996) School values report to back marriage and the family. 20 December, p. 4.

Dearing, R. (1994) *The National Curriculum and Its Assessment: Final Report*. London: School Curriculum and Assessment Authority.

Dearing, R. (1996) To begin at the beginning. Paper delivered to SCAA Conference on 'Education for Adult Life', 15 January. London: School Curriculum and Assessment Authority.

Dennis, N. and Erdos, G. (1993) *Families Without Fatherhood* (2nd edn). London: Institute of Economic Affairs Health and Welfare Unit.

DES (Department of Education and Science) (1977a) *The Curriculum 11–16*. London: HMSO.

DES (Department of Education and Science) (1977b) *Supplement to The Curriculum 11–16*. London: HMSO.

DFE (Department for Education) (1994a) *Education Act 1993: Sex Education in Schools*. Circular 5/94, 6 May.

DFE (Department for Education) (1994b) *Our Children's Education: The Updated Parent's Charter*. London: HMSO.

Dickens, C. (1907) *Little Dorrit*. London: Chapman and Hall (The Popular Edition).

Donald, J. (1992) *Sentimental Education: Schooling, Popular Culture, and the Regulation of Liberty*. London: Verso.

Durkheim, E. (1964) *The Division of Labour in Society*. New York: The Free Press/London: Collier-Macmillan.

Edgerton, D. (1996a) *Science, Technology and the British Industrial 'Decline' 1870–1970*. Cambridge: Cambridge University Press.

Edgerton, D. (1996b) Myths of decline. *Prospect*, August/September, pp. 28–31.

Eliot, T. S. (1931) A commentary. *The Criterion* **XI**(42)

Eliot, T. S. (1948) *Notes Towards the Definition of Culture*. London: Faber and Faber.

Esland, G. (1996) Knowledge and nationhood: the New Right, education and the global market. In Avis, J., Bloomer, M., Esland, G., Gleeson, D. and Hodkinson, P. *Knowledge and Nationhood: Education, Politics and Work*. London: Cassell.

Evans, K. (1995) Competence and citizenship: towards a complementary model for times of critical social change. *British Journal of Education and Work* **8**(2), 14–27

Everett, N. (1994) *The Tory View of Landscape*. New Haven and London: Yale University Press.

Fairclough, N. (1992) *Discourse and Social Change*. Cambridge: Polity Press.

Foot, P. (1996) Handsomely paid up to play the game. *Guardian,* 8 April, p. 13.

Ford, F. M. (1925) *No More Parades*. London: Duckworth.

Ford, F. M. (1926) *A Man Could Stand Up*. London: Duckworth.
Foucault, M. (1972) *The Archeology of Knowledge*. London: Tavistock Publications.
Foucault, M. (1976) *Discipline and Punish: The Birth of the Prison*. London: Allen Lane.
Foucault, M. (1991) On governmentality. In Burchell, G., Gordon, C. and Miller, P. (eds) *The Foucault Effect: Studies in Governmental Rationality*. Brighton: Harvester Press.

Galbraith, J. K. (1996) The war against the poor. *Observer* (*Business*), 29 September, p. 4.
Gallie, W. B. (1995) Essentially contested concepts. *Proceedings of the Aristotelian Society* **56**, 167–98.
Galston, W. (1989) Civic education and the liberal state. In Rosenblum, N. L. (ed.) *Liberalism and the Moral Life*. Cambridge, MA: Harvard University Press.
Gamble, A. (1983) Thatcherism and Conservative politics. In Hall, S. and Jaques, M. (eds) *The Politics of Thatcherism*. London: Lawrence and Wishart, pp. 109–31.
Gardiner, J. (1996) The chief inspector rounds on his critics. *Times Educational Supplement*, 1 March.
Garfinkel, H. (1967) *Studies in Ethnomethodology*. Englewood Cliffs, NJ: Prentice-Hall Inc.
Garrett, J. (1996) Gaming and leisure should not be left to chance. *The Times*, 6 July, p. 28.
Gellner, E. (1983) *Nations and Nationalism*. Oxford: Blackwell.
Gellner, E. (1988) *Plough, Sword and Book: The Structure of Human History*. Routledge: London.
Gellner, E. (1992a) *Postmodernism, Reason and Religion*. London: Routledge.
Gellner, E. (1992b) *Reason and Culture: The Historic Role of Rationality and Rationalism*. Oxford: Blackwell.
Giddens, A. (1982) *Profiles and Critiques in Social Theory*. London: Macmillan.
Giddens, A. (1990) *The Consequences of Modernity*. Cambridge: Polity Press.
Giddens, A. (1991) *Modernity and Self-Identity: Self and Society in the Late Modern Age*. Cambridge: Polity Press.
Giddens, A. (1992) *The Transformation of Intimacy: Sexuality, Love and Eroticism in Modern Societies*. Cambridge: Polity Press.
Giddens, A. (1994a) *Beyond Left and Right: The Future of Radical Politics*. Cambridge: Polity Press.
Giddens, A. (1994b) Living in a post-traditional society. In Beck, U., Giddens, A. and Lash, S. *Reflexive Modernization: Politics, Tradition and Aesthetics in the Modern Social Order*. Cambridge: Polity Press.
Giddens, A. (1994c) Replies and critiques: risk, trust and reflexivity. In Beck, U., Giddens, A., and Lash, S. *Reflexive Modernization: Politics, Tradition and Aesthetics in the Modern Social Order*. Cambridge: Polity Press.
Gilbert, R. (1995) Education for citizenship and the problem of identity in post-modern political culture. In Ahier, J. and Ross, A. (eds) *The Social Subjects Within the Curriculum*. London: Falmer.
Gilliat, P. (1996) Spiritual education and public policy 1944–1994. In Best, R. (ed.) *Education, Spirituality and the Whole Child*. London: Cassell.
Gilligan, C. (1982) *In a Different Voice: Psychological Theory and Women's Development*. Cambridge, MA: Harvard University Press.
Gilroy, P. (1987) *'There Ain't No Black in the Union Jack'*. London: Hutchinson.
Gilroy, P. (1992) The end of antiracism. In Donald, J. and Rattansi, A. (eds) *'Race', Culture and Difference*. London: Sage Publications in association with the Open University.
Goalen, P. (1966) The history curriculum and national identity: exploring children's perceptions of national identity in England. Unpublished manuscript.
Graham, D. with Tytler, D. (1993) *A Lesson for Us All: The Making of the National Curriculum*. London: Routledge.
Gray, J. (1995) Bite of the New Right. *Independent*, 24 October.
Gray, J. (1996) Testing market for the middle classes. *Guardian*, 17 April.
Green, K. (1995) *The Woman of Reason: Feminism, Humanism and Political Thought*. Cambridge: Polity Press.
Guardian (1995) Teach children to be British idea stirs up a storm. 19 July.

Guardian (1996) Marriage is added to schools' moral code. 20 December, p. 4.

Guardian (1996) Moral education could lead to improved exam results. 20 December, p. 5.

Guardian (1996) How Santa rewards the City. 24 December, p. 11.

Guardian (1996) Bosses pay rises fastest: director–worker gap is 4 per cent says TUC. *Guardian*, 27 December, p. 20.

Gunn, S. (1988) The 'failure' of the Victorian middle-class: a critique. In Wolff, J. and Seed, J. (eds) *The Culture of Capital: Art, Power and the Nineteenth Century Middle-Class*. Manchester: Manchester University Press.

Gusfield, J. R. (1967) Moral passage: the symbolic process in public designations of deviance. *Social Problems* **15**(2), 174–88.

Gutman, A. (1987) *Democratic Education*. Princeton, NJ.: Princeton University Press.

Gutman, A. (1989) Undemocratic education. In Rosenblum, N. L. (ed.) *Liberalism and the Moral Life*. Cambridge, MA: Harvard University Press.

Habermas, J. (1975) *Legitimation Crisis*. London: Heinemann.

Hardy, J. and Vieler-Porter, C. (1990) Race, schooling and the 1988 Education Reform Act. In Flude, M. and Hammer, M. (eds) *The Education Reform Act 1988: Its Origins and Implications*. Basingstoke: The Falmer Press.

Hardy, T. (1895) *Jude the Obscure*. London: Macmillan (1903). (St Martin's Library Edition, 1957.)

Hargreaves, D. H. (1994) *The Mosaic of Learning: Schools and Teachers for the Next Century*. London: Demos.

Hargreaves, D. H. (1995) Inspection and school improvement. *Cambridge Journal of Education* **25**(1), 117–25.

Heater, D. (1990) *Citizenship: The Civic Ideal in World History, Politics and Education*. Harlow: Longman.

Heelas, P. (1991) Enterprise and the characters of Thatcherism. In Keat, R. and Abercrombie, N. (eds) *Enterprise Culture*. London: Routledge.

Heelas, P., Lash, S. and Morris, P. (eds) *Detraditionalization: Critical Reflections on Authority and Identity*. Oxford: Blackwell Publishers.

Hickox, M. (1995) The English middle-class debate. *British Journal of Sociology* **46**(2).

Hillgate Group (1987) *The Reform of British Education*. London: The Claridge Press.

Hindess, B. (1987) *Freedom, Equality and the Market: Arguments on Social Policy*. London and New York: Tavistock Publications.

Hirst, P. H. (1974) *Knowledge and the Curriculum: A Collection of Philosophical Papers*. London, Routledge and Kegan Paul.

Hirst, P. H. and Peters, R. S. (1970) *The Logic of Education*. London: Routledge and Kegan Paul.

Hobsbawm, E. (1994) *The Age of Extremes: The Short Twentieth Century*. London: Michael Joseph.

Huckle, J. (1983) Environmental education. In Huckle, J. (ed.) *Geographical Education: Reflection or Action?* Milton Keynes: The Open University Press.

Hurd, D. (1988) Citizenship in the Tory democracy. *New Statesman*, 29 April.

Hurd, D. (1989) Freedom will flourish where citizens accept responsibility. *Independent*, 13 September.

Hutton, W. (1995a) *The State We're In*. London: Jonathan Cape.

Hutton, W. (1995b) High risk: the 30:30:40 society. *Guardian*, 30 October.

Huxley, A. (1946) *The Perennial Philosophy*. London: Chatto and Windus.

Huxley, A. (1954) *The Doors of Perception*. London: Chatto and Windus.

Independent (1996) Plea to curb Hollywood violence. 12 December, p. 6.

Institute of Fiscal Studies (1995) *The Distribution of UK Household Expenditure 1979–92*. London: Institute of Fiscal Studies.

International Herald Tribune (1991) Interview with Sir Geoffrey Howe, 17 January.

Johnson, P. (1996) The *only* guidelines our children need. *Daily Mail,* 31 October, p. 8.

Jones, K. (1989) *Right Turn: The Conservative Revolution in Education*. London: Hutchinson Radius.

Joseph, Sir Keith (1984) History's unique contribution. *Times Educational Supplement*, 17 February.

Joseph, Sir Keith (1985) Exploring the complex political areas. *Times Educational Supplement*, 21 June 1985, p. 12.

Khanum, S. (1995) Education and the Muslim girl. In Blair, M., Holland, J. and Sheldon, S. (eds) *Identity and Diversity: Gender and the Experience of Education*. Clevedon: Multilingual Matters Ltd in association with the Open University.

Klein, J. (1965) *Samples from English Cultures*, Vol. I. London: Routledge and Kegan Paul.

Kogan, M. (1978) *The Politics of Educational Change*. Manchester: Manchester University Press and Fontana (paperback edition).

Lambourn, D. (1996) 'Spiritual' minus 'personal-social' = ?: a critical note on an empty category. In Best, R. (ed.) *Education, Spirituality and the Whole Child*. London: Cassell.

Lash, S. (1994) Reflexivity and its doubles: structure, aesthetics, community. In Beck, U., Giddens, A. and Lash, S. *Reflexive Modernization: Politics, Tradition and Aesthetics in the Modern Social Order*. Cambridge: Polity Press.

Lawton, D. (1994) *The Tory Mind on Education 1979–94*. London: The Falmer Press.

Leavis, F. R. (1930) *Mass Civilization and Minority Culture*. Cambridge: Cambridge University Press, republished as an appendix in Leavis, F. R. (1979) *Education and the University*. Cambridge: Cambridge University Press.

Leavis, F. R. (1972) Elites, oligarchies and an educated public. In Leavis, F. R. *Nor Shall My Sword*. London: Chatto and Windus.

Leavis, F. R. and Thompson, D. (1993) *Culture and Environment*. London: Chatto and Windus.

le Carré, J. (1995) *Our Game*. London: Hodder and Stoughton.

Letwin, O. (1992) *The Anatomy of Thatcherism*. London: Fontana.

Macedo, S. (1990) *Liberal Virtues: Citizenship, Virtues and Community in Liberal Constitutionalism*. Oxford: Clarendon Press.

McLaughlin, T. H. (1992) Citizenship, diversity and education: a philosophical perspective. *Journal of Moral Education* 21(3), 235–50.

McLaughlin, T. H. (1995a) Liberalism, education and the common school. *Journal of Philosophy of Education* 29(2), 239–55.

McLaughlin, T. H. (1995b) Public values, private values and educational responsibility. In Pybus, E. and McLaughlin, T. H. *Values, Education and Responsibility*. St Andrews: Centre for Philosophy and Public Affairs, University of St Andrews, pp. 19–32.

McLennan, G. (1992) The Enlightenment Project revisited. In Hall, S., Held, D. and McGrew, T. (eds) *Modernity and Its Futures*. Cambridge: Polity Press.

MacLeod, D. (1996) Teachers reject moral classes. *Guardian*, 14 August, p. 8.

Maier, D. (1982) Education and enterprise: a positive approach. In Anderson, D. (ed.) *Educated for Employment?* London: The Social Affairs Unit.

Malcolm, N. (1996) Mountains of paper. *Prospect*, August/September, pp. 12–13.

Marquand, D. (1995) Flagging fortunes. *Guardian*, 3 July, p. 13.

Marr, A. (1996) Interview with the Archbishop of Canterbury. *Independent*, 24 June, p. 14.

Marshall, T. H. (1950) *Citizenship and Social Class*. Cambridge: Cambridge University Press.

Mathieson, M. and Bernbaum, G. (1988) The British disease: a British tradition? *British Journal of Educational Studies* **XXVI**(2).

Mercer, D. (1983) Economic awareness in the primary school. *Education 3–13* **16**(1), March.

Millett, A. (1996) Teaching: just another subject? *Times Higher Educational Supplement*, 5 July.

Moore, R. (1994a) Competence, professionality and culture change. Unpublished paper delivered to an ESRC Seminar on 'Competence', British Education Research Association, Oxford, September.

Moore, R. (1994b) Professionalism, expertise and control in teacher training. In Wilkin, M. and Sankey, D. (eds) *Collaboration and Transition in Initial Teacher Training*. London: Kogan Page.

Moore, R. (1996) *Educational Discourse and Social Change*. Open University Course Unit, EU 208, Block 4, Unit 5. Milton Keynes: The Open University.

Morris, P. (1991) Freeing the spirit of enterprise: the genesis and development of the concept of enterprise culture. In Keat, R. and Abercrombie, N. (eds) *Enterprise Culture*. London: Routledge.

Nairn, T. (1988) *The Enchanted Glass: Britain and Its Monarchy*. London: Radius Books.

National Curriculum Council (1990a) *Curriculum Guidance 8: Education for Citizenship*. London: National Curriculum Council.

National Curriculum Council (1990b) *Curriculum Guidance 4: Education for Economic and Industrial Understanding*. London: National Curriculum Council.

National Curriculum Council (1990c) *Curriculum Guidance 7: Environmental Education*. London: National Curriculum Council.

National Curriculum Council (1993) *Spiritual and Moral Development: A Discussion Paper*. London: National Curriculum Council.

Nisbet, J. (1982) The school curriculum: in pursuit of industrial relevance. In Anderson, D. (ed.) *Educated for Employment?* London: The Social Affairs Unit.

Norman, E. R. (1977) The threat to religion. In Cox, C. B. and Boyson, R. *Black Paper 1977*. London: Maurice Temple Smith.

OFSTED (1994) *Spiritual, Moral, Social and Cultural Development: A Discussion Paper*. London: Office for Standards in Education.

OFSTED (1995) *The OFSTED Handbook: Guidance on the Inspection of Secondary Schools*. London: HMSO.

OFSTED (1996) *Reporting on Particularly Good or Poor Teaching: The Code of Practice*. London: Office for Standards in Education.

Ollman, B. (1971) *Alienation: Marx's Conception of Man in Capitalist Society*. Cambridge: Cambridge University Press.

Parsons, T. (1959) The school class as a social system: some of its functions in American society. *Harvard Educational Review* **29**(4).

Peters, R. S. (1966) *Ethics in Education*. London: Allen and Unwin.

Pope, J. A. (1979) The role of universities in a changing technologically based industrial society. *Journal of the Royal Society of Arts* **CXXVII**(5278), September.

Pring, R. (1989) *The New Curriculum*. London: Cassell.

Pyke, N. (1996) Stop blurring lines in arts, says Tate. *Times Educational Supplement*, 16 February.

Reeder, D. A. (1977) Predicaments of city children: late Victorian and Edwardian perspectives on education and urban society. In Reeder, D. A. (ed.) *Urban Education in the Nineteenth Century*. Leicester: Leicester University Press.

Reeder, D. (1979) A recurring debate – education and industry. In Bernbaum, G. (ed.) *Schooling in Decline*. London: Macmillan.

Richards, C. (1996) At the hinge of history. *Times Educational Supplement*, 19 April, p. 22.

Rose, N. (1993) Government, authority and expertise in advanced liberalism. *Economy and Society* **22**(3), August, 283–300.

Rosenblum, N. L. (1989) Introduction. In Rosenblum, N. L. (ed.) *Liberalism and the Moral Life*. Cambridge, MA: Harvard University Press.

Routledge, P. (1996) God may be dead – but not if you're a Conservative MP. *Independent on Sunday*, 12 April, p. 6.

Rubinstein, W. D. (1977 Wealth, elites and the class structure of modern Britain. *Past and Present* **76**, 99–126.

Sarup, M. (1993) *An Introductory Guide to Post-Structuralism and Postmodernism* (2nd edn). New York: Harvester-Wheatsheaf.

SCAA (1996a) *Inform – News from the School Curriculum and Assessment Authority*. London: School Curriculum and Assessment Authority, June.

SCAA (1996b) *The National Forum for Values Education and the Community: Consultation on Values in Education and the Community*. School Curriculum and Assessment Authority, Ref. COM/96/608.

Schama, S. (1995) *Landscape and Memory*. London: HarperCollins.

Scheffler, I. (1960) *The Language of Education*. Springfield, IL; Charles C. Thomas.

Schwartz, B. (1984) The language of constitutionalism: Baldwinite Conservatism. In O'Shea, A. (ed.) *Formations of Nations and People*. London: Routledge and Kegan Paul.

Scruton, R. (1987) The myth of cultural relatism. In Palmer, E. (ed.) *Anti-Racism: The Assault on Education and Value*. London: The Sherwood Press.

Simon, B. (1987) *Bending the Rules: The Baker 'Reform' of Education*. London: Lawrence and Wishart.

Smith, A. D. (1991) *National Identity*. London: Penguin Books.

Smith, A. D. (1995) Gellner on nationalism. *Prospect*, December.

Somerville, J. (1992) The New Right and family politics. *Economy and Society* **21**(2), 93–128.

Spencer, D. and Whitehead, M. (1996) Plans laid for 'moral curriculum'. *Times Educational Supplement,* 18 October, p. 12.

Sun (1996) The Sun says 'right muddle'. 6 July.

Tate, N. (1994) Off the fence on common culture. *Times Educational Supplement*, 29 July.

Tate, N. (1996a) Education for adult life: spiritual and moral aspects of the curriculum. Paper delivered to SCAA Conference on 'Education for Adult Life', 15 January. London: School Curriculum and Assessment Authority.

Tate, N. (1996b) Curriculum, culture and society. Paper delivered to SCAA Conference on 'Curriculum, Culture and Society', 7 February. London: School Curriculum and Assessment Authority.

Tate, N. (1996c) To the lighthouse. *Times Educational Supplement,* 1 March.

Tate, N. (1996d) Letter to all members of the National Forum for Values in Education and the Community, School Curriculum and Assessment Authority, 28 October.

Tate, N. (1996e) Values and identity. Paper delivered to a conference of the Independent Schools Association Incorporated, 11 October. London: School Curriculum and Assessment Authority.

Taylor Fitz-Gibbon, C. (1996) Judgements must be credible and fair. *Times Educational Supplement*, 29 March.

Thompson, E. P. (1980) *Writing by Candlelight*. London: The Merlin Press.

Thompson, J. B. (1990) *Ideology and Modern Cultures*. Cambridge: Polity Press.

The Times (1995) Pupils of 14 may be sent out to work. 19 July.

The Times (1996) Morality debate: Carey urges parents and teachers to set an ethical example for all. 6 July, p. 9.

Times Educational Supplement (1984) Shun TVEI, Labour tells authorities. 15 June.

Times Educational Supplement (1982) MSC threatens l.e.a.s with rival technical school system. 19 November.

Turner, B. S. (1990) Outline of a theory of citizenship. *Sociology* **24**(2), 189–217.

Tylor, E. B. (1871) *Primitive Culture*. Holt.

Weber, M. (1968) *Economy and Society* (3 vols, ed. Roth, G. and Wittich, C.). Bedminster Press.

Weinstock, Sir Arnold. (1976) I blame the teachers. *Times Educational Supplement*, 23 January.

White, J. (1988) An unconstitutional National Curriculum. In Lawton, D. and Chitty, C. (eds) *The National Curriculum*. Bedford Way Papers 33. London: University of London Institute of Education.

White, J. (1996) Education, spirituality and the whole child: a humanist perspective. In Best, R. (ed.) *Education, Spirituality and the Whole Child*. London: Cassell.

White, P. (1988) Countering the critics. In Hicks, D. (ed.) *Education for Peace: Issues, Principles, and Practice in the Classroom*. London: Routledge, pp. 36–50.

White, P. (1993) Citizenship & 'spiritual & moral development'. *Citizenship – The Journal of the Citizenship Foundation* **15**(1).

Whitty, G. (1990) The New Right and the National Curriculum. In Flude, M. and Hammer, M. (eds) *The Education Reform Act 1988: Its Origins and Implications*. Basingstoke: The Falmer Press.

Wiener, M. J. (1981) *English Culture and the Decline of the Industrial Spirit, 1850–1980*. Cambridge: Cambridge University Press.

Williams, R. (1961) *The Long Revolution*. London: Chatto and Windus. (Penguin Books 1965.)

Williams, R. (1973) *The Country and the City*. London: Chatto and Windus. (Paladin Books, 1975; all references are to the Paladin edition.)

Willis, P. (1977) *Learning to Labour: How Working Class Kids Get Working Class Jobs*. Farnborough: Saxon House.

Winterson, J. (1991) *Oranges Are Not The Only Fruit*. London: Pandora Press/Vintage paperback edition.

Wolff, J. and Seed, J. (1988) *The Culture of Capital: Art, Power and the Nineteenth Century Middle-Class* (Introduction). Manchester: Manchester University Press.

Woodhead, C. (1995a) *A Question of Standards: Finding the Balance*. London: Politea.

Woodhead, C. (1996) *The Annual Report of Her Majesty's Chief Inspector of Schools: Standards and Quality in Education 1994/95*. London: HMSO.

Wringe, C. (1992) The ambiguities of education for active citizenship. *Journal of Philosophy of Education* **26**(1), 29–38.

Young, M. F. D. (ed.) (1971) *Knowledge and Control: New Directions for the Sociology of Education*. London: Collier Macmillan.

Name Index

Subject Index